Student Interactive

myView®

LITERACY

4

SAVVAS
LEARNING COMPANY

ISBN-13: 978-0-134-90885-4
ISBN-10:   0-134-90885-6

13   23

Julie Coiro, Ph.D.

Jim Cummins, Ph.D.

Pat Cunningham, Ph.D.

Elfrieda Hiebert, Ph.D.

Pamela Mason, Ed.D.

Ernest Morrell, Ph.D.

P. David Pearson, Ph.D.

Frank Serafini, Ph.D.

Alfred Tatum, Ph.D.

Sharon Vaughn, Ph.D.

Judy Wallis, Ed.D.

Lee Wright, Ed.D.

Diversity

UNIT 4

CONTENTS

Impacts

Features

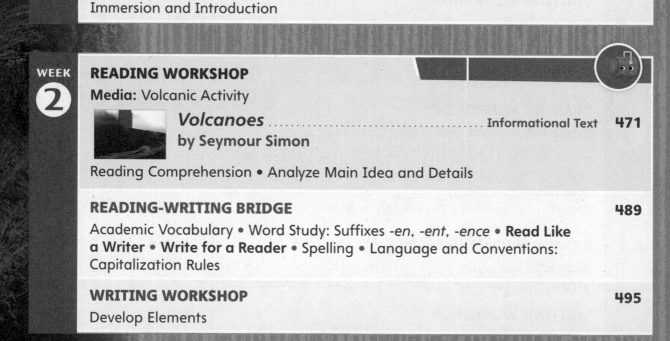

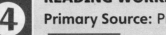

Diversity

Essential Question

How can we reach new understandings through exploring diversity?

 **Watch**

"A World of Differences"

TURNand**TALK**

How you would define diversity?

SAVVAS
realıze™

Go ONLINE for
all lessons.

 VIDEO

 AUDIO

 INTERACTIVITY

 GAME

 ANNOTATE

 BOOK

 RESEARCH

READING WORKSHOP

READING-WRITING BRIDGE

- Academic Vocabulary • Word Study
- **Read Like a Writer • Write for a Reader**
- Spelling • Language and Conventions

WRITING WORKSHOP

- Introduce and Immerse • Develop Elements   **Realistic Fiction**
- Develop Structure • Writer's Craft
- Publish, Celebrate, and Assess

PROJECT-BASED INQUIRY

- Inquire • Research • Collaborate

Independent Reading

In this unit, you will read with your teacher. You will also read on your own. To get the most out of your independent reading, choose a text in a genre that interests you.

Reading for longer, or sustained, periods of time can build your stamina and make you a better reader. The more you read, the better you become.

Set some goals to increase the time you spend reading. Keep track of how long you read.

Step 1 Identify your purpose for reading. Decide which genre best matches your purpose.

> I want to read something in the
> _____ genre.

Step 2 Select a book and examine it. If the book does not match your chosen genre, keep looking. If it does match your chosen genre, start reading!

The topic of this book is _____.
Other books about this topic are usually in the genre _____.
The design and images on the cover of this book tell me it is
_____.
This book has lots of (dialogue / text features / _____).
This book is (factual / imaginative).
This author (has / has not) written other books I know about.
This author writes books that are _____.
The genre of this book is _____.

Independent Reading Log

Date	Book	Genre	Pages Read	Minutes Read	My Ratings
					☆☆☆☆☆

Unit Goals

Shade in the circle to rate how well you meet each goal now.

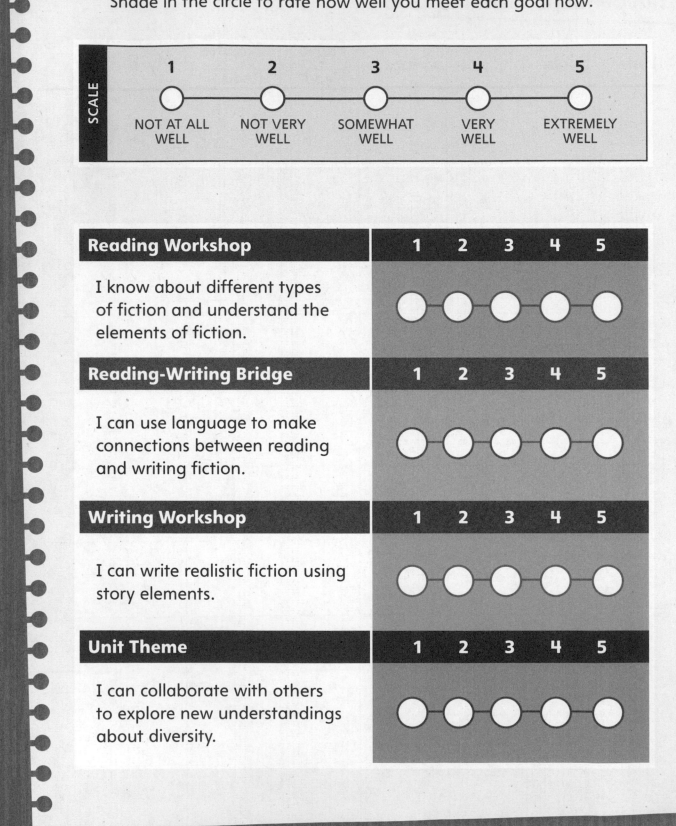

Academic Vocabulary

Use these words to talk and write about this unit's theme, *Diversity*: *accomplish*, *challenge*, *conflict*, *expand*, and *participate*.

TURN and TALK With a partner, review the five academic vocabulary words. Ask your partner, *Where have you heard or seen this word before? What does this word mean to you? What are some related words?* Finally, discuss how the word relates to diversity. During your discussion, take notes using a graphic organizer like this one.

Academic Vocabulary Word

Seen or Heard	Meaning and Related Words	How Word Relates to Diversity

INTERACTIVITY

DIVERSE WAYS
We Communicate

SIGN LANGUAGE People who are deaf or hard of hearing use sign language to communicate. Motions of the hands stand for words, phrases, or ideas. There are over 250 different sign languages in the world.

This gesture means "Why?"

CARRIER PIGEONS can find their way home over long distances. They were used during both World Wars. A soldier wrote a message and inserted it into a tube attached to the pigeon's leg or body. Because the enemy could intercept radio transmissions, pigeons offered another way to deliver messages.

SMOKE SIGNALS Smoke signals are among the oldest means of communication. The ancient Chinese, Greeks, Native Americans, and others used them to send messages over long distances. Torches or piles of vegetation were placed on high ground and set on fire. The smoke from the fires could be seen from far away.

BRAILLE Louis Braille became blind when he was very young. When he was 11, he decided to create a way for blind people to communicate with each other. He then modified "night writing," an alphabet system of raised bumps that Charles Barbier had created in the 1800s.

Cell Phone

More and more, people use their phone's computer technology to text their friends and family rather than make phone calls.

SPEECH-GENERATING DEVICE

People who are unable to speak or write might use a speech-generating device (SGD). These devices allow people to communicate with text or synthesized speech by using a touch keypad or joystick or by tracking a person's eye movements. Stephen Hawking is a famous scientist who has written books and given lectures using an SGD.

Hello

Weekly Question

Why do people communicate in diverse ways?

Quick Write What are some different ways you communicate?

Spotlight on Genre

Realistic Fiction

Realistic fiction is a made-up story that could really happen. This type of fiction contains the same literary elements as other fictional texts. It includes

- **Setting,** or the time and place a story occurs
- **Characters,** or the people and animals involved
- **Plot,** or the series of events
- **Theme,** or message

When you recognize these characteristics in a text, you will know that you are reading fiction.

Do you think I could be in a realistic fiction story?

TURN and TALK Describe a character from a favorite story to a partner. Use the anchor chart to tell how you know whether the story is realistic fiction. Take notes on your discussion.

My NOTES _____

_____

_____

_____

_____

_____

_____

REALISTIC FICTION ANCHOR CHART

Purpose:

To entertain or tell a story

Elements:

Setting: Where? When?

*seems real

Characters: Who?

*behave like real people *often change over the course of the story

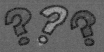

Plot: What?

*events could take place in real life

Theme:

*message about an important topic *usually not stated in the story
*has to be inferred by the reader

Sharon M. Draper has often wondered about what is going on in the minds of people who cannot share their thoughts. The question holds special meaning to her because her own daughter has a disability. She is also the author of *Double Dutch*.

from

Out of My Mind

Preview Vocabulary

As you read *Out of My Mind*, pay attention to these vocabulary words. Notice how they provide clues to the characters and help you understand the story.

frustrated	cool	confused
irritable	bothered	

Read

Before you begin reading the assigned text, establish a purpose. Active readers of **realistic fiction** follow these strategies when they read a text the first time.

Notice
who the story is about and what happens.

Generate Questions
before, during, and after reading to deepen understanding and gain information.

First Read

Connect
ideas within the selection to what you already know and have read.

Respond
by marking parts you find interesting or surprising.

from out of my mind

by Sharon M. Draper

BACKGROUND

Melody has a physical disability called cerebral palsy. She cannot walk or speak and has very little control of her body. However, Melody is one of the smartest students in her school. In this excerpt, Melody describes some of her experiences.

AUDIO

ANNOTATE

21

Analyze Characters

Underline details that tell about the challenges Melody faces.

1   Once I started school, however, I discovered I had a much bigger problem than just falling out of my chair. I needed words. How was I supposed to learn anything if I couldn't talk? How was I supposed to answer questions? Or ask questions?

2   I knew a lot of words, but I couldn't read a book. I had a million thoughts in my head, but I couldn't share them with anybody. On top of that, people didn't really expect the kids in H-5 to learn much anyway. It was driving me crazy!

3   I couldn't have been much more than six when Mrs. V figured out what I needed. One afternoon after school, after a snack of ice cream with caramel sauce, she flipped through the cable channels and stopped at a documentary about some guy named Stephen Hawking.

4   Now I'm interested in almost anything that has a wheelchair in it. Duh! I even like the Jerry Lewis telethon! Turns out Stephen Hawking has something called ALS, and he can't walk or talk, and he's probably the smartest man in the world, and everybody knows it! That is so cool.

frustrated feeling annoyed at being unable to change something

5   I bet he gets really frustrated sometimes.

6   After the show went off, I got real quiet.

7   "He's like you, sort of, isn't he?" Mrs. V asked.

8   I pointed to yes on my board, then pointed to **no**.

9   "I don't follow you." She scratched her head.

10   I pointed to **need** on my board, then to **read**. **Need/read. Need/read.**

11   "I know you can read lots of words, Melody," Mrs. V said.

12   I pointed again. **More**. I could feel tears coming. **More. More. More.**

13   "Melody, if you had to choose, which would you rather be able to do—walk or talk?"

14   **Talk**. I pointed to my board. I hit the word again and again. **Talk. Talk. Talk.**

15   I have so much to say.

16   So Mrs. V made it her new mission to give me language. She ripped all the words off my communication board and started from scratch. She made the new words smaller, so more could fit. Every single space on my talking board got filled with names and pictures of people in my life, questions I might need to ask, and a big variety of nouns and verbs and adjectives, so I could actually compose something that looked like a sentence! I could ask, *Where is my book bag?* or say, *Happy Birthday, Mom,* just by pointing with my thumb.

17   I have magic thumbs, by the way. They work perfectly. The rest of my body is sort of like a coat with the buttons done up in the wrong holes. But my thumbs came out with no flaws, no glitches. Just my thumbs. Go figure.

Make Inferences About Characters

Highlight phrases that help you support an inference about what Melody thinks and wants.

the blue will fish run away

CLOSE READ

Make Inferences About Characters

Highlight evidence that helps you make inferences about Melody.

cool interesting or stylish

18   Every time Mrs. V would add new words, I learned them quickly, used them in sentences, and was hungry for more. I wanted to READ!

19   So she made flash cards.

20   Pink for nouns.

21   Blue for verbs.

22   Green for adjectives.

23   Piles and piles of words I learned to read. Little words, like *fish* and *dish* and *swish*. I like rhyming words—they're easy to remember. It's like a "buy one, get the rest free" sale at the mall.

24   I learned big words, like *caterpillar* and *mosquito*, and words that follow crazy rules, like *knock* and *gnome*. I learned all the days of the week, months of the year, all the planets, oceans, and continents. Every single day I learned new words. I sucked them in and gobbled them up like they were Mrs. V's cherry cake.

25   And then she would stretch out the cards on the floor, position me on a big pillow so I could reach them, and I'd push the cards into sentences with my fists. It was like stringing the beads of a necklace together to make something really cool.

26   I liked to make her laugh, so I'd put the words into wacky order sometimes.

27   *The blue fish will run away. He does not want to be dinner.*

28   She also taught me words for all the music I heard at home. I learned to tell the difference between Beethoven and Bach, between a sonata and a concerto. She'd pick a selection on a CD, then ask me the composer.

29   **Mozart**. I'd point to the correct card from the choices she'd set in front of me. Then I'd point to the color blue on my board.

30   "Huh?" she asked.

31   When she played a selection from Bach, I'd point to the correct composer, then once again touch the color blue on my board. I also touched purple.

32   She looked confused. I searched around for the right words to explain what I meant. I wanted her to understand that music was colorful when I heard it. I finally realized that even Mrs. V couldn't figure out everything in my head. We kept going.

33   Sometimes she'd play hip-hop music, sometimes oldies. Music, and the colors it produced, flowed around her as easily as her clothing.

34   Mrs. V took me outside in all kinds of weather. One day she actually let me sit outside in the rain. It was steaming hot, and I was sticky and irritable.

CLOSE READ

Analyze Characters

Underline the details that tell how Melody experiences music.

confused unable to understand

irritable easily made angry or annoyed

Analyze Characters

Underline details that help you understand how Melody interacts with Mrs. V.

bothered annoyed or upset with

35   It must have been about ninety degrees outside. We were sitting on her porch, watching the storm clouds gather. She told me the names of all the clouds and made up stories about them. I knew that later she'd have the names of every kind of cloud on word cards for me.

36   "Big old Nimbus up there—he's black and powerful and can blow all the other clouds out of the sky. He wants to marry Miss Cumulus Cloud, but she's too soft and pretty to be bothered with such a scary guy. So he gets mad and makes storms," she told me.

37   Finally, old Nimbus got his way, and the rain came down around me and Mrs. V. It rained so hard, I couldn't see past the porch. The wind blew, and the wet coolness of the rain washed over us. It felt so good. A small leak on Mrs. V's porch let a few drops of rain fall on my head. I laughed out loud.

38   Mrs. V gave me a funny look, then hopped up. "You want to feel it all?" she asked.

39   I nodded my head. *Yes, yes, yes.*

40   She rolled me down the ramp Dad had built, both of us getting wetter every second. She stopped when we got to the grass, and we let the rain drench us. My hair, my clothes, my eyes and arms and hands. Wet. Wet. Wet. It was awesome. The rain was warm, almost like bath water. I laughed and laughed.

41   Eventually, Mrs. V rolled me back up the ramp and into the house, where she dried me off, changed my clothes, and gave me a cup of chocolate milk. She dried off my chair, and by the time Dad came to pick me up, the rain had stopped and everything was dry once more.

42   I dreamed of chocolate clouds all night.

CLOSE READ

Vocabulary in Context

Context clues are words and sentences around a word that help readers understand the word's meaning.

Use context clues beyond the sentence to determine the meaning of *drench*. Underline the context clues that support your definition.

Develop Vocabulary

In realistic fiction, authors use precise words to create specific descriptions. These words help the reader visualize and connect with the characters and events.

My TURN Add the vocabulary word from the word bank to complete the Synonym Sandwich. Then choose a character or object that best matches the word and write an example sentence.

Word Bank

bothered   confused   cool   frustrated   irritable

Synonym Sandwich	Who or What Is...	My Example Sentence
discouraged ⎯⎯⎯⎯ disappointed		
puzzled ⎯⎯⎯⎯ perplexed		
annoyed ⎯⎯⎯⎯ exasperated		
troubled ⎯⎯⎯⎯ agitated		
interesting ⎯⎯⎯⎯ stylish		

Check for Understanding

My TURN Look back at the text to answer the questions.

1. Name three details from the text that make it realistic fiction.

2. Why does Sharon Draper use boldface for some words?

3. What do you notice about Mrs. V's character?

4. Explain how Mrs. V changes her perspective on Melody's communication needs based on Melody's reaction to a documentary.

Analyze Characters

You can learn about a **character** through his or her thoughts, feelings, actions, and interactions with other characters. To learn more about a character, look at the details that the author chooses to include about a character. Examine the character's interactions with other characters. Then use these details to analyze and explain how characters develop in a story.

1. **My TURN** Go to the Close Read notes in *Out of My Mind*. Underline the parts that help you understand Melody, her character traits, and the changes she undergoes.

2. **Text Evidence** Use the parts you underlined to complete the chart.

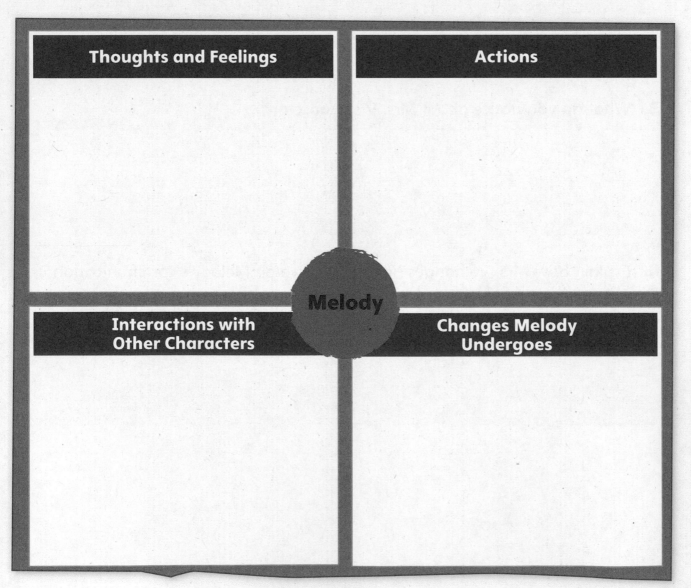

Thoughts and Feelings	Actions

Melody

Interactions with Other Characters	Changes Melody Undergoes

Make Inferences About Characters

While reading, you can make **inferences**, or figure out information that is not stated directly. To make an inference, combine what you read in the text with what you already know from your own life or from other texts you have read. When you connect this information, you deepen your understanding of the text.

1. **My TURN** Go back to the Close Read notes and highlight evidence that helps you make inferences about Melody.

2. **Text Evidence** Use your highlighted text to make inferences, and use evidence to support your understanding of the text.

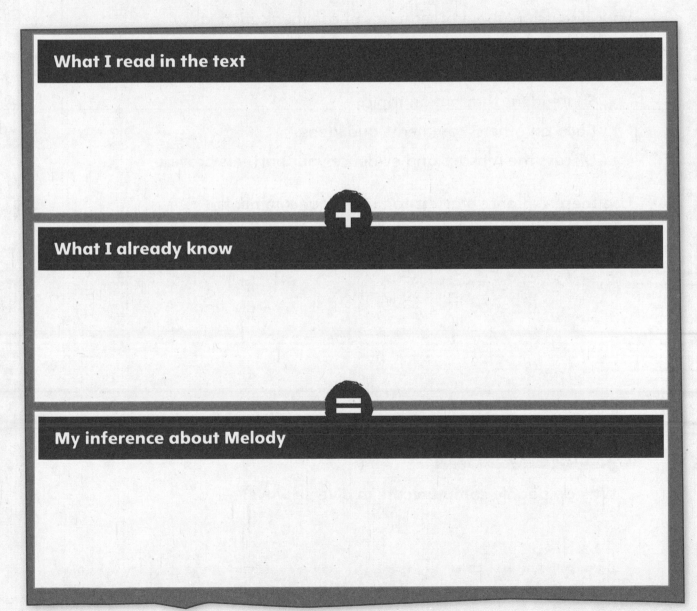

What I read in the text

+

What I already know

=

My inference about Melody

Reflect and Share

Talk About It Mrs. V helped Melody overcome her inability to communicate by teaching her new words using a communication board. What other forms of communication that you read about this week might have helped Melody communicate? Use examples from the text to support your response.

Ask Questions and Make Thoughtful Comments During your discussion about other forms of communication, ask questions and make comments that are related to the topic.

- Ask questions when you need more information.
- Share ideas that are on topic.
- Build on others' comments and ideas.
- Discuss the reasons and evidence your partners provide.

Use these sentence starters to guide your comments.

> You used _____ as evidence for your point. Why do you think . . .

> I agreed with you when you said . . .

Weekly Question

Why do people communicate in diverse ways?

Academic Vocabulary

Learning Goal

I can develop knowledge about language to make connections between reading and writing.

Related words are forms of a word that share roots or word parts. They can have different meanings based on the form of the word, such as *character*, *characters*, and *characterization*.

My TURN For each sentence,

1. **Use** print or digital resources, such as a glossary, dictionary, or thesaurus, to find related words.

2. **Add** an additional related word in the box.

3. **Choose** the correct form of the word to complete the sentence.

Word	Related Words	Correct Form of the Word
conflict	conflicts conflicted _____	I cannot play today because the game _____ with my doctor's appointment.
accomplish	unaccomplished accomplishment _____	I _____ everything I needed to do today.
expand	expands expanded _____	Could you _____ on what you mean?
challenge	challenging unchallenged _____	The heavyweight boxer faced his _____ with a smile.
participate	participates participation _____	Everyone was required to _____ in the school play.

Related Words

Related words are forms of a word that share roots or word parts, but they can have different meanings depending on their parts of speech.

The word *compose* in paragraph 16 of *Out of My Mind* is a verb that means "to create or make up." If you know what *compose* means, you can figure out the meaning of the noun form of the word, *composition*. A *composition* is "a putting together of words" or "a creation of musical works."

My TURN Read each word in the chart. Then complete the chart using related words from *Out of My Mind* or other texts you have read.

Word	Related Words
select	
frustration	
perfection	
communicate	

High-Frequency Words

High-frequency words are words that you will see in texts over and over again. Sometimes they do not follow regular sound-spelling patterns. Read these high-frequency words: *belong, guess, either, country, everything, already.* Try to identify them in your independent reading.

Read Like a Writer

Authors use figurative language to make writing interesting and to develop characters. One form of figurative language is repetition. Writers use repetition when they repeat words and phrases within a text.

Model ! Read this text from *Out of My Mind*.

Wet. Wet. Wet. It was awesome. The rain was warm, almost like bath water. I laughed and laughed.

repeated words

1. **Identify** Sharon Draper repeats *wet* and *laughed*.
2. **Question** How does the repetition help me understand Melody?
3. **Conclude** Repetition of *wet* and *laughed* emphasizes two important ideas: Melody is getting soaked, and the rain makes her happy.

Read the text.

Piles and piles of words I learned to read. Little words, like *fish* and *dish* and *swish*. I like rhyming words—they're easy to remember.

My TURN Follow the steps to analyze the passage. Describe how the author uses repetition.

1. **Identify** Sharon Draper repeats _____.
2. **Question** How does the repetition help me understand Melody?
3. **Conclude** Repetition of _____ emphasizes

_____

Write for a Reader

Writers use elements of craft to develop an engaging idea with relevant details. By repeating language, writers signal to readers that an event or idea is important.

Use repetition to emphasize ideas in your writing.

My TURN Think about how Sharon Draper's use of repetition in *Out of My Mind* affects you as a reader. Now identify how you can use repetition to influence your own readers by developing an idea with relevant details.

1. If you were trying to develop a character who is excited, what words, expressions, or actions might you repeat?

_____

_____

_____

2. Write a fictional passage about an imaginary character. Use repetition to emphasize your character's excitement.

_____

_____

_____

_____

_____

_____

_____

_____

Spell Related Words

Related words have word parts that are spelled the same. The words are often pronounced differently. To spell related words, look at the word parts that are the same, and then add endings when needed. For example, the words *tutoring* and *tutorial* contain the same base word, *tutor*. Spell *tutorial* by spelling the base word *tutor* and then adding the ending *-ial*.

My TURN Read the words, and find the related pairs. Spell the word pairs side by side.

SPELLING WORDS

tutor	breath	crumb	breathe
production	triple	health	relate
medical	imagine	medic	triplet
compose	heal	composition	image
crumble	relative	tutorial	product

_____   _____

_____   _____

_____   _____

_____   _____

_____   _____

_____   _____

Prepositions and Prepositional Phrases

A **preposition** is a word used to show the relationship of a noun or pronoun to another word in the sentence. A **prepositional phrase** is a group of words beginning with a preposition and usually ending with a noun or pronoun.

Type	Prepositions	Prepositional Phrases
Location and Direction	at, below, behind, by, in, inside, outside, near, on, across, down, from, over, to, around	She sat **on** the porch.
Time	after, at, before, during, until	She went home **after** the storm.
Description	in, with, for	Mrs. V was the one **in** the dress.

My TURN Edit this draft by replacing prepositions and changing the meaning of the prepositional phrases.

There is a lot of activity in my neighborhood after school. Boys and girls play basketball on the courts behind the school. Dogs run back and forth on the field. Trucks deliver packages to houses down the street. This all happens around my house.

Understand Realistic Fiction

Learning Goal

I can use elements of narrative writing to write a realistic fiction story.

Realistic fiction is imagined, but it includes believable people, places, and events.

My TURN Fill in the boxes using a story you have read.

Characters are the people and animals in a story.

What do you notice about the characters in the story?

The **setting** is the time and place a story occurs.

What words does the author use to describe the setting?

The **plot** is the series of events.

What are the most important events in the story?

Identify Parts of the Plot

A fictional **plot** is a believable series of events. Writers use a **conflict**, or main problem, to build a plot. The parts of a plot include an introduction of the conflict, rising action, climax or turning point, falling action, and resolution. The **resolution** offers a conclusion or a solution to the conflict.

My TURN Think about a story you have read. Read about conflict and resolution. Fill in the boxes using the story you read.

> The **conflict** is the main problem in the story.
>
> **What main obstacle do the characters face?**
>
>
>
> The **resolution** is how the problem is solved.
>
> **How do the characters overcome the obstacle?**

Recognize Elements of Fiction

As you learned, realistic fiction includes realistic **characters**, a **setting** that is a real place or based on a real place, and a believable **plot**. Realistic fiction also includes a **conflict**, or problem that is at the center of the story, and a **resolution** of the conflict.

My TURN Work with a partner. Read a new story from your classroom library. Give evidence from the text that shows that it is realistic fiction.

Realistic Fiction

Characters

Setting

Plot

Conflict

Resolution

Brainstorm a Topic

Authors think of ideas before they begin drafting a story. The process of gathering ideas is called **brainstorming**. When brainstorming, write every idea that comes to mind. Then use the checklist to evaluate your choices and choose a single topic.

My TURN Complete the sentences to brainstorm a topic for your realistic fiction story.

My story could be about games I like to play, such as _____

_____ .

My story could be about places I've gone, such as _____

_____ .

My story could be similar to books I've read, such as _____

_____ .

Use this checklist to decide on a topic for your realistic fiction story.

NARROW YOUR TOPIC:

☐ My audience will be interested in this topic.

☐ This story idea is not too complicated and not too simple.

☐ The characters, setting, and plot are believable and exciting.

☐ I will enjoy writing about this topic.

Plan Your Realistic Fiction Story

Writers map out their ideas to plan their stories. Telling a story aloud before writing can highlight details to focus on in the written draft.

My TURN Think about the topic of your story. Use the organizer to map your realistic fiction story. Tell your story to your Writing Club, using your map to organize your events and details. Use your partners' feedback to revise your story plan.

To begin planning your story, think about your **characters**. **CHARACTERS**

- ◎ What do they do that will help you tell your story?
- ◎ How do the characters change over the story?

Your story might be about a specific **setting**, or you may need to decide on a setting. **SETTING**

- ◎ What effect does the setting have on the story?
- ◎ Can you imagine your characters in this place?

The **conflict** is often the central focus of the story. **CONFLICT**

- ◎ What problem are the characters trying to solve?
- ◎ What obstacles stand in the way of the characters overcoming the conflict?

The end of the story describes how the conflict is **resolved**. **RESOLUTION**

- ◎ What solution do the characters find for the conflict?
- ◎ How is the story different after the conflict is resolved?

INTERACTIVITY

Meals

At Amir's house, bread is soft and flat.
We scoop up rice and vegetables
from a round metal plate, kneeling on a mat.
I taste these good things with a finger.
Amir laughs and says, "That's ginger!"
The meal is hot and rich with spice,
and so delicious, I dip into the platter twice.

At my house, Amir eats with a fork
while our table talk spins around
soccer wins and losses in the park.
I help him to some cherry pie,
and my friend gives a contented sigh.
Oh, but what about his African home?

So I ask, because I'm curious,
about his home. He remembers markets
and dusty desert storms, thick and furious.
"This is *Ayat*,*" Amir says and shows me a picture.
In it, a man stands proudly in a market teeming
   with camels.
Some day, Amir and I will visit them under the sun.

*grandfather

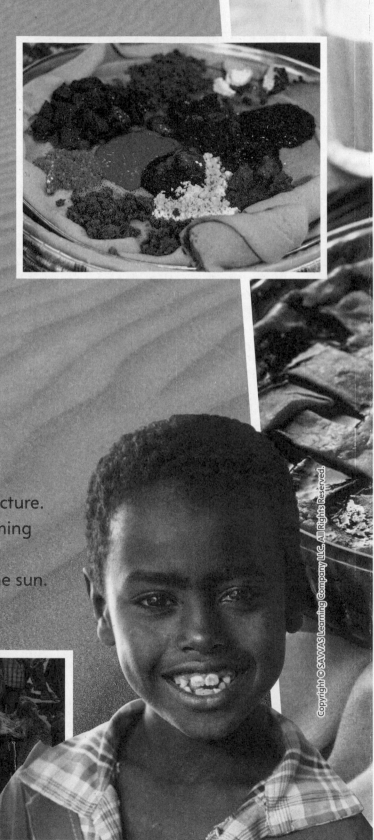

Weekly Question

How do our experiences help us see the world differently?

Illustrate and Describe

Write and illustrate a descriptive paragraph to show a custom that you have recently learned about or that you would like to teach a friend.

Learning Goal

I can learn about fiction by analyzing plot and setting.

Spotlight on Genre

Realistic Fiction

In realistic fiction, the **plot**, or series of events, is believable. You can use the Plot Anchor Chart, or something similar, to analyze a story's plot. Look for

- **Introduction**
- **Rising action**
- **Climax**
- **Falling action**
- **Resolution**

Establish Purpose One **purpose** for reading realistic fiction is to be entertained. You could also read fiction to determine how events are influenced by the setting, or location, of the story.

Does an event show a turning point for the character? That's the story's climax!

TURN and TALK With a partner, establish a purpose for reading *Mama's Window*. For example, you may want to find out how the author builds tension or how characters encounter and respond to challenges. Make a plan to read with this purpose in mind.

My **PURPOSE** _____

_____

_____

_____

Plot Anchor Chart

Climax
Turning point of the conflict

Rising Action
Develops the conflict

Falling Action
Events after the climax

Introduction
Introduces the characters, setting, and conflict

Resolution
Conclusion or solution to the conflict

Lynn Rubright has won awards for her storytelling. Known for her energetic, humorous performance style, she is also an educator and the cofounder of a children's theater.

from
Mama's Window

Preview Vocabulary

As you read *Mama's Window*, pay attention to these vocabulary words. Notice how they help you better understand the plot.

subsided	dedication	impulsively
	trance	grudge

Read

Scan *Mama's Window* and use what you know about the genre to make predictions about what will happen. Record your predictions. As you read, use genre clues, such as setting and plot, to confirm or correct your predictions. Follow these strategies when you read this **realistic fiction** text.

Notice

the plot and its structure as you make and confirm or correct predictions.

Generate Questions

as you read by annotating confusing parts.

First Read

Connect

ideas within the selection to ideas in other texts you have read.

Respond

by discussing your thoughts about the text as you read.

from

MAMA'S WINDOW

by Lynn Rubright

 AUDIO

 ANNOTATE

BACKGROUND

After Sugar's mother passes away, he is sent to live with his uncle. They live near a swamp in the Mississippi Delta. While Sugar's mother was alive, she saved enough money to pay for a beautiful window for her church. Sugar is upset to learn the money for Mama's window will be used instead to buy bricks.

49

CLOSE READ

Analyze Plot

The conflict, or main problem, is part of the rising action in a story. <u>Underline</u> words or phrases that help you identify a conflict between characters as the plot develops.

subsided stopped; died down

1   Furious at the church folks and mad at his uncle, Sugar stood on the dock and watched Uncle Free pole out of the swamp into the bayou. Then Sugar stormed back inside. He plopped down on his cot and began picking at the frayed fishnet.

2   After a few minutes Sugar got up and looked inside the box of clothes. *Clothes jus' like Mama would've bought for Christmas or Easter*, he thought. Tears filled his eyes. With a sudden sweep of his arm, Sugar flung the box on the floor. Shirt, pants, shoes, socks, and underwear went flying. He collapsed onto his cot and wept.

3   "You actin' like a baby," Sugar said to himself as his sobbing subsided. "Jus' feelin' sorry for yourself." He picked up the clothes from the floor and laid them out on the cot. Then he walked over to the old lead sink, took off his overalls, and began pumping icy spring water over his head.

4   "Whew!" Sugar said, shivering. He scrubbed his hair, face, ears, neck, and arms with Uncle Free's lye soap. He rubbed himself dry in a hurry to get warm.

5   Quickly Sugar put on his new underwear, shirt, and pants. He glanced in the mirror as he brushed his hair. Uncle Free had insisted on trimming Sugar's hair a few days ago.

6   "Why you gotta mess with my hair," Sugar had complained. "Nobody care how long it gets."

7   "I care," Uncle Free had said.

8   "So that's why Uncle Free wanna cut my hair," Sugar said. "So it look nice for the dedication."

9   Sugar grabbed his new shoes, stuffing the socks into the toes as he ran out the door. He placed the shoes in the bow of his boat where they wouldn't get wet. Swiftly he untied the boat from the dock and climbed into the stern. He shoved off with his pole, careful not to splash water on his new clothes.

10   Sugar wasn't sure why he was all dressed up, hurrying toward Cypress Grove. He didn't want to go to the dedication of the new Sweet Kingdom Church. Conflicting emotions bubbled up inside him. Nevertheless, he poled forward quickly and smoothly.

11   As he approached Cypress Grove, Sugar could see the new brick church nestled among the trees. *Maybe Uncle Free be right, thinkin' Mama might agree with the trustee committee,* Sugar thought.

CLOSE READ

Confirm or Correct a Prediction

Highlight phrases and sentences that you can use to confirm a prediction you made about a plot event.

dedication an official ceremony for something created for a special purpose

CLOSE READ

Vocabulary in Context

Context clues can help you determine word meanings. Some context clues have the same meaning as an unfamiliar word. Words with the same meaning are called **synonyms**.

Look for words that describe the action or behavior of the crowd of people entering the church. Underline two synonyms in paragraphs 12–15 for *march*.

12   Rounding the bend, Sugar saw the crowd gathered near the shoreline of Sun Lake. They were getting ready to parade up the path into the church for the sermon and singing part of the ceremony.

13   Nobody seemed to notice Sugar enter the cove and slip under the weeping willow branches. He poled alongside Uncle Free's boat and rolled up his pant legs so they wouldn't get wet when he stepped into the shallow water. He pulled the bow of his boat onto the grass, adjusted his clothes, and put on his new socks and shoes.

14   "Ouch!" Sugar said when he stood up. "Uncle Free got everythin' right 'cept these shoes. They too tight."

15   Sugar watched the procession of folks in their Sunday best from behind the canopy of willow fronds. *At least I be dressed like Mama would have wanted, IF I was goin' to the dedication, he thought. Which I ain't.*

16   Pastor Williams led the way, followed by the choir, dressed in their flowing scarlet robes, singing "Walking Up the King's Highway." *Mama's favorite hymn,* thought Sugar.

17   Then came the church members, singing along with the choir. Girls in starched, ruffled frocks, white socks, and Sunday shoes and boys in pressed pants and shirts and freshly shined shoes marched proudly with their parents. Bringing up the rear was Mr. Pearson and the trustee board members, followed by Mrs. Pearson with Stewie in tow.

18   Sugar noticed Uncle Free was lagging behind, limping along slowly but looking good in his new store-bought clothes in spite of his bent body. *Uncle Free ain't no swamp rat,* he thought. *No matter what Stewie Pearson say.*

19   Sugar watched the last of the congregation enter the church before he shot out from under the willow branches and raced up the path. He rushed past his uncle, around toward the front of the church where the stained glass window should have been.

20   Impulsively Sugar reached down and grabbed a rock. His new shoes pinched, but he barely noticed. He thrust back his arm and aimed at the center of the window.

Confirm or Correct a Prediction

Highlight something Sugar does on this page that confirms or corrects a prediction you made about the plot.

impulsively suddenly; without careful thought about the consequences

Confirm or Correct a Prediction

Highlight text in paragraphs 21–26 that tells what happens to Sugar as a result of his action. Determine whether this evidence confirms your prediction.

21   Then abruptly Sugar dropped the rock. He spun around and almost crashed into Uncle Free, who had run after him, bad leg and all. Uncle Free grabbed Sugar with his good arm.

22   "It was Mama," Sugar sobbed, pressing his face against Uncle Free's shoulder. "I wanted to break that plain glass window, but Mama wouldn't let me do it."

23   Uncle Free held the trembling boy close. "That don' surprise me, son," Uncle Free said. "I told you she jus' might want you to go to the dedication, not to wreck the church window, even a plain glass one."

24 Uncle Free pulled his handkerchief from his pocket and wiped Sugar's face. "I see you did a good job washin' up, but now your face all stain with tears," said Uncle Free, examining Sugar. "New clothes fit nice. Look good too. Let's go on inside."

25 "But, Uncle Free, I don' wanna go to the dedication. Can' we jus' go back home?" Sugar pleaded. "Please."

26 Uncle Free gently but firmly grabbed Sugar's arm and led him toward the front door to the church. "Sometimes we gotta do things we don' wanna do, James Earle. This here's one of them times." There was no arguing with Uncle Free when he spoke in that tone of voice.

27 Sugar and Uncle Free entered through the heavy oak doors that framed the entrance to the new Sweet Kingdom Church. The choir and congregation were harmonizing on the last stanza of "Great Day! Great Day! The Righteous Marching, Great Day!"

28 Pastor Wilson looked up from the freshly varnished pulpit and saw Free McBride and Sugar standing behind the last pew. He beckoned them to come down front. Sugar, staring at the black curtain in front of the window, was frozen in his spot.

29 Uncle Free squeezed Sugar's arm and nudged him to move, but Sugar resisted and tried to pull away. Uncle Free bent down and whispered, "James Earle, we goin' to the front of the church. I know you don' wanna, but you ain't got no choice."

30 There was no breaking away from Uncle Free. Together they made their way down the aisle.

CLOSE READ

Analyze Setting

Underline descriptive details that are important to the setting.

Analyze Setting

Underline details that help you understand how characters feel about the place where Sugar lives.

Explain how the settings of the church and the swamp influence the plot of the story.

trance dreamlike state

31   "Swamp rats!" hissed Stewie, wedged between his mama and daddy.

32   "Hush, boy!" Mr. Pearson's voice was as sharp as a viper's tongue.

33   Uncle Free pressed his fingers around Sugar's arm. "Ignore that, son," he whispered. Sugar didn't turn around. He kept walking as if in a trance.

34   There were two empty chairs in the front row where the deacons sat. Pastor Williams gestured them to the seats of honor. Sugar didn't feel like being honored. All he wanted was to escape back to Uncle Free's shack in the swamp.

35   *Stewie's right,* Sugar thought, *I'm a swamp rat. I don' deserve to be in a fancy church like this. Maybe when Mama was alive, but no more. It don' matter that I'm wearin' nice new clothes. I'm nothin' but a swamp rat like Uncle Free.*

36   Sugar was so deep in thought, he barely heard Pastor Williams's sermon, which was about understanding and loving one another and the importance of having dreams.

37   Then the pastor called Mr. Pearson to come forward to say a few words. Making his way to the pulpit, he cast a friendly look in Sugar's direction. Sugar turned away, not wanting to face Mr. Pearson.

38   "James Earle," said Mr. Pearson, looking directly at Sugar. "Your mama, Ida Mae Martin, had a dream."

39   *Yeah,* thought Sugar, *and y'all stole it!* He stared up at the black curtain draped in front of where Mama's window should have been.

40   "But it was Ida Mae's son, James Earle, who kept his mama's dream for a stain glass window alive when the rest of us lost sight of it," Mr. Pearson went on. "James Earle, would you please step up here?"

41   *What's all this talk 'bout dreams,* Sugar was thinking when Uncle Free nudged him. "Get up, son," whispered Uncle Free. "Mr. Pearson callin' you up to the front." Feeling numb, Sugar walked toward the pulpit.

42   "James Earle," said Mr. Pearson, "would you please pull this cord?"

43   Pastor Williams put a thin rope in Sugar's palm. It was attached to the black curtain on a pulley. Mr. Pearson and Pastor Williams nodded, and Sugar tugged.

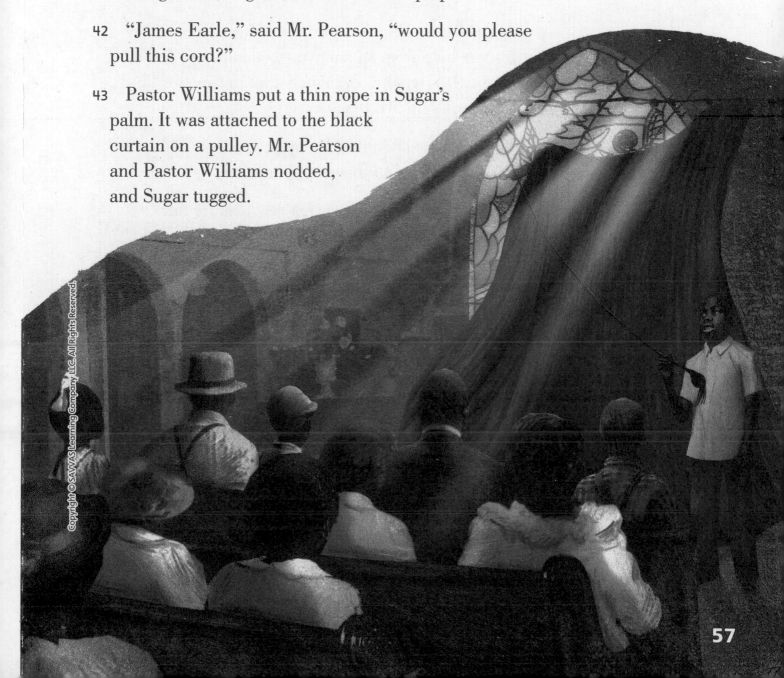

CLOSE READ

Confirm or Correct a Prediction

Highlight details Lynn Rubright includes to build suspense and details of an event that leads up to the climax. Determine if these details confirm or correct your prediction.

57

Analyze Plot

Underline the sentence that shows the climax of the plot. Why is it the turning point?

44   Suddenly the curtain fell to the floor, revealing a window with the sun shining through red, pink, purple, green, yellow, and blue stained glass. Black angels floated up and down a shimmering staircase that reached into a heaven of blue and white clouds.

45   There were gasps from the congregation as folks jumped to their feet and burst into applause. Sugar couldn't take his eyes off the beautiful window. Stumbling, he returned to his seat next to Uncle Free.

46   When folks settled down, Mr. Pearson continued. Sugar was barely listening.

47   "It was James Earle's faith in Ida Mae's dream, with some help from an anonymous donor, that led to the stain glass window bein' installed in time for this dedication," said Mr. Pearson.

48   Sugar jolted to attention. Anonymous donor? *Who that be?* he wondered. *And why they wanna keep it a secret?*

49   "The trustee board knew what was best for our physical well-bein' by buildin' a church outta brick," said Mr. Pearson. "But it was Ida Mae who knew what was best for our souls. James Earle knew it too. James Earle was even willin' to fight for it." Then Mr. Pearson led the congregation in a fresh round of applause sprinkled with loud, joyous shouts of "Amen," "Glory Be," and "Praise the Lord."

50   Pastor Williams nodded, and the choir started to sing "Glory Alleluia! A Great Day Is A-Coming." The congregation began to chant the Amen chorus. All Sugar could do was sit there staring at Mama's window.

51   Before he knew it, Sugar was swept outside onto the lawn with Uncle Free and folks from the congregation. Church women served everyone platters of fried chicken, barbecued ribs, greens, potato salad, coleslaw, baked beans, watermelon slices, fresh apple pies, and jugs of lemonade and iced tea. Mama's old friends fussed over Sugar as if he was some kind of hero.

52   While the grown-ups visited, the children ran off and played statues and tag. Sugar joined them. Stewie hung back.

53   "Hey, Stewie," Sugar hollered. "Come on."

54   Reluctantly Stewie entered into the games. Sugar acted as if nothing bad had happened between them. He knew this was not a time to hold a grudge.

55   Now and again Sugar heard Uncle Free's laugh above the din of the crowd. It reminded Sugar of how Uncle Free and Mama used to laugh together.

CLOSE READ

Analyze Plot

<u>Underline</u> the details that show how the main character responds as the falling action of the plot moves toward a resolution.

grudge a strong feeling of dislike toward someone who treated you badly

Analyze Plot
and Setting

Underline the change
Uncle Free sees in
Sugar as the falling
action moves toward
a resolution.

56   Finally Uncle Free came over and called to Sugar, "We gotta get back 'fore dark, son." They pulled themselves away from the crowd and waved good-bye.

57   "Hey, Sugar," one of the children called after them. "You promised us a ride in your boat."

58   "Someday soon," Sugar called back.

59   Uncle Free and Sugar slipped under the great weeping willow. They removed their shoes and socks, waded into the shallow water, and hopped into their boats.

60   Sugar led the way across Sun Lake. As he maneuvered into the bayou, Sugar shouted, "Look, Uncle Free! Swamp vine bloomin' there on that cypress tree."

61   "So it is, Sugar," called Uncle Free. "You noticin' all sort of things you never paid no mind to 'fore now."

62   It was true. Sugar pointed to a great blue heron daintily tiptoeing along the edge of the water. Then he looked up, and through the canopy of cypresses he saw an eagle circling high above. Sugar also noticed how the sun shining through the overhanging mosses made delicate patterns on the water and how the water sparkled in the dappled light.

63   Sugar rowed along in silence. After a while he called out, "Uncle Free! There's somethin' else I noticed. You seem to know all 'bout the stain glass window bein' in place for the dedication."

64   "Well," said Uncle Free. "I know what you know. Some anonymous donor pay for the window so it be put in the church. That's all there was to it."

65   "That ain't all there was to it, and you know it."

66   "Maybe somebody jus' want it to be a secret," said Uncle Free.

67   "That somebody be *you*!" Sugar exclaimed.

68   Uncle Free didn't say a word.

69   "Mama knew jus' what she was doin' when she sent me to live with you, didn' she, Uncle Free?" said Sugar.

70   "She sure did, son. She knew exactly what she was doin'. Lots more than I knew what she was doin'." Uncle Free let out a laugh that echoed all the way to Cypress Grove. Sugar laughed too, sounding just like Uncle Free.

71   As the sun set over the swamp, the shack came into view. "We almos' there, Uncle Free," said Sugar. "We almos' home."

CLOSE READ

Analyze Plot and Setting

Underline words and phrases that show how the setting is an important part of the plot's resolution.

Develop Vocabulary

In realistic fiction, authors use precise words to develop a story's plot. These words help the reader connect to the rising and falling action in the story.

My TURN Use a print or digital dictionary to determine the definition of the underlined words. Then explain how the words help you better understand the plot of *Mama's Window*.

Rising Action   "Impulsively Sugar reached down and grabbed a rock."

Definition:

_____

How did Sugar pick up the rock?

_____

_____

_____

Falling Action   "[Sugar] knew this was not a time to hold a grudge."

Definition:

_____

What was Sugar *not* going to do to Stewie?

_____

_____

_____

Check for Understanding

My TURN Look back at the text to answer the questions.

1. What two elements in this story help you identify it as realistic fiction?

2. How does Lynn Rubright's word choice develop your understanding of the characters?

3. Explain how one of the settings, either the church or the swamp, influences the plot.

4. Compare how Sugar feels about his life with Uncle Free by synthesizing text evidence from two or more scenes in the story.

Analyze Plot and Setting

Plot is the structure of a story's events. Plot includes **rising action**, **conflict**, **climax**, **falling action**, and **resolution**, or conclusion. A story's **setting** is the location and time in which story events take place. Setting can influence the plot because it affects how characters live and where the action takes place.

1. **My TURN** Go to the Close Read notes in *Mama's Window* and underline parts that help you analyze the elements of plot and setting.

2. **Text Evidence** Use your evidence to complete the diagram.

Event	Setting
Conflict Sugar is "furious at the church folks and mad at his uncle"	• Uncle Free's shack in the swamp • Sweet Kingdom Church
Climax	
Resolution	
How Setting Impacts Plot	

Confirm and Correct Predictions

You can use what you know about realistic fiction to make predictions about the plot. For example, characters usually face a conflict that must be resolved. As you read, you can find evidence to confirm or correct your predictions.

1. **My TURN** Go back to the Close Read notes. Highlight evidence about the plot, characters, or setting that helped you confirm or correct predictions.

2. **Text Evidence** Use your highlighted text to complete the chart. Add a check mark if your prediction was confirmed. Add an X if you corrected your prediction.

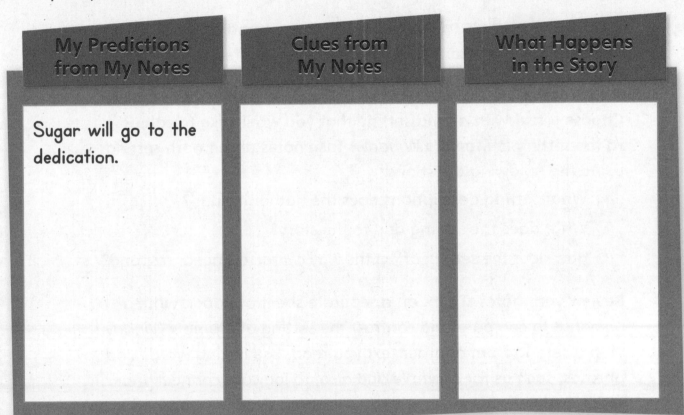

My Predictions from My Notes	Clues from My Notes	What Happens in the Story
Sugar will go to the dedication.		

3. With a partner, talk about a prediction that was not confirmed by story events. How could you use text evidence to correct or revise the prediction?

_____

_____

_____

Reflect and Share

Write to Sources In *Mama's Window*, you read about events that were directly influenced by the story's setting. Think back to texts you have read this week. What settings did you read about? How did the characters respond to those settings? Use the following process to compare and contrast the setting of *Mama's Window* with the setting of another text.

- -

Compare and Contrast Ideas Compare and contrast information in different texts to analyze how different authors develop fictional elements such as setting.

Choose a text with a vivid setting that you would like to compare to the setting in *Mama's Window*. Take notes about both settings using the following questions.

- What setting descriptions does the author include?
- What does the setting add to the story?
- How does the setting affect the way characters act or respond?

Review your notes. Then, on a separate sheet of paper, write a response to compare and contrast the setting of *Mama's Window* with a setting from another text you read. Use linking words and phrases, such as *for example* and *also*, to logically connect your ideas. End your response with a concluding statement or section that restates your ideas.

- -

Weekly Question

How do our experiences help us see the world differently?

Academic Vocabulary

Learning Goal

I can develop knowledge about language to make connections between reading and writing.

Synonyms and Antonyms A **synonym** is a word that has the same or nearly the same meaning as another word. An **antonym** is a word that means the opposite of another word. A thesaurus is a resource that can be used to check if a pair of words are synonyms or antonyms.

My TURN For each sample thesaurus entry,

1. **Define** the entry word.

2. **Choose** two synonyms and two antonyms for each word.

3. **Confirm** your definitions, synonyms, and antonyms using a print or digital dictionary or thesaurus.

Thesaurus Entries

challenge, *noun* <u>a thing that requires skill or thought</u>

Synonyms: <u>problem</u> _____

Antonyms: <u>answer</u> _____

expand, *verb* _____

Synonyms: _____ _____

Antonyms: _____ _____

conflict, *noun* _____

Synonyms: _____ _____

Antonyms: _____ _____

r-Controlled Vowels

An **r-controlled vowel** is a vowel that is followed by the letter *r*. The letter *r* influences the sound of the vowel, which is neither long nor short.

The letters *ar* can spell the vowel sound you hear in the word *car*. The letters *er, ir,* and *ur* can spell the vowel sound you hear in the word *herd*. The letters *or, ore,* and *oar* can spell the vowel sound you hear in the word *for*.

My TURN Use these activities to apply your knowledge of *r*-controlled vowels.

1. Read these words with *r*-controlled vowels: *discard, format, conserve, purchase, cardboard, confirm, margin.*

2. Write three sentences using a word with an *r*-controlled vowel.

_____

_____

_____

_____

_____

Read Like a Writer

Proverbs are a type of figurative language. They state common truths or observations and generally give advice. For example, "Two wrongs don't make a right." **Adages** are similar, but they are also very old sayings, such as "Seek and you shall find."

Model ! Read the text.

> Soren scowled when he saw that Jane was in line ahead of him. "The early bird gets the worm!" Jane said.

proverb

1. **Identify** Jane says, "The early bird gets the worm!"

2. **Question** What does the proverb tell me about what is happening in the story?

3. **Conclude** The proverb tells me that Jane got in line before Soren, so he might miss out on an opportunity.

Read the text.

> "Cleo, when you take the test," Mom said, "don't worry when others finish before you do. Slow and steady wins the race."

My TURN Follow the steps to analyze the adage and explain its meaning.

1. **Identify** Mom said _____

   and _____

2. **Question** What does the adage tell me about the story?

3. **Conclude** The adage tells me that _____

   _____.

Write for a Reader

Does using adages seem hard? Appearances are deceiving!

Adages and **proverbs** are common sayings that express general truths or observations. They also give advice or warnings. Adages are very old proverbs.

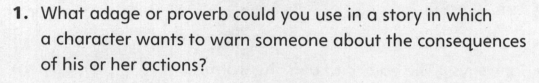 **My TURN** Think about how the use of adages and proverbs affects you as a reader. Now identify how you can use adages and proverbs to entertain and connect with your own audience.

1. What adage or proverb could you use in a story in which a character wants to warn someone about the consequences of his or her actions?

_____

_____

_____

2. Write a dialogue for the story, using the adage or proverb you chose.

_____

_____

_____

_____

_____

_____

_____

_____

_____

Spell Words with *r*-Controlled Vowels

In words with **r-controlled vowels,** the letter *r* changes the vowel sound. The letters *ar* can spell the vowel sound you hear in the word *car*. The letters *er*, *ir*, and *ur* can spell the vowel sound you hear in the word *herd*. The letters *or*, *ore*, and *oar* can spell the vowel sound you hear in the word *for*. Use what you have learned to successfully spell words with *r*-controlled vowels in your writing.

My TURN Read the words. Then spell and alphabetize the words. Make sure to spell each *r*-controlled vowel sound correctly.

SPELLING WORDS			
discard	margin	marvel	remark
orchard	portrait	foreign	dormant
format	permanent	nervous	thermal
purchase	conserve	confirm	absurd
ardent	rehearse	versus	converse

_____   _____

_____   _____

_____   _____

_____   _____

_____   _____

_____   _____

_____   _____

_____   _____

_____   _____

_____   _____

My TURN When you edit drafts of your writing, use what you know about *r*-controlled vowels to correctly spell words with those patterns.

Subject-Verb Agreement

Subject-verb agreement occurs when the form of a verb agrees, or works with, the subject. Use these subject-verb agreement rules to form the present tense.

Rule	Sample Sentences
When the subject is a **singular noun**, add *-s* or *-es* to the **verb**.	• **Sugar** stands on the dock.
When the subject is a **plural noun**, do not add an ending to the **verb**.	• **They** sing along with the choir.
When the verb is a form of *be* and the subject is named, use • *is* to agree with a **singular noun**. • *are* to agree with a **plural noun**.	• **Sugar** is happy about Mama's window. • The **congregation members** are happy about Mama's window.
When the verb is a form of *be* and the subject is a **pronoun**, use • *am* to agree with *I*. • *is* to agree with *he*, *she*, and *it*. • *are* to agree with *we*, *you*, and *they*.	• **I** am glad I read *Mama's Window*. • **He** is a young boy like me. • **We** are glad we did!

My TURN Edit this draft to correct the subject-verb agreement.

Sugar are furious when he finds out that Mama's money will be used for bricks instead of a window. Sugar go to the dedication anyway. There the congregation learn that an anonymous donor had given money so now there are a stained glass window.

Compose a Character Description: External

Learning Goal

I can use elements of narrative writing to write a realistic fiction story.

Describe the characters in a story using sensory images that convey how a character looks, sounds, and smells. In addition, describe the actions and words spoken by each character.

My TURN Read the paragraph and fill in the chart. Then complete the sentence to compose another description.

> Yan stood up and stretched. She yawned. "I need to move!" she said. Hopping up and down at the window, she added, "It has been raining for two whole days." Sita, who had been reading, stood up too. "We could do some jumping jacks," she suggested with a smile.

Character	Actions	Words
Yan		
Sita		

Yan replied with a _____

_____

_____

My TURN Include sensory details to describe characters as you compose your realistic fiction story.

Compose a Character Description: Internal

Create narrators who reveal the thoughts and feelings a character has.

- If the narrator is a character in the story, he or she may reveal personal thoughts and feelings through an internal monologue.
- If the narrator is outside of the story, he or she may reveal a character's thoughts and feelings through descriptions and through the character's actions and words.

My TURN Read the first paragraph. Notice the underlined words and phrases that reveal Beth's thoughts and feelings. Then, compose a paragraph that reveals the thoughts and feelings of a character who is with Beth. The first sentence has been done for you.

Beth caught her breath. The pony gave a snort and began backing up. <u>"What is that rustling in the leaves?" Beth wondered.</u> Her heart beat faster and faster. She patted the pony's neck and forced herself to start breathing again. <u>"I'm sure it's nothing," she thought.</u>	I was surprised to see Beth's pony backing up.

My TURN When drafting your realistic fiction story in your writing notebook, use internal monologues to describe your characters.

Compose Information About the Setting

The **setting** of a realistic fiction story consists of a real **time** and **place** at which events take place. You may reveal features of the setting while writing about characters and events.

> Lakeesha left her **bedroom** door open so she could hear the music. Her **parents were doing dishes** [1] and singing songs from the musical they all saw **last week**. Hearing that music again, here **at home in El Paso** [2], carried her back to her family's **great spring break trip** [3].
>
> [1] The character is in her bedroom after a meal.
>
> [2] The character lives in El Paso.
>
> [3] The scene takes place a week after spring break.

My TURN Think of how you would turn a place you know well into the setting of a realistic fiction story. Write details of the setting on the lines.

Sights

_____

_____

Sounds

_____

_____

Smells

_____

_____

Time of Year

_____

_____

My TURN Include details that reveal the time and place of your realistic fiction story when you compose a draft in your writing notebook.

Compose a Plot: Develop a Problem

At the beginning of a realistic fiction story, the main character faces a problem. This might be a conflict with another character. It might be a problem inside the character. The character responds to this problem through the story's events.

My TURN Read the first paragraph. Notice the underlined sentences about Lee's problem. Then, complete a new paragraph that develops the problem and Lee's response to it.

Lee hunted through the supplies around the workshop. There was plenty of cardboard, tape, and glue. However, Lee needed wood. She wanted the walls and the roof of the model to be wood. <u>Where could she get supplies at this late hour? Why had she waited to complete the project until the night before it was due?</u>

Lee could see the model in her mind, but she could not make it the way she had planned to.

My TURN Develop a problem and a character's response to it when you draft a realistic fiction story in your writing notebook.

Help readers imagine what it feels like to have the main character's problem.

Compose a Plot: Develop a Resolution

The **resolution** is how a problem is solved at the end of a story. Telling your story aloud can help you make sure you have provided enough closure.

My TURN Read the problem and the responses in the first two boxes. In the third box, complete the conclusion with the resolution to the problem.

Problem

Tai and Silvio promise to help the Smiths clean out their garage on Saturday afternoon. Then Sapra invites them to his birthday party at the same time.

How Characters Respond

Tai says, "We should tell the Smiths we need to come next Saturday instead." Silvio replies, "No—we already told the Smiths we would help this Saturday, so we have to say 'no' to Sapra."

How the Problem Is Solved

"Let's tell the Smiths about our problem," Tai suggests.

My TURN Develop a resolution as you draft the conclusion of a realistic fiction story in your writing notebook. Tell your story aloud to your Writing Club, providing descriptive details about your problem and solution.

INTERACTIVITY

MAKING MUSIC
Together

Music is a universal language that brings together people throughout the world. Through a rich variety of music, we can learn about many cultures and customs. Watch the video clip, view the images, and read the captions. How do different styles of music appeal to people?

Watch

Musician Troy Andrews's greatest inspiration is the brass band music in his hometown of New Orleans, Louisiana.

Hip-hop musicians draw crowds with their lyrical skill and danceable beats.

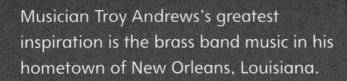

Weekly Question

How does music bring people together?

Take Notes As you view the media and review the text, write your responses on a separate sheet of paper. Describe what you see and hear, and connect the media to your personal experiences.

Samba music and dance are the main attraction of Brazil's Carnival festival, which draws more than two million people each year.

Violins, trumpets, and guitars are the ingredients of a versatile mariachi band.

Autobiography

Autobiography is one type of **narrative nonfiction**. Narratives recount events, tell a story, and use literary elements. Nonfiction is factual and tells events that really happened. An **autobiography** is a true story about a real person's life, written by that person.

- It is written in **first-person point of view**.
- The **sequence of events** is usually in chronological, or time, order.
- The author includes **facts** and **details** to create a portrait of his or her life.
- The author describes personal **thoughts**, **feelings**, and **reactions** to experiences.

An autobiography is a true story about the author's life.

TURN and TALK Tell your partner how an autobiography is similar to and different from a realistic fiction story. Use details from the anchor chart to compare and contrast. Take notes on your discussion.

My NOTES _____

_____

_____

_____

_____

Autobiography Anchor Chart

Newspaper article

Diary or journal

Narrative Nonfiction

Biography

Autobiography

- Pronouns: I, me, mine, my, myself, we, us, our

- Signal Words: first, on (date), at (time) when, until, before, after, first, second, then, finally, lastly

- Important events and people in author's life

Troy "Trombone Shorty" Andrews started playing trombone at age four. Practicing constantly, he led his own band when he was just eight! Today, he and his outstanding band, Orleans Avenue, perform for audiences all over the world. Troy Andrews says, "My trombone is my passport."

Trombone Shorty

Preview Vocabulary

As you read *Trombone Shorty*, pay attention to these vocabulary words. Notice how they add detail to Troy Andrews's life story.

> inspiration   create   heritage
>
> festival   performance

Read

Before you read, preview the text and art in *Trombone Shorty*. Set a **purpose** for reading based on your preview. Then follow these strategies as you read the **autobiography**.

Notice
details about Troy Andrews's experiences.

Generate Questions
that will help you evaluate the truth of statements.

First Read

Connect
what you read about Troy Andrews's experiences with your own experiences.

Respond
by telling a partner what you did and did not like about the text.

TROMBONE SHORTY

by TROY "TROMBONE SHORTY" ANDREWS

illustrated by Caldecott Honor winner
BRYAN COLLIER

AUDIO

ANNOTATE

Explain Author's Purpose

<u>Underline</u> one or more sentences that show why Troy Andrews is writing this text.

1 WHERE Y'AT?

2 WHERE Y'AT?

3 We have our own way of living down here in New Orleans, and our own way of talking, too. And that's what we like to say when we want to tell a friend hello.

4 So, WHERE Y'AT?

5 Lots of kids have nicknames, but I want to tell you the story of how I got mine. Just like when you listen to your favorite song, let's start at the beginning. Because this is a story about music.

6   But before you can understand how much music means to me, you have to know how important it is to my hometown, my greatest inspiration.

7   I grew up in a neighborhood in New Orleans called Tremé. Any time of day or night, you could hear music floating in the air.

8   And there was music in my house, too. My big brother, James, played the trumpet so loud you could hear him halfway across town! He was the leader of his own band, and my friends and I would pretend to be in the band, too.

9   "FOLLOW ME," James would say.

CLOSE READ

Explain Author's Purpose

Underline the detail Troy Andrews wants readers to understand first about his life.

inspiration something that gives someone the desire to do something

85

CLOSE READ

Make Connections

Highlight a detail that you can relate, or connect, to your own life.

10   There's one time every year that's more exciting than any other: Mardi Gras! Parades fill the streets, and beaded necklaces are thrown through the air to the crowd.

11   I loved the brass bands, with their own trumpets, trombones, saxophones, and the biggest brass instrument of them all, the tuba—which rested over the musician's head like an elephant's trunk!

12   WHERE Y'AT?

13   WHERE Y'AT? the musicians would call.

14   All day long I could see brass bands parade by my house while my neighbors danced along. I loved these parades during Mardi Gras because they made everyone forget about their troubles for a little while. People didn't have a lot of money in Tremé, but we always had a lot of music.

CLOSE READ

Explain Author's Purpose

Underline a sentence that gives important information about Tremé.

Vocabulary in Context

Context clues are words and sentences around a word that you can use to determine the word's meaning. These clues can appear in the same sentence or in surrounding sentences.

Define the word *gumbo*. Then <u>underline</u> context clues that support your definition of *gumbo*.

create make or produce something

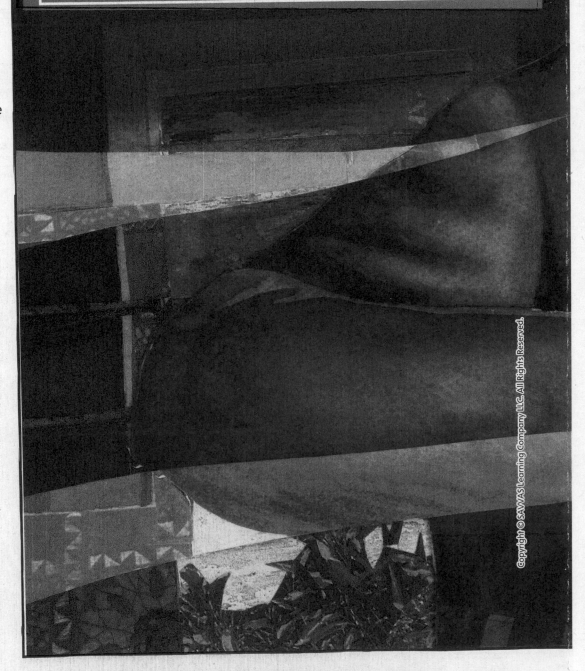

15   I listened to all these sounds and mixed them together, just like how we make our food. We take one big pot and throw in sausage, crab, shrimp, chicken, vegetables, rice—whatever's in the kitchen— and stir it all together and let it cook. When it's done, it's the most delicious taste you've ever tried. We call it gumbo, and that's what I wanted my music to sound like—different styles combined to create my own *musical* gumbo!

Make Connections

Highlight details in the text that you can connect to your own life.

Explain Author's Purpose

Underline the sentence that tells how Troy Andrews earned his nickname.

16   But first I needed an instrument. The great thing about music is that you don't even need a real instrument to play. So my friends and I decided to make our own.

17   We might have sounded different from the real brass bands, but we felt like the greatest musicians of Tremé. We were making music, and that's all that mattered.

18   Then one day I found a broken trombone that looked too beaten up to make music anymore. It didn't sound perfect, but finally with a real instrument in my hand, I was ready to play.

19   The next time the parade went by my house, I grabbed that trombone and headed out into the street. My brother James noticed me playing along and smiled proudly.

20   "TROMBONE SHORTY!" he called out, because the instrument was twice my size!

21   WHERE Y'AT?

Make Connections

Highlight details that you can use to make a connection to your own experiences.

22   From that day on, everyone called me Trombone Shorty! I took that trombone everywhere I went and never stopped playing. I was so small that sometimes I fell right over to the ground because it was so heavy. But I always got back up, and I learned to hold it up high.

23   I listened to my brother play songs over and over, and I taught myself those songs, too. I practiced day and night, and sometimes I fell asleep with my trombone in my hands.

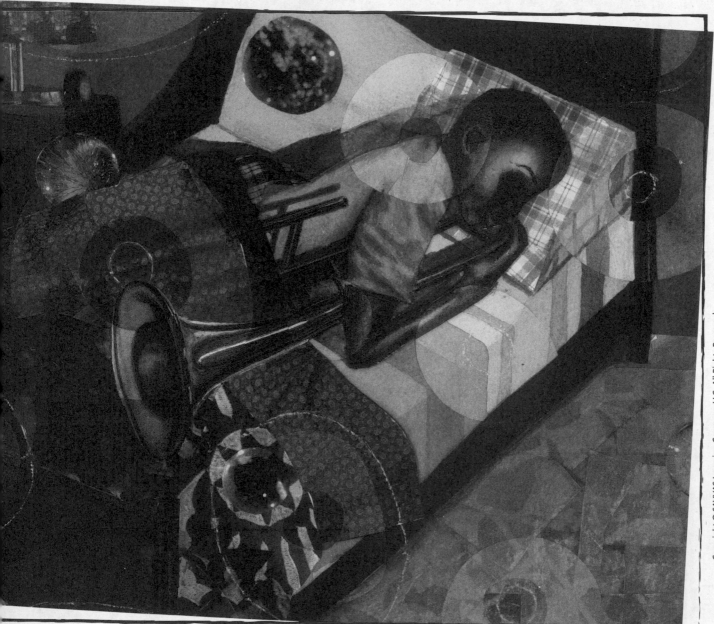

24   One day my mom surprised me with tickets to the New Orleans Jazz & Heritage Festival, the best and biggest music festival in town. We went to see Bo Diddley, who my mom said was one of the most important musicians of all time. As I watched him onstage, I raised my trombone to my lips and started to play along. He stopped his band in the middle of the song and asked the crowd, "Who's that playing out there?"

25   Everyone started pointing, but Bo Diddley couldn't see me because I was the smallest one in the place! So my mom held me up in the air and said, "That's my son. Trombone Shorty!"

26   "Well, TROMBONE SHORTY, come on up here!" Bo Diddley said.

27   The crowd passed me overhead until I was standing on the stage next to Bo Diddley himself! I walked right up to the microphone and held my trombone high up in the air, ready to blow.

28   "What do you want to play?" Bo Diddley asked.

29   "FOLLOW ME," I said.

Explain Author's Purpose

Underline sentences that tell you why this event was important in Troy Andrews's life.

Make Connections

30   After I played with Bo Diddley, I knew I was ready to have my own band. I got my friends together, and we called ourselves the 5 O'Clock Band, because that was the time we went out to play each day after finishing our homework.

31   We played all around New Orleans. I practiced and practiced, and soon my brother James asked me to join his band. When people wondered who the kid in his band was, he'd proudly say, "That's my little brother, TROMBONE SHORTY!"

32   WHERE Y'AT?

CLOSE READ

Explain Author's Purpose

<u>Underline</u> details that Troy Andrews repeats in order to support his purpose for writing.

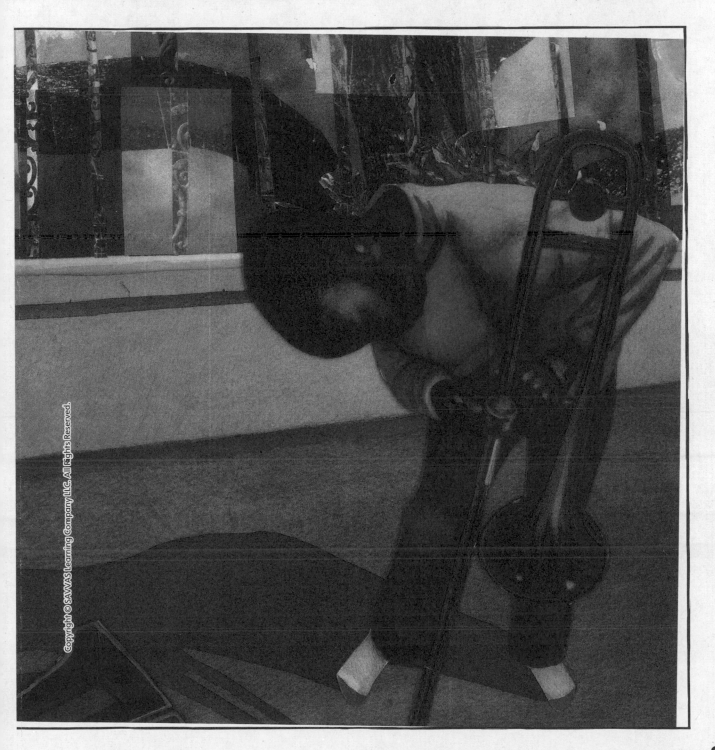

33   And now I have my own band, called Trombone Shorty & Orleans Avenue, named after a street in Tremé. I've played all around the world, but I always come back to New Orleans. And when I'm home, I make sure to keep my eyes on the younger musicians in town and help them out, just like my brother did for me.

Explain Author's Purpose

Underline details that relate to information Troy Andrews introduced at the beginning of the text.

34   Today I play at the same New Orleans jazz festival where I once played with Bo Diddley. And when the performance ends, I lead a parade of musicians around, just like I used to do in the streets of Tremé with my friends.

35   WHERE Y'AT? WHERE Y'AT?

36   I still keep my trombone in my hands, and I will never let it go.

Explain Author's Purpose

Underline details that Troy Andrews includes to show readers a connection between his current life and his childhood experiences.

performance a public presentation to entertain an audience

Develop Vocabulary

In autobiographies, authors use precise language and vivid details to describe their life stories and engage readers.

My TURN Demonstrate the meanings of the words by completing the sentences. Make connections between the pairs of words that help you visualize the life events described in *Trombone Shorty*.

Heritage and **festival** are connected because

_____

_____

Festival and **performance** are connected because

_____

_____

Inspiration and **create** are connected because

_____

_____

Heritage and **inspiration** are connected because

_____

_____

Check for Understanding

My TURN Look back at the texts to answer the questions.

1. How is autobiography different from realistic fiction? Use *Trombone Shorty* and *Out of My Mind* as examples in your answer.

2. Why does Troy Andrews compare the music in Tremé to gumbo?

3. How is the structure of this text similar to the structure of a song? Cite evidence from the text to support your answer.

4. Do you think repetition is an effective literary technique for an autobiography? Support your evaluation with details from *Trombone Shorty*.

Explain Author's Purpose

An **author's purpose**, or reason for writing, may be to inform, entertain, persuade, or express ideas and feelings. Authors often have more than one purpose for writing.

1. **My TURN** Go to the Close Read notes in *Trombone Shorty*. Underline the parts that help you explain the author's purpose.

2. **Text Evidence** Use the parts you underlined to complete the chart and explain the author's purpose.

Identify Author's Purpose

Text Evidence	Text Evidence	Text Evidence

Explain how the text evidence you chose supports the author's purpose.

Make Connections

You can make connections when reading a text by identifying details that relate to your own life or to ideas in other texts you have read. Making these connections can help you identify the **author's message**, or the big idea the author wants readers to understand. The message is communicated through details in the text.

1. **My TURN** Go back to the Close Read notes and highlight the parts that you connected with personally.

2. **Text Evidence** Use the text evidence you highlighted to complete the chart and explain the author's message.

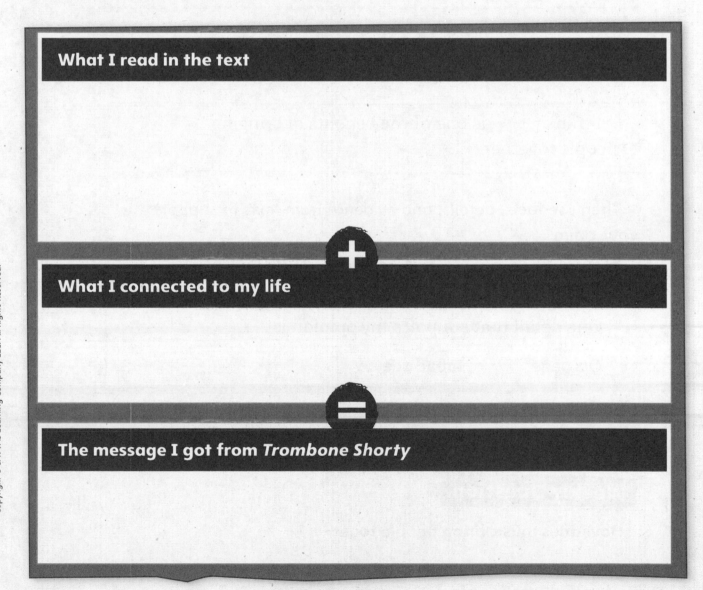

What I read in the text

+

What I connected to my life

=

The message I got from *Trombone Shorty*

Reflect and Share

Write to Sources In *Trombone Shorty*, music brings performers together in bands, listeners together in parades, and schoolchildren and jazz legends together on stage. What other texts have you read that describe something that brings people together? On a separate sheet of paper, state an opinion about the benefits of bringing people together. Use examples from more than one text to support your response.

- -

State and Support a Claim When writing argumentative texts, begin by identifying the opinion, or claim, you will support.

> I think _____ is one of the benefits of bringing people together.

Then use facts, details, and evidence from texts to support your claim.

> The text says . . .
>
> One detail that supports my opinion is . . .
>
> On page _____ , I read that . . .

- -

Weekly Question

How does music bring people together?

Academic Vocabulary

Learning Goal

I can develop knowledge about language to make connections between reading and writing.

Context clues are words and phrases in a sentence or surrounding sentences that help you determine the meaning of unfamiliar words.

My TURN For each sentence or sentences,

1. **Underline** the academic vocabulary word.

2. **Highlight** the context clue or clues.

3. **Write** a synonym of the word based on the clues.

The coach rotated through the team roster throughout the game so that everyone had a chance to participate.

Synonym: _____

As the number of users grew, the social network expanded to include more and more people.

Synonym: _____

During the debate, one side presented an argument, and then the other side gave a different perspective. The conflicting points of view left the audience with many questions.

Synonym: _____

Although the climb itself was difficult, the biggest challenge for the climbers was trying to stay warm as they climbed higher and higher.

Synonym: _____

After winning the story competition, Maria knew this accomplishment would motivate her to keep writing.

Synonym: _____

Final Stable Syllables

Each syllable has one vowel sound. A **final stable syllable** is an ending syllable. These are examples of final stable syllables: consonant plus -le, -tion, and -sion. In the word table, the letters ble spell the sound you hear in the word bull. The letters tion and sion spell the sound you hear in the words shun, nation, and decision. When you come to a word with one of these final stable syllables, you will be able to read it.

My TURN Read each word with a final stable syllable. Then divide the word into syllables. To determine correct syllabication, use a print or digital dictionary.

Words with Final Stable Syllables	Words Divided into Syllables
trouble	trou / ble
solution	
allusion	
people	
nation	
decision	
middle	
connection	

Read Like a Writer

Writers include graphic features, such as illustrations, to convey information in a visual way. Illustrations can support text details, clarify complex ideas, or contribute to the meaning and beauty of a text.

Model ! Reread paragraph 17 from *Trombone Shorty* and look at the related illustration.

1. Identify The illustration shows Trombone Shorty and his friends with imaginary crowns on their heads.

2. Question How does the illustration help me understand why this event is important?

3. Conclude The illustration helps me understand that making music made Trombone Shorty and his friends feel proud and confident, like kings.

Reread paragraph 33 and look at the illustrations that surround it.

My TURN Follow the steps to closely read the text. Then analyze Troy Andrews's use of graphic features.

1. Identify The illustration shows _____

_____

2. Question How does the illustration help me understand why this event is important?

3. Conclude The illustration helps me understand _____

_____

_____

Write for a Reader

Illustrations show details of important events.

Authors add graphic features to a text to engage readers, to visually express information, and to add meaning. Illustrations often complement the ideas and events in a text, which gives readers a deeper understanding than reading the words alone.

My TURN Think about how the illustrations in *Trombone Shorty* support the meaning of events. Now identify how you could use illustrations to show meaning in your own writing.

1. If you were writing about a proud moment in your life, what illustrations could you include to help the reader understand how you felt?

_____

_____

2. Create an illustration of a proud moment in your life. Then, write a short paragraph about that moment.

_____

_____

_____

_____

Spell Words with Final Stable Syllables

Final stable syllables include *-tion*, *-sion*, and a consonant plus *-le*. Some words, such as *nation* and *table*, already have these final syllables. In other cases, the spelling of the base word may change when a final stable syllable is added. For example, drop the final *se* in *confuse* and add *-sion* to spell *confusion*.

My TURN   Read the words. Sort and spell the words by their final stable syllables.

SPELLING WORDS

pollute	pollution	revolve	revolution
generate	generation	decorate	decoration
confuse	confusion	erode	erosion
conclude	conclusion	timetable	castle
adorable	stifle	stable	vehicle

---

consonant + *le*

_____

_____

_____

_____

-*tion*

_____

_____

_____

-*sion*

_____

_____

_____

no final stable syllable

_____

_____

_____

_____

Irregular Verbs

Regular verbs add -ed to show the past tense. **Irregular verbs**, however, change their spelling in the simple past tense. Learn the past-tense forms of irregular verbs or look them up in a dictionary. This will help you correctly use and spell these verbs in your own writing.

Regular	Irregular	Present Tense	Past Tense
x		pick(s)	picked
x		walk(s)	walked
	x	know(s)	knew
	x	make(s)	made
	x	go(es)	went
	x	take(s)	took
	x	fall(s)	fell

My TURN Edit this draft to change the verbs from present tense to past tense. Make sure to use the correct spelling for each regular or irregular verb.

Trombone Shorty knows he wants to play in a band. He takes an old trombone and fixes it up. He and his friends go out in the street and play music. Trombone Shorty falls in love with performing. Later, Trombone Shorty and his band go all over the world to perform.

Compose from a Point of View

Learning Goal

I can use elements of narrative writing to write a realistic fiction story.

A narrator who tells a story from the first-person point of view is one of the characters in the story. That narrator uses the first-person pronouns: *I, me, my, mine, we, us, our, ours.*

A narrator who is not a character in the story speaks from the third-person point of view. That narrator refers to characters using the third-person pronouns: *he, him, his, she, her, hers, they, them, their, theirs.*

My TURN If a sentence is written from the first-person point of view, rewrite it from the third-person point of view. If a sentence is written from the third-person point of view, rewrite it in the first-person point of view.

1. I told my friend that we should buy hats. _____

_____

2. Bobby and Ray shook hands before the match. _____

_____

3. We took our seats. _____

_____

4. The contestants took their places. _____

_____

My TURN Write consistently from one point of view when you draft a realistic fiction story in your writing notebook.

Compose an Event Sequence

The events in a realistic fiction story take place one after the other, in a natural and believable sequence. Use transitional words and phrases to make the sequence clear.

Sample Transition Words		Sample Transition Phrases	
first	therefore	in addition	due to
next	so	at the beginning	for example
then	because	in the end	in response

My TURN Read the following events and determine a natural sequence. In your writing notebook, rewrite the events in order using transitional words and phrases.

_____1_____ Gem and Meena need a project for the science fair.

_____ Gem and Meena decide to use a cactus and a tomato plant.

_____ They ask their teacher for help planning the experiment.

_____ They decide to do an experiment about plants and water.

_____ The teacher suggests giving two different plants the same amount of water.

My TURN Compose a natural event sequence when you draft a realistic fiction story in your writing notebook.

Compose Dialogue

Dialogue is a written conversation between people. It is written as quotations. Speakers take turns. With each new speaker, the dialogue begins a new line.

Lael asked, "Where can I see the tigers?"

"In the big cat building," the zookeeper replied.

Characters can express their own thoughts through an internal monologue, which can be written the same way as regular dialogue.

Lael wondered, "When will I ever see tigers?"

My TURN Rewrite the text as dialogue. Follow the example of the first two lines.

Without Dialogue	With Dialogue
Ike asked Ije to pass the potatoes. Ije asked if she could take some first. Ike said no, but then Dad told Ike to let Ije have some. Ike complained that Ije always took too much. Mom lifted the bowl of potatoes off the table and said she would put a fair amount on each child's plate.	"Ije, would you please pass the potatoes?" Ike said. "Only after I take some first," Ije replied.

My TURN Compose dialogue as you write the draft of a realistic fiction story in your writing notebook.

115

Plan Illustrations

Realistic fiction stories may include illustrations that help readers visualize characters, settings, and events. Often, the illustrations build on specific descriptions in the text.

My TURN Read the paragraph. In the box, draw or describe an illustration that reflects and builds on the text.

> Deshawn wondered how he could fit his little brothers and sisters into the two red wagons. He needed to pull more than the children to the library. He had to take their blankets in case they got cold, their snacks in case they got hungry, their juice in case they got thirsty, and their stuffed animals in case they got tired!

My TURN Build on specific descriptions in the text when you plan illustrations for the draft of a realistic fiction story in your writing notebook.

Select a Genre

Writers can decide on a genre for the topic they choose and consider the purpose and audience for their writing to help them plan their first draft. For example, you might want to write a book review for your classmates so they can learn more about a book you read. Brainstorming or mapping can help you decide on your topic, purpose, and audience. Writers can choose from many genres. Each major genre has many subgenres. The following table shows just some.

Poetry	Narrative		Opinion	Informational Text
Free Verse	Fiction	Nonfiction	Argument	Essay
Narrative Poetry	Realistic Fiction	Biography	Persuasive Essay	Feature Article
Limerick	Fables and Folktales	Autobiography	Persuasive Speech	News Article
Sonnet	Myths and Legends	Personal Narrative	Book Review	Book Review
Song	Historical Fiction	Narrative Nonfiction	Letter to the Editor	Research Report
Lyric Poetry	Science Fiction	Personal Reflection	Editorial	How-to Essay

My TURN Identify a topic, purpose, and audience. Then select any genre, and plan a draft by freewriting your ideas in your writing notebook.

NEW PLACES
Affect How We Eat

HOW DO WE GET OUR FOOD

GLOBAL MARKETS Trade between countries brings us foods we do not grow at home. Approximately 15 percent of our food supply is imported.

NARROW FOCUS Three-quarters of the world's food production comes from a dozen plants and five animal species.

GO WITH THE GROW Farming in the United States depends heavily on migrant seasonal workers. These workers move from place to place as different agricultural products become ready for harvest.

What do you call a plant that you can use as kindling, lunch, or shampoo? Or one that you can use to write a letter, sail a ship, or make a shirt? Many cultures have grown multipurpose crops like these.

Different climates produce different food crops. Sugarcane and coffee are grown in the tropical region of Brazil, and much of the world's rice comes from warm, humid regions in China. Cold weather is required for the majority of the wheat grown in the United States.

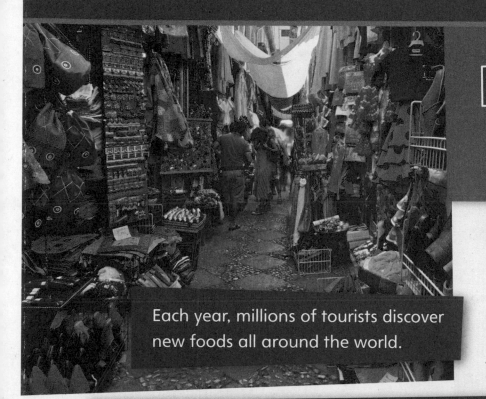

Each year, millions of tourists discover new foods all around the world.

Weekly Question

How do new places influence us?

TURN and TALK What countries do you think are involved in producing the food you eat every day? How might your diet be different if all of your food came from your own region?

In the United States, the demand is growing for skilled chefs and head cooks. These professionals combine ingredients from all over the world to make delicious and unique creations.

Spotlight on Genre

Fiction and Realistic Fiction

Fiction is a story involving made-up characters and events. **Realistic fiction** describes characters and events that could be real. The perspective from which a fictional story is told is the narrative **point of view**.

- In **first-person point of view**, the narrator, or storyteller, describes events from his or her own perspective using pronouns such as *I*, *me*, *we*, and *us*.
- In **third-person point of view**, the narrator is outside the action and describes events and the thoughts and feelings of characters using pronouns such as *he*, *she*, *they*, and *them*.
- The **voice** of the narrator, developed through an author's word choice, gives the story a unique "sound."

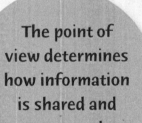

The point of view determines how information is shared and presented.

TURN and TALK With a partner, discuss different purposes for reading *Weslandia* and "The Circuit." For example, you may want to compare the effects of narrators' points of view. Set your purpose for reading these texts.

My PURPOSE _____

_____

_____

	FIRST-PERSON	**THIRD-PERSON**
NARRATOR	a character in the story who is involved in the action	an outsider who is not involved in the action
EFFECTS OF POINT OF VIEW	limits information to one person's view · allows readers to connect more closely to narrator · requires readers to determine whether narrator is reliable or trustworthy	provides information on one or more characters · allows readers to understand behaviors and motivations of one or many characters

Paul Fleischman has a fascination with history. In fact, he once lived in a house with wood heating, no electricity, and no phone. He likes to learn historical facts about how people used to dress, eat, and work. He often brings these kinds of facts into his storytelling.

Weslandia

Preview Vocabulary

As you read *Weslandia*, pay attention to these vocabulary words. Notice how the narrator uses these words to describe characters' thoughts and feelings.

miserable	thrilling

Read

To read with **purpose**, ask yourself, *How can I identify point of view in this text?* Before reading, preview *Weslandia*. Then follow these strategies as you read.

Notice	**Generate Questions**
the literary point of view from which the story is told.	about what the author wants you to understand.

First Read

Connect	**Respond**
what you read in this text to what you have experienced in your own community.	by discussing what you thought about as you read.

Weslandia

by PAUL FLEISCHMAN

 AUDIO

 ANNOTATE

Compare and Contrast Point of View

<u>Underline</u> pronouns that help you identify the narrator's point of view.

miserable deeply unhappy or uncomfortable

1   "Of course he's miserable," moaned Wesley's mother. "He sticks out."

2   "Like a nose," snapped his father.

3   Listening through the heating vent, Wesley knew they were right. He was an outcast from the civilization around him.

4   He alone in his town disliked pizza and soda, alarming his mother and the school nurse. He found professional football stupid. He'd refused to shave half his head, the hairstyle worn by all the other boys, despite his father's bribe of five dollars.

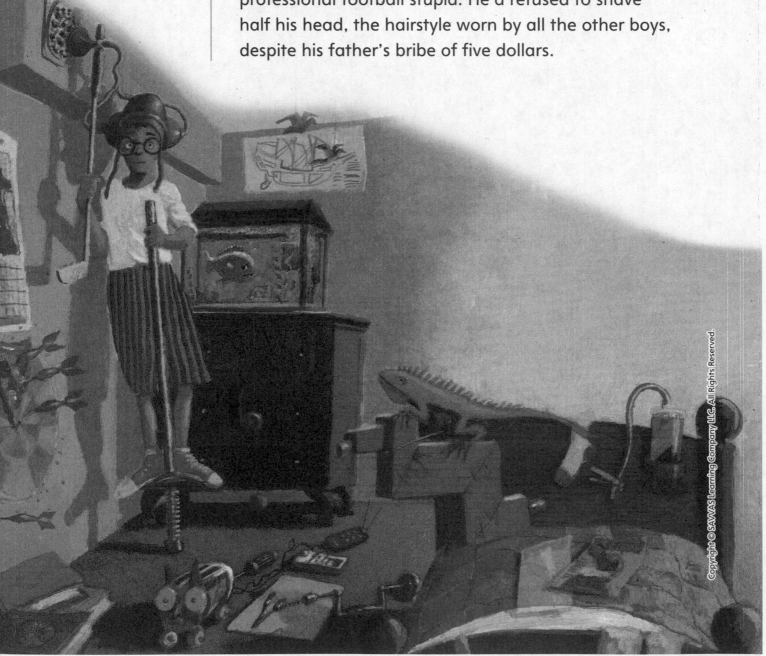

5   Passing his neighborhood's two styles of housing—garage on the left and garage on the right—Wesley alone dreamed of more exciting forms of shelter. He had no friends, but plenty of tormentors.

6   Fleeing them was the only sport he was good at.

7   Each afternoon his mother asked him what he'd learned in school that day.

8   "That seeds are carried great distances by the wind," he answered on Wednesday.

9   "That each civilization has its staple food crop," he answered on Thursday.

10   "That school's over and I should find a good summer project," he answered on Friday.

11   As always, his father mumbled, "I'm sure you'll use that knowledge often."

Generate Questions

Highlight a detail that helps you form a question about the difference between the story's narrator and main character.

Compare and Contrast Point of View

Underline sentences that show how the narrator reveals Wesley's inner thoughts.

12   Suddenly, Wesley's thoughts shot sparks. His eyes blazed. His father was right! He could actually use what he'd learned that week for a summer project that would top all others. He would grow his own staple food crop—and found his own civilization!

13   The next morning he turned over a plot of ground in his yard. That night a wind blew in from the west. It raced through the trees and set his curtains snapping. Wesley lay awake, listening. His land was being planted.

14   Five days later the first seedlings appeared. "You'll have almighty bedlam on your hands if you don't get those weeds out," warned his neighbor.

15   "Actually, that's my crop," replied Wesley. "In this type of garden there are no weeds."

16   Following ancient tradition, Wesley's fellow gardeners grew tomatoes, beans, Brussels sprouts, and nothing else. Wesley found it thrilling to open his land to chance, to invite the new and unknown.

17   The plants shot up past his knees, then his waist. They seemed to be all of the same sort. Wesley couldn't find them in any plant book.

18   "Are those tomatoes, beans, or Brussels sprouts?" asked Wesley's neighbor.

19   "None of the above," replied Wesley.

Compare and Contrast Point of View

Underline text details that give you insight into Wesley's thoughts and responses.

20   Fruit appeared, yellow at first, then blushing to magenta. Wesley picked one and sliced through the rind to the juicy purple center. He took a bite and found the taste an entrancing blend of peach, strawberry, pumpkin pie, and flavors he had no name for.

21   Ignoring the shelf of cereals in the kitchen, Wesley took to breakfasting on the fruit. He dried half a rind to serve as a cup, built his own squeezing device, and drank the fruit's juice throughout the day.

22   Pulling up a plant, he found large tubers on the roots. These he boiled, fried, or roasted on the family barbecue, seasoning them with a pinch of the plant's highly aromatic leaves.

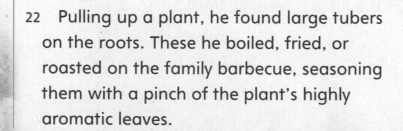

23   It was hot work tending to his crop. To keep off the sun, Wesley wove himself a hat from strips of the plant's woody bark. His success with the hat inspired him to devise a spinning wheel and loom on which he wove a loose-fitting robe from the stalks' soft inner fibers.

24   Unlike jeans, which he found scratchy and heavy, the robe was comfortable, reflected the sun, and offered myriad opportunities for pockets.

Generate Questions

Highlight words that you can use to ask or answer a question about the narrative point of view.

Generate Questions

Highlight details that help you ask or answer a question about how Wesley gets along with others.

25   His schoolmates were scornful, then curious. Grudgingly, Wesley allowed them ten minutes apiece at his mortar, crushing the plant's seeds to collect the oil.

26   This oil had a tangy scent and served him both as suntan lotion and mosquito repellent. He rubbed it on his face each morning and sold small amounts to his former tormentors at the price of ten dollars per bottle.

27 "What's happened to your watch?" asked his mother one day.

28 Wesley admitted that he no longer wore it. He told time by the stalk that he used as a sundial and had divided the day into eight segments—the number of petals on the plant's flowers.

29 He'd adopted a new counting system as well, based likewise upon the number eight. His domain, home to many such innovations, he named "Weslandia."

Generate Questions

Highlight text evidence that you can use to ask or answer a question about how the narrator reveals the thoughts and feelings of Wesley's mother.

Compare and Contrast Point of View

How does the narrator help the reader understand Wesley's motivation? Underline text evidence.

30   Uninterested in traditional sports, Wesley made up his own. These were designed for a single player and used many different parts of the plant. His spectators looked on with envy.

31   Realizing that more players would offer him more scope, Wesley invented other games that would include his schoolmates, games rich with strategy and complex scoring systems. He tried to be patient with the other players' blunders.

32   August was unusually hot. Wesley built himself a platform and took to sleeping in the middle of Weslandia. He passed the evenings playing a flute he'd fashioned from a stalk or gazing up at the sky, renaming the constellations.

33 His parents noted Wesley's improved morale. "It's the first time in years he's looked happy," said his mother.

34 Wesley gave them a tour of Weslandia.

35 "What do you call this plant?" asked his father. Not knowing its name, Wesley had begun calling it "swist," from the sound of its leaves rustling in the breeze.

36 In like manner, he'd named his new fabrics, games, and foods, until he'd created an entire language.

37 Mixing the plant's oil with soot, Wesley made a passable ink. As the finale to his summer project, he used the ink and his own eighty-letter alphabet to record the history of his civilization's founding.

38 In September, Wesley returned to school . . .

39 He had no shortage of friends.

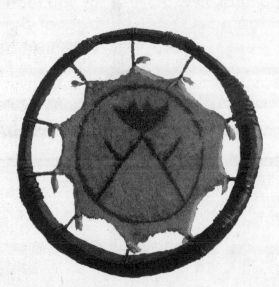

Compare and Contrast Point of View

Underline a sentence in which the narrator describes a change in the characters' feelings.

Francisco Jiménez wrote "The Circuit" based on his own experiences. As a child, he worked with his parents in California fields. Jiménez writes inspiring books for children and teens to help others achieve their own successes. He writes in both Spanish and English.

The Circuit

Preview Vocabulary

As you read "The Circuit" from *The Circuit*, pay attention to these vocabulary words. Notice how the narrator uses these words to describe his own thoughts and feelings.

recover	instinctively	savoring

Read and Compare

To read with **purpose**, ask yourself, *How does the narrative point of view in this text compare to the previous text?* Active readers of **fiction** follow these strategies when they read a text the first time.

Notice the point of view of the narrator.

Generate Questions as you read to keep track of characters' responses to events.

First Read

Connect this text to other texts. How are the texts similar?

Respond by describing the narrator.

The CIRCUIT

by Francisco Jiménez

Compare and Contrast Point of View

Underline the pronouns that help you identify whether the point of view in this selection is first or third person.

1 It was that time of year again. Ito, the strawberry sharecropper, did not smile. It was natural. The peak of the strawberry season was over and the last few days the workers, most of them *braceros,* were not picking as many boxes as they had during the months of June and July.

2 As the last days of August disappeared, so did the number of *braceros.* Sunday, only one—the best picker—came to work. I liked him. Sometimes we talked during our half-hour lunch break. That is how I found out he was from Jalisco, the same state in Mexico my family was from. That Sunday was the last time I saw him.

3   When the sun had tired and sunk behind the mountains, Ito signaled us that it was time to go home. "*Ya esora*," he yelled in his broken Spanish. Those were the words I waited for twelve hours a day, every day, seven days a week, week after week. And the thought of not hearing them again saddened me.

4   As we drove home Papá did not say a word. With both hands on the wheel, he stared at the dirt road. My older brother, Roberto, was also silent. He leaned his head back and closed his eyes. Once in a while he cleared from his throat the dust that blew in from outside.

5   Yes, it was that time of year. When I opened the front door to the shack, I stopped. Everything we owned was neatly packed in cardboard boxes. Suddenly I felt even more the weight of hours, days, weeks, and months of work. I sat down on a box. The thought of having to move to Fresno and knowing what was in store for me there brought tears to my eyes.

6   That night I could not sleep. I lay in bed thinking about how much I hated this move.

7   A little before five o'clock in the morning, Papá woke everyone up. A few minutes later, the yelling and screaming of my little brothers and sister, for whom the move was a great adventure, broke the silence of dawn. Shortly, the barking of the dogs accompanied them.

CLOSE READ

Compare and Contrast Point of View

Underline details the narrator uses to describe his emotional reactions to moving. How do the details support the author's use of point of view?

CLOSE READ

Vocabulary in Context

Context clues are words and phrases that can be used to define other words in a text.

<u>Underline</u> words that provide context clues to the meaning of *jalopy*.

8   While we packed the breakfast dishes, Papá went outside to start the "*Carcachita.*" That was the name Papá gave his old black Plymouth. He bought it in a used-car lot in Santa Rosa. Papá was very proud of his little jalopy. He had a right to be proud of it. He spent a lot of time looking at other cars before buying this one. When he finally chose the *Carcachita,* he checked it thoroughly before driving it out of the car lot. He examined every inch of the car. He listened to the motor, tilting his head from side to side like a parrot, trying to detect any noises that spelled car trouble. After being satisfied with the looks and sounds of the car, Papá then insisted on knowing who the original owner was. He never did find out from the car salesman, but he bought the car anyway. Papá figured the original owner must have been an important man because behind the rear seat of the car he found a blue necktie.

9   Papá parked the car out in front and left the motor running. "*Listo*," he yelled. Without saying a word Roberto and I began to carry the boxes out to the car. Roberto carried the two big boxes and I carried the two smaller ones. Papá then threw the mattress on top of the car roof and tied it with ropes to the front and rear bumpers.

CLOSE READ

Compare and Contrast Point of View

Underline a sentence that tells you how the narrator feels about this move.

10   Everything was packed except Mamá's pot. It was an old large galvanized pot she had picked up at an army surplus store in Santa Maria. The pot had many dents and nicks, and the more dents and nicks it acquired the more Mamá liked it. "*Mi olla*," she used to say proudly.

11   I held the front door open as Mamá carefully carried out her pot by both handles, making sure not to spill the cooked beans. When she got to the car, Papá reached out to help her with it. Roberto opened the rear car door and Papá gently placed it on the floor behind the front seat. All of us then climbed in. Papá sighed, wiped the sweat from his forehead with his sleeve, and said wearily: "*Es todo*."

12   As we drove away, I felt a lump in my throat. I turned around and looked at our little shack for the last time.

Generate Questions

Highlight details you can use to compare and contrast events described by this narrator to events described by the narrator of *Weslandia*.

13   At sunset we drove into a labor camp near Fresno. Since Papá did not speak English, Mamá asked the camp foreman if he needed any more workers. "We don't need no more," said the foreman, scratching his head. "Check with Sullivan down the road. Can't miss him. He lives in a big white house with a fence around it."

14   When we got there, Mamá walked up to the house. She went through a white gate, past a row of rose bushes, up the stairs to the house. She rang the doorbell. The porch light went on and a tall husky man came out. They exchanged a few words. After the man went in, Mamá clasped her hands and hurried back to the car. "We have work! Mr. Sullivan said we can stay there the whole season," she said, gasping and pointing to an old garage near the stables.

15   The garage was worn out by the years. It had no windows. The walls, eaten by termites, strained to support the roof full of holes. The dirt floor, populated by earth worms, looked like a gray road map.

16   That night, by the light of a kerosene lamp, we unpacked and cleaned our new home. Roberto swept away the loose dirt, leaving the hard ground. Papá plugged the holes in the walls with old newspapers and tin can tops. Mamá fed my little brothers and sister. Papá and Roberto then brought in the mattress and placed it on the far corner of the garage. "Mamá, you and the little ones sleep on the mattress. Roberto, Panchito, and I will sleep outside under the trees," Papá said.

17   Early the next morning Mr. Sullivan showed
us where his crop was, and after breakfast, Papá,
Roberto, and I headed for the vineyard to pick.

18   Around nine o'clock the temperature had risen
to almost one hundred degrees. I was completely
soaked in sweat and my mouth felt as if I had been
chewing on a handkerchief. I walked over to the
end of the row, picked up the jug of water we had
brought, and began drinking. "Don't drink too
much; you'll get sick," Roberto shouted. No sooner
had he said that than I felt sick to my stomach. I
dropped to my knees and let the jug roll off my
hands. I remained motionless with my eyes glued on
the hot sandy ground. All I could hear was the drone
of insects. Slowly I began to recover. I poured water
over my face and neck and watched the dirty water
run down my arms to the ground.

CLOSE READ

Compare and Contrast Point of View

How does this narrator experience heat? <u>Underline</u> descriptions the narrator uses.

recover return to normal health or strength

Generate Questions

Highlight a detail you can use to ask or answer a question about why the narrator and his brother hide.

instinctively without thinking about how to do it

19   I still felt dizzy when we took a break to eat lunch. It was past two o'clock and we sat underneath a large walnut tree that was on the side of the road. While we ate, Papá jotted down the number of boxes we had picked. Roberto drew designs on the ground with a stick. Suddenly I noticed Papá's face turn pale as he looked down the road. "Here comes the school bus," he whispered loudly in alarm. Instinctively, Roberto and I ran and hid in the vineyards. We did not want to get in trouble for not going to school. The neatly dressed boys about my age got off. They carried books under their arms. After they crossed the street, the bus drove away. Roberto and I came out from hiding and joined Papá. "*Tienen que tener cuidado,*" he warned us.

20   After lunch we went back to work. The sun kept beating down. The buzzing insects, the wet sweat, and the hot dry dust made the afternoon seem to last forever. Finally the mountains around the valley reached out and swallowed the sun. Within an hour it was too dark to continue picking. The vines blanketed the grapes, making it difficult to see the bunches. "*Vámonos*," said Papá, signaling to us that it was time to quit work. Papá then took out a pencil and began to figure out how much we had earned our first day. He wrote down numbers, crossed some out, wrote down some more. "*Quince*," he murmured.

21   When we arrived home, we took a cold shower underneath a water hose. We then sat down to eat dinner around some wooden crates that served as a table. Mamá had cooked a special meal for us. We had rice and tortillas with *"carne con chile,"* my favorite dish.

22   The next morning I could hardly move. My body ached all over. I felt little control over my arms and legs. This feeling went on every morning for days until my muscles finally got used to the work.

Vocabulary in Context

Context clues can help you understand what a narrator means by using figurative language.

Underline figurative language in paragraph 20 that helps you understand what *blanketed* means.

Copyright © SAVVAS Learning Company LLC. All Rights Reserved.

CLOSE READ

Generate Questions

Highlight details you can use to ask or answer questions about why the narrator does not want to look at his brother.

savoring completely enjoying

23   It was Monday, the first week of November. The grape season was over and I could now go to school. I woke up early that morning and lay in bed, looking at the stars and savoring the thought of not going to work and of starting sixth grade for the first time that year. Since I could not sleep, I decided to get up and join Papá and Roberto at breakfast. I sat at the table across from Roberto, but I kept my head down. I did not want to look up and face him. I knew he was sad. He was not going to school today. He was not going tomorrow, or next week, or next month. He would not go until the cotton season was over, and that was sometime in February. I rubbed my hands together and watched the dry, acid stained skin fall to the floor in little rolls.

24   When Papá and Roberto left for work, I felt relief. I walked to the top of a small grade next to the shack and watched the *Carcachita* disappear in the distance in a cloud of dust.

25   Two hours later, around eight o'clock, I stood by the side of the road waiting for school bus number twenty. When it arrived I climbed in. Everyone was busy either talking or yelling. I sat in an empty seat in the back.

26 When the bus stopped in front of the school, I felt very nervous. I looked out the bus window and saw boys and girls carrying books under their arms. I put my hands in my pant pockets and walked to the principal's office. When I entered I heard a woman's voice say: "May I help you?" I was startled. I had not heard English for months. For a few seconds I remained speechless. I looked at the lady who waited for an answer. My first instinct was to answer her in Spanish, but I held back. Finally, after struggling for English words, I managed to tell her that I wanted to enroll in the sixth grade. After answering many questions, I was led to the classroom.

CLOSE READ

Compare and Contrast Point of View

Underline details that help you understand how the narrator feels.

Compare and Contrast Point of View

Underline details that give the reader information that other characters in the story would not have.

27 Mr. Lema, the sixth grade teacher, greeted me and assigned me a desk. He then introduced me to the class. I was so nervous and scared at that moment when everyone's eyes were on me that I wished I were with Papá and Roberto picking cotton. After taking roll, Mr. Lema gave the class the assignment for the first hour. "The first thing we have to do this morning is finish reading the story we began yesterday," he said enthusiastically. He walked up to me, handed me an English book, and asked me to read. "We are on page 125," he said politely. When I heard this, I felt my blood rush to my head; I felt dizzy. "Would you like to read?" he asked hesitantly. I opened the book to page 125. My mouth was dry. My eyes began to water. I could not begin. "You can read later," Mr. Lema said understandingly.

28 During recess I went into the rest room and opened my English book to page 125. I began to read in a low voice, pretending I was in class. There were many words I did not know. I closed the book and headed back to the classroom.

29 Mr. Lema was sitting at his desk correcting papers. When I entered he looked up at me and smiled. I felt better. I walked up to him and asked if he could help me with the new words. "Gladly," he said.

30 The rest of the month I spent my lunch hours working on English with Mr. Lema, my best friend at school.

31   One Friday during lunch hour Mr. Lema asked me to take a walk with him to the music room. "Do you like music?" he asked me as we entered the building. "Yes, I like *corridos*," I answered. He then picked up a trumpet, blew on it, and handed it to me. The sound gave me goose bumps. I knew that sound. I had heard it in many *corridos*. "How would you like to learn how to play it?" he asked. He must have read my face because before I could answer, he added: "I'll teach you how to play it during our lunch hours."

32   That day I could hardly wait to tell Papá and Mamá the great news. As I got off the bus, my little brothers and sister ran up to meet me. They were yelling and screaming. I thought they were happy to see me, but when I opened the door to our shack, I saw that everything we owned was neatly packed in cardboard boxes.

Compare and Contrast Point of View

Underline details that show the feelings of the main character.

Develop Vocabulary

In literary texts, authors use precise words to describe characters' actions and speech. These words can help the reader make connections to the characters' thoughts and feelings.

My TURN Complete the sentences to demonstrate the word meanings. Then use each word to describe a character in *Weslandia* or "The Circuit."

If a character **recovers**, he or she . . .

Something **thrilling** is something that is . . .

A person who is **miserable** is . . .

When you are **savoring** a thought, you are . . .

Check for Understanding

My TURN Look back at the texts to answer the questions.

1. What traits of fiction do *Weslandia* and "The Circuit" include?

2. Contrast the circumstances in which characters in *Weslandia* and "The Circuit" pick crops.

3. What predictions can you make based on the last images and paragraphs of *Weslandia*?

4. Synthesize details from both texts to create a dialogue in which Wesley and Panchito discuss a topic, such as *school*.

Compare and Contrast Point of View

Authors of narratives shape the reader's experience by developing the **point of view**. With **first-person point of view**, the story is told by a character inside the story. This point of view helps readers relate to the narrator, who uses the pronouns *I*, *me*, *my*, *mine*, *we*, *us*, *our*, and *ours*. With **third-person point of view**, the narrator is not a character in the story and uses the pronouns *he*, *him*, *his*, *she*, *her*, *hers*, *they*, *them*, *their*, and *theirs*.

1. **My TURN** Go to the Close Read notes in *Weslandia* and "The Circuit." Underline text evidence that helps you compare and contrast points of view.

2. **Text Evidence** Use your evidence to complete the chart.

	Weslandia	"The Circuit"
Detail that reveals the main character's feelings		
Point of view		
Contrast how point of view connects me to the main character		

Generate Questions

You can generate questions before, during, and after reading to deepen understanding and gain information. Being able to answer *who*, *what*, *when*, and *where* questions about a text shows that you are noticing necessary details. Asking and answering *why* and *how* questions also helps you identify and understand how point of view affects a text.

1. **My TURN** Go back to the Close Read notes. Highlight details that help you generate questions about point of view in *Weslandia* and "The Circuit."

2. **Text Evidence** Use your evidence to complete the chart and answer the questions.

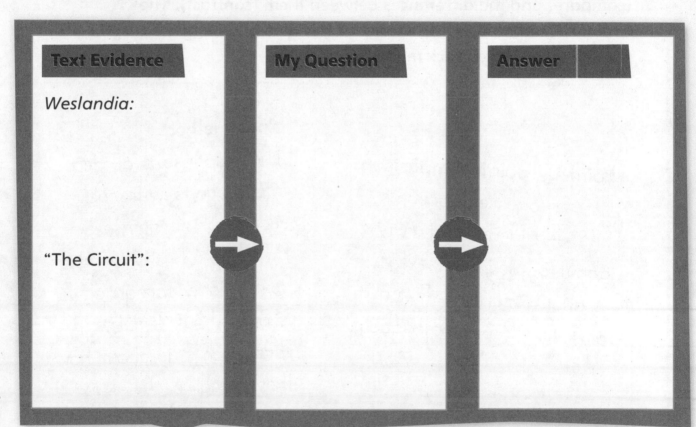

Text Evidence	My Question	Answer
Weslandia:		
"The Circuit":		

How does asking questions help you understand points of view?

Reflect and Share

Write to Sources In *Weslandia* and "The Circuit," you read about young people who feel different. Think about other main characters and how they do (or do not) belong to a group. What happens when people do or do not "fit in"? Compare and contrast ideas from multiple sources to write your response.

- -

Compare and Contrast When writing about ideas from two or more sources, be clear about what the texts have **in common (compare)** and the **differences** between them **(contrast).** The two most common text structures for this type of writing are **point-by-point** and **block method.**

Point-by-point comparison: One-to-one relationships between ideas. Text A is about apples, <u>but</u> Text B is about oranges. Text A and Text B are both about fruits.

Block method: The response is divided into sections, with each section about one text. Paragraph 1 is only about Text A, and paragraph 2 is only about Text B. Paragraph 3 is about how they are alike.

- -

Weekly Question

How do new places influence us?

Academic Vocabulary

Learning Goal

I can develop knowledge about language to make connections between reading and writing.

Figurative language is any language that gives words a meaning beyond their usual, literal definition. Some figurative language creates comparisons. **Similes** are comparisons of two unlike things using *like* or *as*, and **metaphors** are comparisons that do not use *like* or *as*.

My TURN For each sentence,

1. **Underline** the simile or metaphor.

2. **Match** a vocabulary word from the word bank with the comparison that relates to its definition.

3. **Use** each comparison and its related academic vocabulary word in a sentence.

WORD BANK

accomplish   expand   challenge

The chipmunk's cheeks filled up like two hot-air balloons.

_____

For Jeremiah, starting at a new school was a towering obstacle.

_____

She sang beautifully for the crowd, like a professional singer at the peak of her career.

_____

_____

_____

_____

Syllable Patterns V/CV and VC/V

Syllable patterns help you divide and read words. If a word has one consonant between two vowels, the syllable pattern could be V/CV or VC/V. The first syllable in the word *finish* ends in a consonant. It has the VC/V pattern: fin/ish. Syllables that end in consonant sounds are closed syllables. The first syllable in the word *tiger* ends in a long vowel sound. It has the V/CV pattern: ti/ger. Syllables that end in vowel sounds are open syllables.

My TURN Use your knowledge of syllable patterns and open and closed syllables to read and divide the words in the chart. Use a print or online dictionary to check for correct syllabication.

Word	Syllable Pattern	Divided Word
habit		
result		
cubic		
modern		
vivid		

Read Like a Writer

An **author's purpose** is his or her reason for writing, such as to inform or to entertain. An author's **message** is the overall idea or lesson the author wants to share. Authors express purpose and message through details.

Model !   Reread paragraph 12 of *Weslandia*.

1. **Identify** The details in this paragraph tell me about Wesley and his plan.

2. **Question** What do these details tell me about the author's purpose? What do the details tell me about Paul Fleischman's message?

3. **Conclude** The details suggest that the author's purpose is to entertain. Paul Fleischman's message seems to be that coming up with a good idea is energizing.

Reread paragraph 23 of "The Circuit."

My TURN Notice important details. Then identify the author's purpose and message.

1. **Identify** The details in this paragraph tell me more about

_____

2. **Question** What do these details tell me about Francisco Jiménez's purpose and message?

3. **Conclude** These details tell me that the author's purpose is

_____ and that his message is _____

_____

Write for a Reader

Evaluate the details in your writing. Make sure they support your purpose and message.

Authors choose specific details to describe characters and events in their stories. These details support the author's **purpose**, or reason for writing, and the author's **message**, or the idea the author wants readers to gain from the story.

My TURN Think about how the details in *Weslandia* and "The Circuit" helped you determine each author's purpose and message. Now identify how you can use details to support your own purpose and message.

1. If you wanted to write a scene about how a new place influenced a character, what purpose and message might you use?

My purpose would be

_____

My message would be

_____

_____

_____

2. Write a short scene about a character who goes to a new place. Include details that support the purpose and message you just identified.

_____

_____

_____

_____

_____

Spell V/CV and VC/V Words

Knowing **syllable patterns** can help you spell words. If a word has one consonant between two vowels, the syllable pattern could be V/CV or VC/V. The first syllable in the word *finish* ends in a consonant. It has the VC/V pattern: fin/ish. Syllables that end in consonant sounds are closed syllables. The first syllable in the word *tiger* ends in a long vowel sound. It has the V/CV pattern: ti/ger. Syllables that end in vowel sounds are open syllables.

My TURN Read the words. Spell and sort the list of words by their syllable patterns.

SPELLING WORDS

hazard	novel	savage	habit
vanish	proper	balance	credit
modern	vivid	result	decent
rival	cubic	vapor	humor
pilot	final	student	focus

V/CV

_____

_____

_____

_____

_____

_____

_____

VC/V

_____

_____

_____

_____

_____

_____

_____

Progressive Verb Tenses

Progressive verb tenses show an ongoing action at some point in time. They can show action in the past, present, or future. To form the progressive tense, use helping verbs and the ending *-ing* with the main verb. Present progressive tense helping verbs are *am*, *is*, and *are*. Past progressive tense helping verbs are *was* and *were*. The future progressive tense helping verbs are *will* and *be*.

My TURN Use your knowledge of verb tenses to complete this chart.

Present Progressive Tense	Past Progressive Tense	Future Progressive Tense
I _____ waiting for my friend.	I _____ waiting for my friend.	I _____ waiting for my friend.
He _____ growing plants in the garden.	He _____ growing plants in the garden.	He _____ growing plants in the garden.
You _____ explaining different points of view.	You _____ explaining different points of view.	You _____ explaining different points of view.

My TURN Edit this draft to change the crossed-out verbs to the progressive tense. Make sure to use the correct helping verb.

Wesley did not have much luck making friends. One day while he talked to his parents, he had a great idea. "I am going to create my own civilization!" he thought. Soon he learned all about growing and using things in a garden. Now his former tormentors looked forward to what he creates next.

Use Irregular Verbs

To show the past tense of **regular verbs**, add *-ed*. **Irregular verbs** have different forms for the past and form the past tense with *has*, *had*, or *have*. Irregular verbs are common, so be sure to learn their spellings.

Learning Goal

I can use elements of narrative writing to write a realistic fiction story.

Present	Past	Past with *has*, *had*, or *have*
ask	asked	has asked
think	thought	had thought
go	went	has gone
sing	sang	have sung
bite	bit	had bitten

My TURN Use a dictionary to find and write the past tense of these irregular verbs. Spell each word correctly.

grow _____

rise _____

see _____

My TURN Check the past tense of irregular verbs when you edit the draft of a realistic fiction story in your writing notebook. Be sure to spell the irregular verbs correctly.

Edit for Punctuation

A **possessive noun** shows ownership. To make a singular noun possessive, add an apostrophe and an *s*. To make a plural noun that ends in *s* possessive, add just an apostrophe.

Javier → Javier's   the girls → the girls'

A **compound sentence** is made of two complete sentences that are joined together with a comma and a conjunction (such as *and*, *so*, or *but*).

Incorrect	Correct
Amy ran and Pablo walked.	Amy ran, and Pablo walked.

Words in quotations and dialogue are called **direct speech**. Enclose direct speech in quotation marks.

Incorrect	Correct
Amy said, I got here first! Well, said Pablo, so you did.	Amy said, "I got here first!" "Well," said Pablo, "so you did."

My TURN Edit the paragraph so that apostrophes, commas, and quotation marks are used correctly.

Lamont cried, The kitten rolled over! How cool is that? The kitten looked at Lamont and then the kitten sat up and looked at Lamonts mother.

My TURN Check apostrophes, commas, and quotation marks when you edit drafts in your writing notebook.

Edit for Prepositional Phrases

A **preposition** is the first word in a group of words called a prepositional phrase. A **prepositional phrase** ends with a noun or pronoun called the **object of the preposition**. Each prepositional phrase tells something about another word in the sentence.

Example	Explanation
I baked cookies **for dessert**.	The prepositional phrase *for dessert* tells why I baked the cookies.
Darrel asked **for twelve cookies**!	The prepositional phrase *for twelve cookies* tells what Darrel asked for.
Sheila got angry **at him**.	The prepostional phrase *at him* tells who Sheila got angry at.
I stayed **in the kitchen** all day.	The prepositional phrase *in the kitchen* tells where I stayed.

My TURN Use each of these prepositions and prepositional phrases once to complete the sentences: *into the family room, of, with her toe, under, until.*

The white rat crept _____. It hid

_____ the corner _____ the rug _____

Celia poked the rug _____.

My TURN Check prepositions and prepositional phrases when you edit the draft of a realistic fiction story in your writing notebook.

Edit for Coordinating Conjunctions

Use the coordinating conjunction **and** to form compound subjects and compound predicates.

The **subject** of a sentence is a noun or a pronoun. Combine two sentences with the same verb into one sentence with a **compound subject**: Socks *and* shoes must be worn at all times.

The **predicate** of a sentence is a verb. Combine two sentences with the same subject into one sentence with a **compound predicate**: Cast members **lined up** *and* **took a bow**.

Use a comma plus the coordinating conjunction **and**, **but**, or *or* to combine whole related sentences into a **compound sentence**.

  The rain fell, *and* the flowers bloomed.
  He grinned at her, *but* she did not smile back.
  We can go home now, *or* we can stay for another hour.

My TURN Turn each pair of sentences into a single sentence by using a coordinating conjunction.

1. Charlotte wrote the best story. James gave the most dramatic reading.

_____

_____

2. The sunrise pierced the clouds. The sunrise woke the birds.

_____

_____

3. On Lewis's farm, chickens eat grain. On Lewis's farm, horses eat grain.

_____

_____

My TURN Use coordinating conjunctions to combine sentences when you edit your drafts in your writing notebook.

Use Pronouns

Pronouns are words that can replace nouns. The five kinds of pronouns are subjective, objective, possessive, reflexive, and relative.

Type of Pronoun	How Writers Use This Type
Subjective	as the subject of a sentence: **I, you, he, she, it, we, they**
Objective	as the object of a verb or a preposition: **me, you, him, her, it, us, them**
Possessive	to show ownership: **my, mine, your, yours, his, her, hers, its, our, ours, their, theirs**
Reflexive	to reflect an action back onto the subject: **myself, yourself, himself, herself, itself, ourselves, themselves**
Relative	to relate two clauses by taking the place of the subject in the second clause: **who, whose, whom, which, that**

My TURN Edit each sentence to make all pronouns correct.

1. Elizabeth looked at myself in the mirror.

2. Her wondered whose could cut her hair.

3. Later, hers dad got home from work, and him saw the scissors on the hall table.

My TURN Edit sentences for pronouns when you draft a realistic fiction story in your writing notebook. Discuss your editing with your Writing Club.

INTERACTIVITY

Approaches to Poetry

Poetry is a part of every culture.

SAY IT LOUD All around the world, the spoken performance of poetry has been a way for people to express what is important to them. Called bards, griots, skalds, or scops, poets who combine cultural values with vivid language are at the heart of many human gatherings.

TRULY EPIC Epic poetry, which tells a dramatic story, dates back thousands of years. Epics often describe the exciting actions of a hero. People from all cultures and walks of life can find something interesting in these poems.

CONTEMPORARY VOICES To find out more about poetry in your community, visit a library or media center. Ask your librarian about poetry readings, open mics, or youth poetry slams near you.

GOLD MEDAL POETRY

Lyric poems were written to celebrate the winners of the earlier Olympic games. Later, in the first half of the twentieth century, epic and lyric poetry "directly inspired by the idea of sport" was eligible for Olympic medals. In 1948, Finnish poet Aale Maria Tynni won a gold medal for her poem "Laurel of Hellas."

How do people with interests different from ours help us grow?

Freewrite You read about ways that poetry connects to different topics. Without stopping, freewrite for a short time about *uncommon interests*.

MEDICINE, MATHEMATICS, AND...POETRY?

Having a love for poetry does not stop people from engaging with their other interests. For instance, famous American poet William Carlos Williams was also a pediatrician for most of his life! Lewis Carroll, the author of *Alice's Adventures in Wonderland*, also wrote numerous poems and published papers about new theories in mathematics.

Poetry

Poetic elements are the techniques that make poems different from prose. **Poetry** can include

- **Verses or stanzas,** or arrangements of lines
- **Imagery,** or vivid descriptive details
- **Figurative language,** or nonliteral language, including similes and metaphors
- **Personification,** or language that gives human traits to animals, objects, or ideas
- **Onomatopoeia,** or words that sound like their meanings
- **Rhyme,** or words with the same ending sounds

Can poetry help you "see" language?

TURN and TALK How do authors express images or ideas in a unique way? With a partner, compare how language is used in poetry and in other kinds of creative writing, such as fiction.

Be a Fluent Reader Poetry contains language that is designed to please the ear as well as the mind's eye.

When you read poetry aloud,

- Slow down or speed up to express the mood, or feeling, of the words.
- Pause only at punctuation, as though you were reading prose.
- Read each word, stopping to sound out unfamiliar words as needed.

Poetry

Purpose:

To entertain, express, or describe in a fresh and inventive way

Elements:

- Language and word choices are precise and vivid.
- Line breaks end a line to emphasize ideas or images.
- Stanzas group lines to keep related ideas together.

Forms:

narrative, lyrical, concrete, free verse, & more!

Gwendolyn Zepeda, the author of "A Day on a Boat," was the very first Latina blogger. She writes about matters close to the heart, such as identity, family, and music. In 2013, she became the first poet laureate of Houston, Texas.

Poetry Collection

Preview Vocabulary

As you read the poetry collection, pay attention to these vocabulary words. Notice how they help you use your imagination to experience what the poems describe.

plunge	trilled	thud
buoy	flocked	

Read

As you read a poem, creating a mental image, or picture in your mind, can help you understand the poem better. Think about the language the poet uses to help create an image in your mind. Use these strategies when you read the poetry collection.

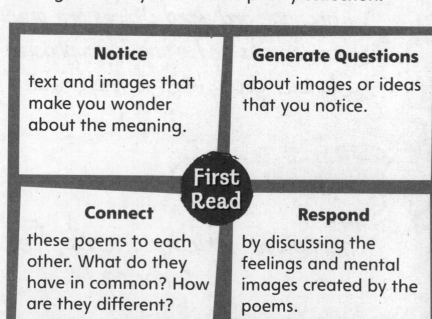

Notice text and images that make you wonder about the meaning.

Generate Questions about images or ideas that you notice.

First Read

Connect these poems to each other. What do they have in common? How are they different?

Respond by discussing the feelings and mental images created by the poems.

170

Poetry Collection

A Day on a Boat
by Gwendolyn Zepeda

I Will Be a Chemist: Mario José Molina
by Alma Flor Ada

I ♥ Mozart
by Dana Crum

AUDIO

ANNOTATE

Examine Poetic Elements

How does Gwendolyn Zepeda create images in this poem?

Underline examples of **figurative language**.

plunge dive; sink rapidly; drop quickly

A Day on a Boat

by Gwendolyn Zepeda

A
day on a boat.
We
float
in the
sun. One
by one the
others plunge
from blue above   to
blue below, like gulls   that
dive. Like fish that fly.   They
call my name and say that   I should
swim. They wish that I could   feel the way
they feel. Like jellyfish or otters.   My sisters and
brothers are eels that love to swirl and   splash around
each other. Knowing if I tried it, I would   like it, just like
they do. They always like the same things   and they wish
I'd
like   them,
too.   A
day   on
a boat, we float in the sun. One by one, I turn the pages of a
book and hear its story in my mind. It's like a world I carry
and can open any time. An ocean where I float to other
times and spy on pirates, mermaids, queens, and
magic stones. I'm swimming through my
story, with the others, but alone.

5

10

15

20

25

I Will Be a Chemist:
Mario José Molina

by Alma Flor Ada

Visualize to Understand

Highlight words and phrases that Alma Flor Ada uses to help you create a mental image of what the character in the poem sees and experiences.

Only a drop of water

but looking under the microscope

I see things that move inside that very drop.

My aunt Esther has given me a chemistry set.

5   She says that everything—water, air, earth,

the trunks of trees and our own skin—

is made of small particles we cannot see.

She explains that even these molecules

are made of chemical elements;

10 just around a hundred elements

combine to make all that exists.

I have started today

in my simple lab in the old unused bathroom

to study these elements.

15 I will know the secrets of the universe.

Visualize to Understand

Highlight a simile that helps you create a mental picture to understand how Phoenix experiences the music.

Examine Poetic Elements

Dana Crum uses **onomatopoeia**, or words that sound like their meaning, to engage the reader's senses. Underline examples of onomatopoeia.

trilled made a pleasant, repetitive, high-pitched sound

thud a dull sound

I ♥ Mozart

by Dana Crum

1 One night in April Phoenix hosted
a sleepover. To pass the time
while friends arrived, he sat
at his desk, opened his PC's music app,
5 and clicked his favorite song:
Mozart's "Gran Partita."
Oboes, clarinets, and basset horns,
horns, bassoons, and bass drifted through
his bedroom like campfire smoke.

10 The doorbell ding-donged. The first arrival had arrived.
A thud and swish as the door opened.
His mother's voice trilled: "Hello, Chase."
"Hi, Mrs. Lippincott."
A swish and thud as the door closed.
15 Chase swaggered into Phoenix's room.
He stopped. He frowned. "What mess
is this you're listening to?" he asked.
"Mozart," Phoenix replied.

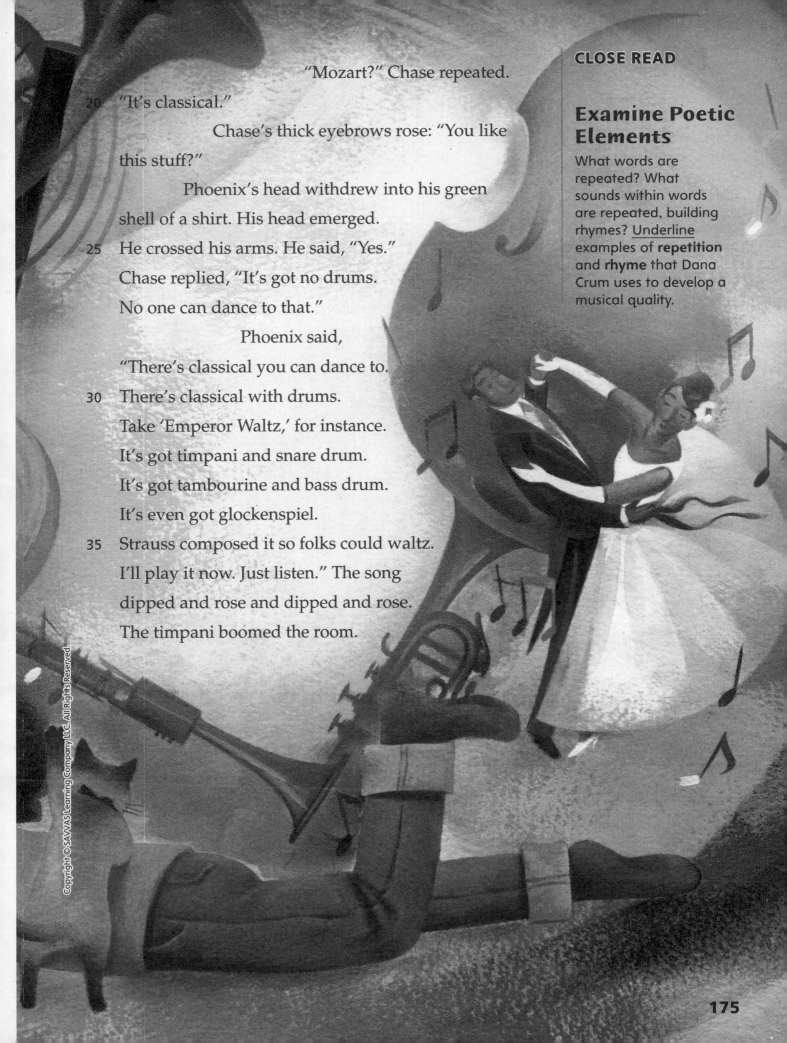

"Mozart?" Chase repeated.

20 "It's classical."

Chase's thick eyebrows rose: "You like this stuff?"

Phoenix's head withdrew into his green shell of a shirt. His head emerged.

25 He crossed his arms. He said, "Yes."
Chase replied, "It's got no drums.
No one can dance to that."

Phoenix said,
"There's classical you can dance to.

30 There's classical with drums.
Take 'Emperor Waltz,' for instance.
It's got timpani and snare drum.
It's got tambourine and bass drum.
It's even got glockenspiel.

35 Strauss composed it so folks could waltz.
I'll play it now. Just listen." The song
dipped and rose and dipped and rose.
The timpani boomed the room.

Examine Poetic Elements

What words are repeated? What sounds within words are repeated, building rhymes? <u>Underline</u> examples of **repetition** and **rhyme** that Dana Crum uses to develop a musical quality.

Visualize to Understand

Highlight a metaphor that helps you create a mental image of a character in the poem.

buoy an object that floats on the surface of water

flocked moved in a group

Chase's round head bobbed, a buoy at sea.

40 He said what his body had already said:

"Okay. I admit it. You can dance to that.

But classical—it's so old."

"So is Shakespeare.

But we read him," Phoenix replied.

45 Chase smirked. "You can't deny that classical

is for snobs."

Phoenix said, "Actually, I can.

Classical was popular in its time. Fans flocked

to Mozart's shows. He was a rock star."

50 "Really?" Chase said.

"Really," Phoenix replied. "If you want to know why, listen to this." He chose the overture of *The Marriage of Figaro*, then clicked play. Cellos, violas, and violins

55 raced, a maddening pace. Flutes and clarinets floated over the din. Oboes and bassoons and trumpets and timpani joined the fray. The song exploded, a playful storm.

Chase declared, "I've heard this before!

60 This is Mozart?"

"This is Mozart," Phoenix replied. Chase's thick eyebrows rose. "This is incredible! I can see why this was popular back then!" "It's popular now, also," Phoenix said. "It's from

65 *The Marriage of Figaro*. He wrote this part just hours before opening night."

"So he was some kind of genius then," Chase said. Phoenix smiled. "That he certainly was."

Vocabulary in Context

Underline context clues, or words and phrases, that help you define *fray*.

Fluency

Read lines 51–61 aloud to a partner. Remember to read at an appropriate rate and with expression so that your partner understands the feeling of the words. Use what you know about sound spelling patterns to read words as needed.

Develop Vocabulary

Words have **denotations,** or definitions found in a dictionary. Each reader will know the same denotation of a word. Words also have connections with ideas, concepts, and other words. These related ideas and words are called **connotations.** A word can have positive, negative, or neutral connotations. Readers may have different, specific connotations for some words depending on their personal experiences.

My TURN Complete the graphic organizer by writing a denotation and a connotation for each word.

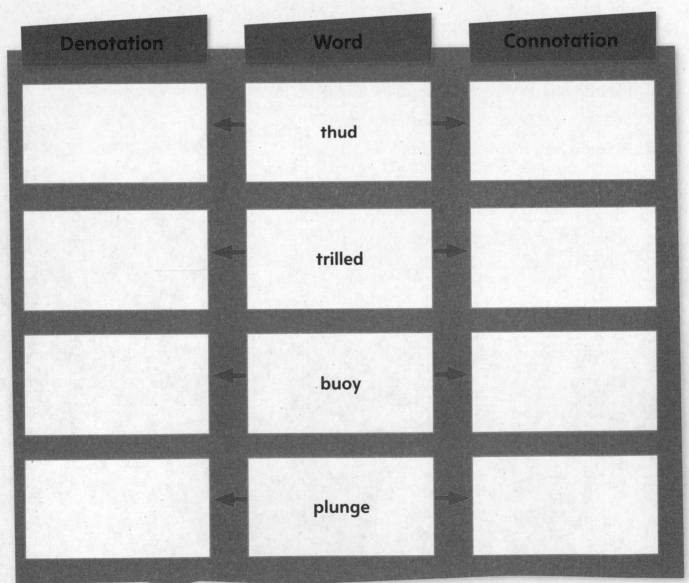

Denotation	Word	Connotation
	thud	
	trilled	
	buoy	
	plunge	

Check for Understanding

My TURN Look back at the texts to answer the questions.

1. What characteristics identify these texts as poetry?

2. How does the use of language in the poems affect the reader?

3. How would you adapt one of the poems to create a short story with most of the same information?

4. Select one of the poems, tell what it is about, and describe the poet's choices. Give examples of strong images from the poem.

Examine Poetic Elements

Poetry often includes **figurative language**, such as **similes** and **metaphors**. Such language adds an extra layer of meaning to the **theme**, or message, of a poem. A simile compares two unlike things using *like* or *as*. A metaphor creates a comparison without those words. **Onomatopoeia** refers to words that imitate the sounds of the action associated with the words. Onomatopoeia, **repetition** (repeated lines or words), and **rhythm** create a musical quality in poems.

1. **My TURN** Go to the Close Read notes in the poetry collection. Underline examples of poetic elements. Then analyze how poetic elements help determine a poem's theme.

2. **Text Evidence** Use your evidence to complete the graphic organizer and explain the effect of poetic elements on the reader.

Element

Effect on Reader

compares _____ to _____

The effect on the reader is

In _____, the poet uses the poetic element _____ .

The effect on the reader is

How do the poetic elements help you determine the theme of "I ♥ Mozart"?

Visualize to Understand

Poets use figurative language, descriptive details, and sensory details, or imagery, to help readers visualize, or create a mental image. Creating a mental picture helps a reader understand what the poet is trying to say. Pay attention to how poets use language to create layers of meaning in their writing. Summarizing a poem can help you explain what you visualize.

1. **My TURN** Go back to the Close Read notes and highlight elements that help you create mental images of the text.

2. **Text Evidence** Use your evidence to complete the graphic organizer. Then write a short summary of a poem.

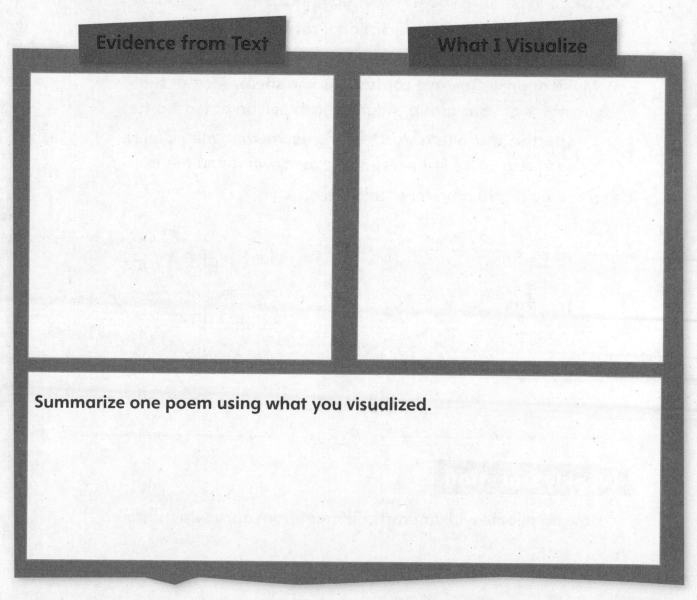

Evidence from Text

What I Visualize

Summarize one poem using what you visualized.

Reflect and Share

Talk About It In the poetry collection, characters describe what they are interested in. What other hobbies, interests, or activities did you read about this week? In a discussion, describe how you would encourage someone to try something new. Use text evidence to support your response.

- -

Speak to Be Heard When expressing an opinion in a discussion, make sure you get your point across.

◎ **Speak at a normal conversational rate.** Choose a speed that makes it easy for listeners to understand you.

◎ **Make appropriate eye contact.** As you speak, look at the members of your group. Address each person at least once.

◎ **Be specific.** Using terms such as *rhyme, rhythm, meter, lines,* and *stanzas* helps listeners know exactly what you mean.

Use these guides to monitor your speech.

Too fast: Listeners miss some ideas.

Just right: Words are spoken clearly so that listeners can comprehend.

- -

Weekly Question

How do people with interests different from ours help us grow?

Academic Vocabulary

Parts of speech are word categories that include nouns, verbs, adjectives, and adverbs. You can use what you know about base words and word endings to create words that function as different parts of speech.

Learning Goal

I can develop knowledge about language to make connections between reading and writing.

My TURN For each sentence,

1. **Underline** the academic vocabulary word.

2. **Identify** the word's part of speech.

3. **Write** your own sentence using the same word but as a different part of speech.

Sentence	Part of Speech	My Sentence
The agent had accomplished a lot in her long career.	verb	Graduating early was a great accomplishment. (noun)
In the film, the characters' opinions often conflicted.		
The test was a challenge for most students.		
The students received ribbons for their participation.		

Silent Letters

In some English words, a letter may appear in the spelling of the word, but the letter is not pronounced. For example, the word *knowing* in line 16 of "A Day on a Boat" contains the **silent letter k.** Other words that begin with the *kn* letter combination also have a silent *k*.

My TURN Review the silent letter chart. Add one or more example words for each silent letter. Use a print or online dictionary if you need help determining pronunciation.

Silent Letters	Words
the *k* in *kn*	_____
the *w* in *wr*	_____
the *g* in *gn*	_____
the *b* in *bt* or *mb* (usually)	_____
the *t* in *st* or *ft* (sometimes)	_____
the *h* in *kh*, *gh*, or *rh*	_____
h at the beginning of a word (sometimes)	_____

Read Like a Writer

Poets often use **figurative language**, or language that gives words meaning beyond their dictionary definitions. **Imagery**, or sensory language, helps readers understand how things look, sound, smell, taste, or feel. **Similes** compare two unlike things using the words *like* or *as*, and **metaphors** compare two unlike things without those words.

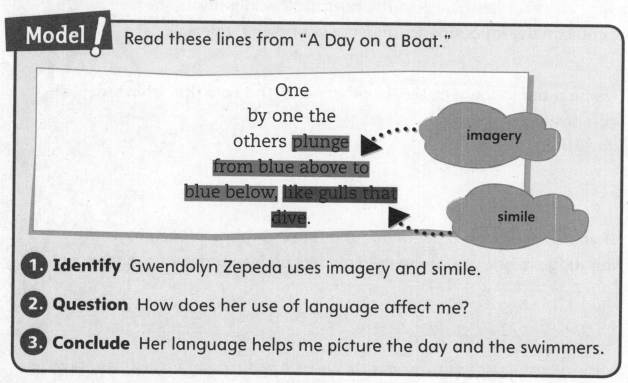

Model ! Read these lines from "A Day on a Boat."

One
by one the
others plunge
from blue above to
blue below, like gulls that
dive.

imagery

simile

1. Identify Gwendolyn Zepeda uses imagery and simile.

2. Question How does her use of language affect me?

3. Conclude Her language helps me picture the day and the swimmers.

Reread lines 7–11 in "I ♥ Mozart."

My TURN Follow the steps to analyze Dana Crum's use of language.

1. Identify Dana Crum uses _____

2. Question How does his use of language affect me?

3. Conclude His language helps me _____

_____

_____

_____

Write for a Reader

How will you create images in a reader's mind?

Poets use imagery, similes, metaphors, and other kinds of **figurative language** to bring their poems to life for readers and help readers visualize their ideas.

My TURN Think about how the poets' language affected the way you visualized ideas in the poems. Now identify how you can use language to influence your own readers.

1. Name a book, song, movie, or other piece of media that affected you positively.

   _____

   _____

2. If you were writing a poem about this text or piece of media, what language might you use to help readers understand your experience?

   _____

   _____

   _____

3. In your writing notebook, write a short poem about how your chosen text or piece of media affected you. Use literary devices to emphasize how you felt.

Spell Words with Silent Letters

In some words, a consonant may not be pronounced. You can accurately spell words by learning which letter combinations produce **silent letters**. For example, the combination *mb* in words like *climb* and *lamb* contains a silent *b*.

My TURN Read the words. Then spell and alphabetize the words. Make sure to include the correct silent letters as you spell each word.

SPELLING WORDS

glisten	sword	subtle	wreckage
wrestle	align	salmon	autumn
aisle	doubt	heir	mortgage
debris	corps	asthma	gourmet
tongue	ballet	condemn	yolk

_____   _____

_____   _____

_____   _____

_____   _____

_____   _____

_____   _____

_____   _____

Auxiliary Verbs

A verb phrase is made up of a main verb and one or more helping verbs. **Main verbs** show action, while **helping verbs** help the main verb show the time of an action. Helping verbs are also called auxiliary verbs.

Examples of Auxiliaries	Meanings	Example Sentences
can could	to be able to to be possible to	I <u>can</u> run for a long time. I <u>could</u> see the stars.
may **might**	to allow to to have possibility to	Yes, you <u>may</u> take a piece of fruit. You <u>might</u> see a comet tonight.
must	to be required to need to to be certain	You <u>must</u> stay inside. The clock <u>must</u> be correct.
shall should	to command to to expect to	You <u>shall</u> pass! You <u>should</u> see me around noon.
will would	to expect to to be possible to	You <u>will</u> see me later. I <u>would</u> like to see you later.

My TURN Complete each sentence with an auxiliary verb from the chart.

1. In "A Day on a Boat," the speaker opens her book, and she _____ hear the story.

2. Her siblings _____ want her to swim.

3. Through her book, the speaker _____ experience adventure.

Rearrange and Combine Ideas

A realistic fiction story is **coherent** when all of its parts fit together. None of the fictional elements or details seem out of place. To determine whether writing is coherent, ask:

- Do any events or details seem out of place?
- Are there so many words that the meaning is hard to find?

A realistic fiction story is **clear** when a reader can understand everything in it. To determine whether writing is clear, ask:

- Will each sentence make sense to a thoughtful reader?
- Does every pronoun refer to a recognizable noun?

My TURN Combine and rearrange words, sentences, and ideas to make this paragraph clear and coherent. Write your version on the lines.

    Beulah watched the snake closely. Last week, Ms. Jones got a new pet for her class. In the tank was a corn snake. She made sure the screen fit tightly over the top of the tank. This job was going to be interesting. The snake stared back at her. Beulah volunteered to care for it.

_____

_____

_____

My TURN Rearrange and combine words, sentences, and ideas for coherence and clarity when you revise the draft of a realistic fiction story in your writing notebook.

Edit for Capitalization

Follow rules for capitalizing words to help readers understand your ideas.

> - Capitalize the main words in names of historical periods, events, and documents.
> - Capitalize the main words in the titles of books, stories, and essays.
> - Capitalize the names of languages.
> - Capitalize the names of races and nationalities.

My TURN Highlight each letter that should be capitalized in this passage.

> Sam and Carlita jogged along. "I need to finish my report on the american revolution," gasped Carlita.
>
> Sam asked, between breaths, "Have you read the chapter in *our country's history* yet?"
>
> "Not yet," said Carlita. "I finished the chapter titled 'heroes of the revolution,' though."
>
> "Did it talk about the help we got from french and polish soldiers?" Sam inquired.
>
> "No," Carlita said, "just about the men who signed the declaration of independence."

My TURN Check for correct capitalization when you edit the draft of a realistic fiction story in your writing notebook.

Capitalize proper nouns, but do not capitalize common nouns.

Publish and Celebrate

Read your realistic fiction story aloud. Decide which is the most dramatic, or exciting, part. Then make an audio recording of yourself reading that part of the story.

My TURN Complete these sentences about your writing experience. Write legibly in cursive.

The characters in my story are realistic because

_____

_____

_____

The problem my characters face is realistic because

_____

_____

_____

I used dialogue in my realistic fiction story to

_____

_____

_____

The next time I write a realistic fiction story, I want to

_____

_____

_____

Prepare for Assessment

My TURN Follow a plan as you prepare to write a realistic fiction story in response to a prompt. Use your own paper.

1. Study the prompt.

You will receive an assignment called a writing prompt. Read the prompt carefully. Highlight the type of writing you must do. Underline the topic you are supposed to write about.

Prompt: Write a realistic fiction story about exploring a diverse community in your life.

2. Freewrite.

For several minutes, write down everything you can think of about the topic, including how people explore and benefit from diversity. Then take a short break. Look at what you wrote and circle ideas you want to include in your story.

3. Map out your realistic fiction story.

Introduction: Characters, Setting, and Problem

Plot: Event 1 → Next Events → Resolution

4. Write your draft.

Remember to make the sequence of events natural and clear.

5. Revise and edit your realistic fiction story.

Apply the skills and rules you have learned to polish your writing.

Be inventive in the way you use realistic details in your story. Make up characters and events that are believable.

Assessment

My TURN Before you write a realistic fiction story for your assessment, rate how well you understand the skills you have learned in this unit. Go back and review any skills you mark "No."

		Yes!	No
Ideas and Organization	◐ I can create a realistic setting.	☐	☐
	◐ I can describe realistic characters inside and out.	☐	☐
	◐ I can develop a clear, natural sequence of events.	☐	☐
	◐ I can write the resolution to a conflict or problem.	☐	☐
	◐ I can select a genre.	☐	☐
Craft	◐ I can choose the narrator's point of view.	☐	☐
	◐ I can think of illustrations.	☐	☐
	◐ I can write dialogue between people.	☐	☐
	◐ I can use transition words and phrases.	☐	☐
	◐ I can rearrange and combine ideas for clarity.	☐	☐
Conventions	◐ I can use irregular verbs correctly.	☐	☐
	◐ I can use reflexive and relative pronouns.	☐	☐
	◐ I can use prepositional phrases.	☐	☐
	◐ I can use coordinating conjunctions.	☐	☐
	◐ I can edit compound sentences for commas, possessives for apostrophes, and dialogue for quotation marks.	☐	☐

COMPARE ACROSS TEXTS

UNIT THEME
Diversity

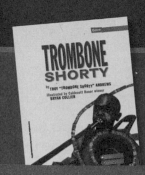

TURNand**TALK** Trait Snapshot

Choose a trait that best describes each
character or person you read about.
Then, talk with your partner about
how these traits relate to the unit
theme of *Diversity*.

WEEK 3

Trombone Shorty

Trombone Shorty is

_____

BOOK CLUB

WEEK 2

from Mama's Window

Sugar is

_____

BOOK CLUB

WEEK 1

from Out of My Mind

Melody is

_____

194

BOOK
CLUB

Weslandia
by PAUL FLEISCHMAN

The
CIRCUIT
by Francisco Jiménez

WEEK 4

Weslandia and "The Circuit"

Wesley is

_____

Panchito is

_____

BOOK CLUB

WEEK 5

Poetry Collection

"A Day on a Boat" narrator is

_____

Mario José Molina is

_____

Poetry Collection
A Day on a Boat
by Gwendolyn Brooks
I Will Be a Chemist:
Mario José Molina
by Alma Flor Ada
I ♥ Mozart
by Diana Cruz

Essential Question

My TURN

In your notebook, answer the Essential Question: How can we reach new understandings through exploring diversity?

BOOK CLUB

WEEK 6

Now it's time to apply what you learned about Diversity in your WEEK 6 PROJECT: Let's All Play!

Let's All PLAY!

Activity

A 2010 law requires all play areas to have playground equipment that is inclusive for people with disabilities. Compose a letter to your principal telling why your school needs to have inclusive playground equipment.

Research Articles

With your partner, read "Playing Together!" to generate questions you have about inclusive playgrounds. Then make a research plan for writing your letter to the principal.

1 Playing Together!

2 Who Needs Recess?

3 Understanding Physical Disabilities: A Path to Support

Generate Questions

COLLABORATE After reading "Playing Together!" generate three questions you have about the article. Then, share your questions with the class.

1. _____

2. _____

3. _____

Use Academic Words

COLLABORATE Work with your partner to add more academic vocabulary words to each category. If appropriate, use this vocabulary when you respond to your principal.

Academic Vocabulary	Word Forms	Related Examples
accomplish	accomplishes accomplished accomplishment	goals
expand	expansive expanding expanded	balloons
conflict	conflicts conflicted conflicting	argument
challenge	challenging challenged challenger	difficult assignments
participate	participates participating participation	swimming

A Matter of Opinion

Every claim has an opinion, but not every opinion is a claim.

People write opinion essays to convince, or persuade, someone to think or do something. When reading opinion essays or argumentative texts, look for

- the claim
- facts and evidence that support the claim
- reasons based on evidence in the text
- the intended audience or reader

COLLABORATE   With a partner, read "Who Needs Recess?" Then, answer the questions about the text.

1. What is the writer's claim?

_____

_____

_____

2. What evidence does the writer use to convince readers?

_____

_____

_____

3. Who is the intended audience or reader for this article? How can you tell?

_____

_____

_____

Plan Your Research

COLLABORATE Before you begin your research, you must come up with a research plan. A research plan will help you decide where to focus your research.

Definition	Examples
CLAIMS A claim is a statement that tries to persuade, argue, or convince a reader to agree with an opinion. A claim • defines your goal, • is specific, and • is supported with evidence. Read the two examples in the next column. Then, with your partner, write a claim statement for your playground project.	I like vegetables. No, this is not a claim. Doctors say that eating vegetables every day can help you live longer. Yes, this is a claim! My playground claim:
EVIDENCE You can support your claims with evidence, such as • facts • statistics • quotations • examples With your partner, plan the types of research you will look for.	**Fact:** Raw broccoli has more dietary fiber than steak. **Statistic:** The average American eats only 2 cups of fruits and vegetables a day. **Quote:** Dr. Jones says, "Vegetables are packed with nutrients." **Examples:** Most kids would rather eat candy than vegetables.

With your partner, list some keywords for finding evidence for your playground research project. With your plan in mind, begin your research.

TOOLS of the TRADE

A **search engine** is an online tool used to gather credible information. Your search results on playgrounds will probably turn up lots of information on your topic, but how do you know whether this information is **credible**? Look for the author!

On most Web pages you have to know where to search to find the author's name. Once you locate the author, you can see if the author has the **expertise** to write about the topic.

STEP 1: Use a student-friendly search engine and enter your keywords for research.

STEP 2: On the homepage, find a phrase, such as About Us or About [organization name] and click on it. It could be at the top or bottom of the page.

STEP 3: Read the information about the author and question whether he or she has the expertise to write about the topic. Remember, you would not want to take advice from someone who does not have the experience or education to speak about the topic.

Martin Houlihan, MD

Director, Center for Children's Allergies

Doctor Martin Houlihan worked for 22 years as a pediatric surgeon before taking the job as director of the Center for Children's Allergies, a nonprofit dedicated to treating young people with allergies.

COLLABORATE With your partner, go online to search for information on your topic. Use the note cards to record your most credible sources on inclusive playgrounds.

Web Address:

Author:

Author's Expertise:

Notes:

Web Address:

Author:

Author's Expertise:

Notes:

Discuss your search results. Do you need to change your keywords to find more specific information?

Take A STAND!

People write **argumentative texts** to convince others to think or act in certain ways. An argumentative letter, such as the one to the principal, makes a claim about a topic and supports it with facts.

Before you begin writing, choose how you will deliver your message. Will you

- mail your written letter to the principal?
- orally read your letter to the principal?
- give a multimedia presentation using videos and images?

COLLABORATE Read the Student Model. Work with your partner to recognize the characteristics of argumentative texts.

Now You Try It!

Discuss the checklist with a partner. Work together to follow the steps as you write your letter.

Make sure your letter

- ☐ identifies the intended audience or reader.
- ☐ states a specific claim that defines your goal.
- ☐ includes facts, statistics, quotes, or examples.
- ☐ uses persuasive language, such as *must*, *should*, or *need* to help convince readers.
- ☐ includes a strong conclusion that restates your claim.

Student Model

February 8

Dear Principal Wehmeyer, ◀···· **Highlight** the intended audience.

We should have more cafeteria offerings to ◀···· **Underline** the claim.
include a more diverse menu to accommodate students
with food allergies. Two kids in our class have peanut
allergies, so they eat lunch in the classroom. We think
they should be able to eat with their friends.

One reason it is important to expand our ◀···· **Highlight** a fact.
menu is because statistics show that 1 in 13 children
have food allergies. So most classrooms probably have
two or more students with allergies! A more important
reason is that eating something you are allergic ◀···· **Underline** persuasive language.
to can make you sick.

Will you join us in helping to make our cafeteria a
safer place for all students? With more menu offerings,
all students can eat lunch in the cafeteria. ◀···· **Highlight** the conclusion.

Sincerely,
Odette Calderón and Rob Shallcross
Ms. Horwitz's Fourth Grade Class

In Your Own Words!

Be sure you recognize the difference between **paraphrasing** and **plagiarism** before using any source materials in your letter.

Plagiarism is using someone else's exact words without giving that person credit. Instead, you should paraphrase or quote information.

Paraphrasing is writing down information in your own words.

> Original sentence: *People have allergies to a wide variety of things, such as foods, medicines, and plants.*
>
> People can be allergic to many different things. ◀ • • • • • **Paraphrasing**

Quoting is copying exactly the words from a source, putting the words in quotation marks, and naming the author.

> Bert Kausal wrote, "People have allergies to a wide ◀ • • • • • **Quoting**
> variety of things, such as foods, medicines, and plants."

RESEARCH

COLLABORATE Read "Understanding Physical Disabilities: A Path to Support." Identify a fact from the article. Then, with your partner, show how you would quote and paraphrase this fact.

Fact from article	
Quote the fact	
Paraphrase the fact	

COLLABORATE Read the paragraph from a research source and answer the questions.

Food Allergies in Children

by Dr. Rowena Vargas

Researchers have found that more and more children have or are developing allergies to different types of foods. These allergies occur in countries around the world. Some young people have allergies to foods such as nuts, dairy, and wheat. Others are sensitive to certain fruits and vegetables. Food scientists are trying to discover what causes these allergies because people who eat foods they are allergic to can become very ill. They may even need to go to the emergency room if the reaction is serious. Discovering what causes these allergies will help all children stay healthy.

1. Paraphrase the first sentence so that it maintains its meaning and logical order.

_____

_____

2. Is the following sentence an example of plagiarizing, paraphrasing, or quoting?

    These allergies occur in countries around the world.

_____

_____

3. Quote a sentence from the paragraph.

_____

_____

Incorporate Media

Writers can make their writing stronger by including different **media**, or formats for sharing information.

Images make your writing interesting and memorable. Photographs, drawings, and paintings help your readers visualize your topic more clearly.

A **diagram** points out special features in a picture. The labels help your readers better understand your topic.

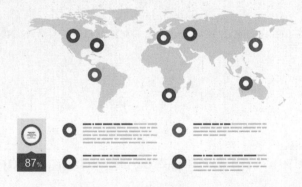

Graphs and **tables** give your readers additional information such as numbers, percentages, and years. They come in many different types.

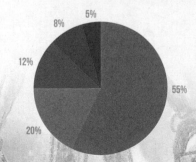 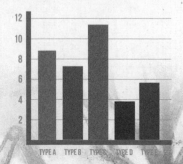 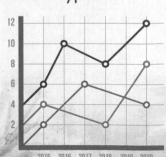

COLLABORATE With your partner, brainstorm media to make your argumentative letter stronger. Then, go online to find relevant information, or information that will support your argument. Gather this information from a variety of sources, such as Web sites and videos. Show that you understood your research by explaining why the information from each source makes your argument more convincing. Decide on how you will present your findings.

Type of Media:

Source:

How would it make the argument more convincing?

Type of Media:

Source:

How would it make the argument more convincing?

Revise

Vocabulary Reread your letter with your partner. Then revise your letter for word choice. Have you included

☐ academic vocabulary from the unit?

☐ domain-specific vocabulary related to the activity?

☐ persuasive language to help convince the reader?

Revise Word Choice

The writers of the Student Model realized that they had not used any academic or domain-specific vocabulary. They revised some sentences to include these words and make their argument more powerful.

expand our
We should ∧ ~~have more~~ cafeteria offerings to include a more diverse menu to accommodate students with food allergies.

A more important reason is that eating something you are allergic to can ∧ ~~make you sick.~~
cause anaphylaxis, which is a severe reaction to the food.

Edit

Conventions Read your letter again and make edits. Have you used correct conventions?

- ☐ spelling
- ☐ punctuation
- ☐ paraphrase or quote information
- ☐ quotation marks for quoted text
- ☐ capitalization of names and places
- ☐ a variety of simple and compound sentences

Peer Review

COLLABORATE Exchange argumentative letters with another group. As you read, try to recognize characteristics of an argumentative text, such as the claim and the intended audience. Then, see if you can identify how the authors have used facts to support their argument.

Time to Celebrate!

COLLABORATE Read your argumentative letter to another group. Be sure to enunciate your words at a natural rate and volume. How did your audience react to your letter? Write some of their reactions.

_____

_____

_____

_____

Reflect on Your Project

My TURN Think about the argumentative letter you wrote. Which parts of your letter do you think are the strongest? Which areas might you improve next time? Write your thoughts here.

Strengths

_____

_____

_____

_____

Areas of Improvement

_____

_____

_____

_____

Reflect on Your Goals

SCALE	1	2	3	4	5
	NOT AT ALL WELL	NOT VERY WELL	SOMEWHAT WELL	VERY WELL	EXTREMELY WELL

Look back at your unit goals.

Use a different color to rate yourself again.

Reflect on Your Reading

What surprised you most about what you read in this unit?

Reflect on Your Writing

What surprised you most about your writing in this unit?

UNIT 4

Impacts

Essential Question

How do our stories shape our world?

▶ **Watch**

"Stories Shape Us"

TURN and TALK

How have stories influenced your life?

SAVVAS
realize™
Go ONLINE for
all lessons.

 VIDEO

 AUDIO

 INTERACTIVITY

 GAME

 ANNOTATE

 BOOK

 RESEARCH

READING WORKSHOP

READING-WRITING BRIDGE

- Academic Vocabulary • Word Study
- **Read Like a Writer** • **Write for a Reader**
- Spelling • Language and Conventions

WRITING WORKSHOP

- Introduce and Immerse • Develop Elements
- Develop Structure • Writer's Craft
- Publish, Celebrate, and Assess

Opinion

PROJECT-BASED INQUIRY

- Inquire • Research • Collaborate

Independent Reading

Building stamina means developing your ability to do an activity for a longer amount of time. Review your Independent Reading Logs for previous units.

- How many pages did you read in one sitting? _____
- What is the longest amount of time you spent reading independently? _____

Use these tips to help you increase your reading stamina.

- Choose books based on what interests you. If a book does not hold your attention, consider choosing a different book.

- Stretch first, if you can. You will find it easier to sit still and read quietly if you have recently done some exercise.

- Pace yourself. Read at a rate that works for you.

- Limit distractions. If possible, choose a location that is quiet and comfortable, where you will not be interrupted.

- Each time you read, aim to read a few more pages, or for a couple more minutes, than you did last time. Small goals lead to big successes!

When I read (book title) _____, I will build

my reading stamina by _____.

Independent Reading Log

Date	Book	Genre	Pages Read	Minutes Read	My Ratings
					☆☆☆☆☆

Unit Goals

Shade in the circle to rate how well you meet each goal now.

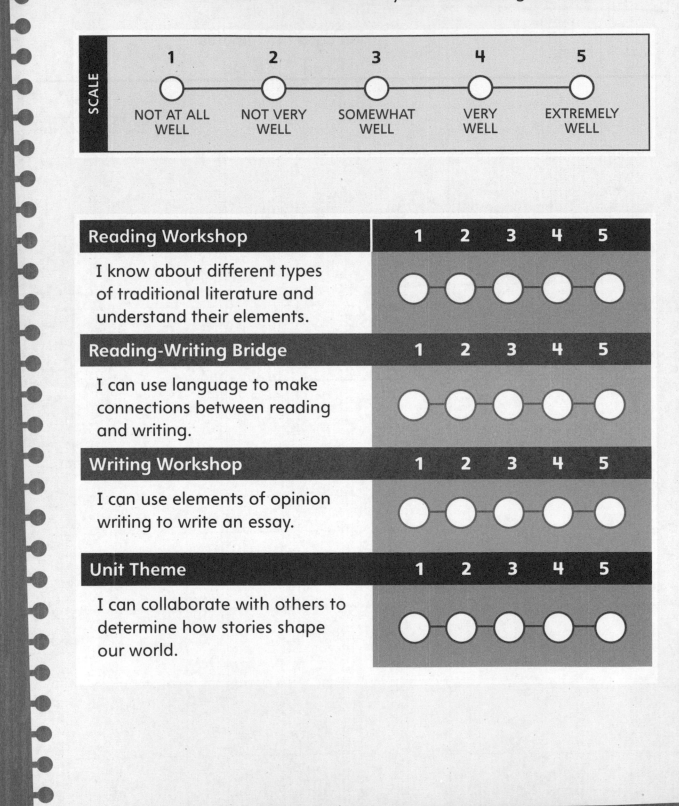

SCALE	1	2	3	4	5
	○	○	○	○	○
	NOT AT ALL WELL	NOT VERY WELL	SOMEWHAT WELL	VERY WELL	EXTREMELY WELL

Reading Workshop	1	2	3	4	5
I know about different types of traditional literature and understand their elements.	○	○	○	○	○

Reading-Writing Bridge	1	2	3	4	5
I can use language to make connections between reading and writing.	○	○	○	○	○

Writing Workshop	1	2	3	4	5
I can use elements of opinion writing to write an essay.	○	○	○	○	○

Unit Theme	1	2	3	4	5
I can collaborate with others to determine how stories shape our world.	○	○	○	○	○

Academic Vocabulary

Talk and write about this unit's theme, *Impact*, using these words:
reveal, traditional, illustrate, interpret, and *predict.*

TURN and TALK Read the sentences with these vocabulary words.
Write a plus (+) for a statement you agree with, or write a minus (–)
for a statement you do not agree with. Explain to a partner why you
agree or disagree with each statement.

Sentence with Academic Vocabulary Word	Agree (+) or Disagree (–)
Stories **reveal**, or make known, how people lived in the past.	
Traditional tales have the same purpose that modern types of stories do.	
Myths often **illustrate**, or show, how gods influence human lives.	
When I **interpret** a story, I figure out the author's exact meaning.	
Reading stories can help me **predict** how real people might respond to future real-life situations.	

INTERACTIVITY

Revealing
SECRETS

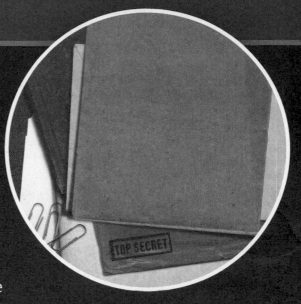

What happens when secrets are revealed? Think about examples in daily life. A surprise birthday party you plan for a friend is secret, but the surprise is lost if the friend finds out before the party. How does that make you feel? How do you think your friend feels?

What about other secrets, like secret clubs, secret treasures, or secret codes? Once a secret is revealed, situations change. Knowledge that used to be protected now belongs to others.

These ideas about secrets are reflected in traditional stories. In many of these stories, a common theme is a secret name. The main character faces an impossible problem. Often a mysterious person offers to help, but that help comes at a great price. The main character has to guess the mysterious person's secret name to avoid paying the price.

▶ Watch

TURN and TALK

What happens when Rumpelstiltskin's secret name is revealed?

Weekly Question

How can revealing a secret make it lose its power?

Quick Write How have you felt when a secret you had was revealed? How have you felt when you learned someone else's secret?

Learning Goal

I can learn about traditional literature by analyzing characters.

Spotlight on Genre

Traditional Literature

Traditional literature has been passed down for generations. Folktales, fables, legends, myths, and tall tales are examples of traditional literature. Sometimes the original author of a traditional tale is unknown. Historically, these tales were spoken instead of written, so they were passed on when people retold them. Traditional literature includes

- **Stock characters,** meaning those who have instantly recognizable traits
- A simple **conflict** between characters
- A **setting** that is easy to recognize
- A fast-moving **plot** that includes repeated actions (usually in threes) and, generally, a happy ending

The characters in traditional literature probably seem familiar to you.

TURN and TALK Describe a favorite story to a partner. Use the anchor chart to decide whether the story is a traditional tale. Take notes on your discussion.

My NOTES _____

_____

_____

_____

_____

_____

TRADITIONAL LITERATURE anchor chart

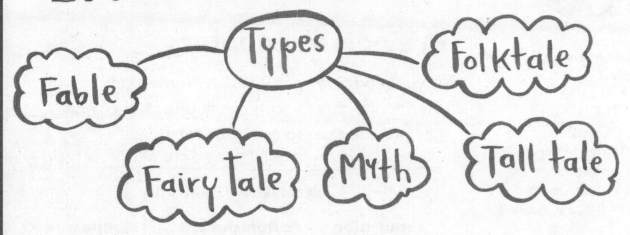

Types

Fable

Folktale

Fairy tale

Myth

Tall tale

CHARACTERS
- Do not change
- One or two traits
  - Wise owl
  - Kind godmother

CONFLICTS
- Fast-paced plot
- Simple and direct
  - Boy defeats giant
  - Woman outsmarts trickster

SETTING
- Does not affect story events
- Can be obviously unrealistic

THEME
- Big idea about human needs or wants
  - "Good triumphs over evil"
  - "Bad deeds are punished"

Judy Sierra got hooked on traditional literature as a child when she discovered her library's fairy tale and folklore section. She now writes picture books and collections of traditional tales. Choosing the perfect topic to write about is important to her. "It has to be something kids are interested in (parents, too)," she says.

from

Can You Guess My Name?

Preview Vocabulary

As you read *Can You Guess My Name?*, pay attention to these vocabulary words. Notice how they provide clues to events and actions.

> **deceived**   **bargain**
>
> **reputation**   **astonishment**   **composure**

Read

Before you begin, establish a purpose for reading. Then follow these strategies as you read these **traditional tales** for the first time.

Notice

character traits and how characters interact.

Generate Questions

before, during, and after reading to clarify understanding of character responses.

First Read

Connect

the selection to other stories you have heard or read.

Respond

by discussing how this text answers the weekly question.

Can You Guess My Name?

by
Judy Sierra

AUDIO

ANNOTATE

Tales Like "Rumpelstiltskin"

Belief in the magical power of names is ancient and wide-spread. According to folk belief, to know a person's name—especially a person's secret name—confers control over him or her. In traditional societies, adults warned children never to tell their names to a stranger, recounting the sad fates of those who did. Tales about guessing names also satisfy keen interest in keeping, telling, and guessing secrets. The secret names in the following tales are made-up nonsense words, and so they are virtually impossible to guess. But everyone knows that secrets are difficult, if not impossible, to keep.

Titeliture
Sweden

Analyze Characters

Underline details that show the daughter's character traits.

1   There was once a poor woman who had an only daughter, and the girl was so lazy that she refused to turn her hand to any work whatsoever. This caused her mother no end of grief. The woman tried time and again to teach her daughter how to spin, but it was of no use. Finally, the mother made the girl sit on the thatched roof of their cottage with her spinning wheel. "Now the whole world can see what a lazy, good-for-nothing daughter you are," said the woman.

2   That very afternoon, the king's son came riding by the house on his way home from the hunt. He was surprised to see such a beautiful young woman sitting on a cottage roof. He asked the girl's mother why she was there.

3   The woman was tongue-tied. How could she tell him the truth? "O-o-oh," she stammered. "My daughter is on the roof because . . . because she is such a clever girl, she can spin the long straw on the roof into pure gold."

Analyze Characters

Underline details that tell what the prince and the queen want from the girl.

deceived caused a person to believe something that is not true

4   "Aha!" cried the prince. "If what you say is true, and this maiden *can* spin gold from straw, she must come to the palace and be my bride." So the girl came down from the roof and mounted the prince's horse behind him, and off they rode.

5   When they reached the palace, the queen led the girl to a small tower room, and gave her a spinning wheel and a great tall pile of straw, and said, "If you can spin this into gold by the time the sun rises, you shall be my son's bride. But if you have deceived us, you will pay with your life."

6   The poor girl was terribly afraid, for of course she had never learned to spin thread, let alone gold. There she sat, her head in her hands, crying bitter tears, when the door to the room slowly opened and in walked an odd-looking little man. He greeted her in a friendly way and asked why she was crying.

7   "I have good reason to cry," answered the girl. "The queen has ordered me to spin this straw into gold before dawn, or I shall pay with my life. No one can spin straw into gold."

8   "No one?" asked the little man. He held out a glove that sparkled and shimmered in the candlelight. "As long as you wear this, *you* will be able to spin it all into gold. But there is a price for using my glove. Tomorrow night I shall return and ask you to guess my name. If you cannot guess it, you must marry me and be my wife."

9   In her despair, the girl made the bargain. As soon
    as the little man disappeared, she put on the glove,
    and sat and spun as if she had been spinning her
    whole life. By sunrise she had spun all the straw into
    the finest gold.

10 Great was the joy of everyone in the palace that
    the prince had found a bride who was so beautiful
    and so skillful. The maiden did not rejoice, though,
    but sat by the window and strained to think what the
    little man's name might be.

11 When the prince returned from the hunt, he sat
    down, and to amuse her he began to tell her of his
    adventures that day. "I saw the strangest thing in the
    forest," he said. "I came to a clearing, and there was
    a little old man dancing round and round a juniper
    bush, singing the most peculiar song."

Copyright © SAVVAS Learning Company, LLC. All Rights Reserved.

CLOSE READ

Analyze Characters

<u>Underline</u> two details that show how the girl feels about the bargain.

bargain an agreement between people about what each will give or receive

Synthesize Information About Characters

Highlight details that show how the girl is able to get what she wants.

Vocabulary in Context

Authors use context clues to help readers determine the correct definition of multiple-meaning words.

Define the word *spun* as it is used in paragraph 15. Underline the context clues that support your definition.

12   "What did he sing?" asked the maiden.

13   The prince replied,

"My bride must sew her wedding dress,

Because she used my magic glove,

And she will never, ever guess

Titeliture's the name of her love."

14   The girl smiled and clapped her hands, and asked the prince to sing the little man's song over and over so that she wouldn't forget. And when the prince left her alone, and night fell, the door to her chamber opened. There stood the little old man, grinning from ear to ear. Before he could say a word, the girl held out the glove, saying, "Here is your glove . . . *Titeliture!*"

15   When the little man heard her speak his name, he shrieked and he spun around and around, and then, with a bang and a great puff of smoke, he shot up through the air and disappeared, taking part of the tower roof with him.

16   The girl and the prince were married, and never again did she have to spin, because, of course, spinning is not proper work for a princess.

How Ijapa the Tortoise Tricked the Hippopotamus

Nigeria: Yoruba

Nigeria

Analyze Characters

Underline a detail that shows how the hippopotamus is similar to Titeliture in the previous tale.

17   The story floats in the air. It hovers. Where will it land? It falls upon Ijapa, the tortoise. He is small, yet he tricked the powerful hippopotamus.

18   Today the hippopotamus lives in the water, where he is ruler of no one. But long ago he lived on dry land and was a mighty chief, second only to the elephant. A curious thing about the hippopotamus was that, apart from his family, no one knew his name. He had seven wives, each as big and plump as he, and his wives were the only ones, besides the hippopotamus himself, who knew what he was called.

19   The hippopotamus and his wives enjoyed nothing more than eating. They would invite all the other animals to dine with them, and then, just as the feasting was about to begin, the hippopotamus would say, "You have come to feed at my table—yes, you have, yes, you have—but who among you knows my name? No one should eat my food or drink my wine if he does not know my name."

Analyze Characters

Underline four verbs that tell you important character traits of Ijapa.

20   Not one of the animals knew the name of the hippopotamus. What could they do? A few of them would guess, but their guesses were always wrong. Time and again, they went away hungry until at last Ijapa the tortoise could stand it no longer.

21   "You say that if we guess your name, you will let us eat your food," said Ijapa. "That is not enough. I think you should do something very big, very important, if we guess your name."

22   "No one will *ever* guess my name!" bellowed the hippopotamus. "But if you do, I promise I will leave the land and go live in the water, and so will all of my family."

23   It was the custom of the hippopotamus and his seven wives to bathe in the river each morning. Ijapa the tortoise hid in the underbrush and watched them come and go, day after day. He noticed that one of the hippo's wives walked more slowly than the rest and was always the last to leave the river.

24   One morning, Ijapa waited for all of the hippos to walk down to the river. Then, while they were washing and drinking, Ijapa dug a hole in the middle of the path. He lowered himself into the hole so that his shell looked like a smooth, worn rock. He waited as the hippo and the first six wives clomped back up the path. Then, before the seventh wife came, he rolled onto his side. His shell stuck up out of the hole. Sure enough, hippo wife number seven tripped on Ijapa's shell. She crashed to the ground and rolled onto her back.

25   "Help!" she shouted. "I can't get up! Isantim, my husband! Come quickly! Help! Isantim!"

26   While the hippopotamus helped wife number seven onto her feet, Ijapa the tortoise walked home, repeating "Isantim, Isantim, Isantim." From morning till night he said the word to himself softly, so that no one else could hear, "Isantim, Isantim, Isantim."

27   At his next feast, the hippopotamus proclaimed as usual, "You have come to feed at my table—yes, you have, yes, you have—but who among you knows my name? No one should eat my food or drink my wine if he does not know my name."

28   Ijapa cleared his throat, *hem, hem.* Then he said, "Be quiet, Isantim, and let me eat."

29   The hippopotamus's mouth dropped open. He was speechless. A cheer went up from all the animals, "Hooray for Ijapa!" They sat down and ate Isantim's food and drank Isantim's palm wine.

30   When the feast was over, Isantim and his wives carried all their belongings to the river. That is where they live today, because Isantim allowed himself to be tricked by Ijapa the tortoise.

CLOSE READ

Synthesize Information About Characters

Highlight three events that are similar to the ones at the end of "Titeliture."

Oniroku

Japan

CLOSE READ

Analyze Characters

Underline two details that show how the builder's qualities are different from those of the girl in "Titeliture."

31   High in the mountains of Japan there flowed a raging river that surged and whirled around rocks and boulders. Since the beginning of time, there had been no way to cross that river, whether on foot, or on horseback, or in a boat. The people who lived near the river had tried again and again to build a bridge, but each time, the river's powerful currents brought their handiwork crashing down.

32   In a faraway city there lived a man who was rumored to be the finest builder in all of Japan. His fame spread throughout the country until at last news of his great skill reached the people who lived in the village beside the river. They sent a messenger, offering whatever price he asked to build a bridge for them.

33   The master builder came at once, eager to test his skill. He stood on the riverbank looking out at the whirlpools and waterfalls that he would have to conquer, and he thought, "There is no bridge that will withstand the power of this river. Yet if I do not build one here, my reputation will be ruined."

reputation the opinion that many people have of someone

34   As the builder pondered his situation, an oni—a hideous horned ogre—arose from the river—*tsaan!* The oni's long, tangled hair swirled about him, and his enormous eyes flashed like lightning.

Synthesize Information About Characters

astonishment a feeling of great surprise

35   "You can never build a bridge here," thundered the oni, "unless you have my help. I bring them all down, yes. I bring them *all* crashing down."

36   The builder began to tremble and shake. Then the oni spoke again: "If you should agree to pay my price, I will not only allow a bridge to be built here, I will build it myself, tonight, while you sleep."

37   How much money would the oni want, the master builder wondered. The people of the village had offered him any price he asked. "Very well," he told the oni, "I will pay your price." Then he went to a local inn for the night, but the uneasy memory of making a bargain with an oni kept him awake for a long time.

38   The next morning, the builder hurried to the spot where he had met the oni. There, to his great astonishment, a magnificent wooden bridge, high and strong, arched above the wild currents of the river. At the foot of the bridge stood the oni, smiling and showing his gruesome yellow tusks.

39   "And now for my payment," he said. "You must give me your eyes!"

40   "My eyes?" the master builder cried out in anguish. "No! No!" How had he fallen into the oni's trap so easily? He dropped to his knees and pleaded with the monster, tears streaming down his cheeks.

41 "Oh, very well," said the oni at last. "Since you carry on in this disgusting manner, I will give you one chance to escape your fate. If by sunset you have learned my name, you may keep your eyes. If not, they are mine!"

42 The oni strode onto the bridge, jumped over the side—*tsaan!*—and sank beneath the swirling rapids.

43 The builder turned and ran into the forest. He had no idea how he could ever discover the name of the oni. Deeper and deeper he plunged into the silent woods.

44 Then he heard the sound of drumming and the footsteps of dancers—*tangura, tangura, tangura, tangura.* He walked toward the noise and found a clearing among the trees where six or seven little oni children were dancing and clapping their paws, and singing,

> "When Oniroku brings the eyes,
>
> How happy we will be!
>
> When Oniroku brings the eyes,
>
> How happy we will be!"

45 The builder's heart pounded with joy and excitement. He turned and ran back to the river.

46 "Oniroku! Oniroku!" he shouted. "Where are you, Oniroku?"

CLOSE READ

Analyze Characters

Underline details in paragraphs 40–43 that show how the builder's reaction to the oni's bargain is different from Ijapa's reaction to Isantim's bargain.

CLOSE READ

Synthesize Information About Characters

Highlight words the oni says that also could have been spoken by Titeliture or Isantim.

composure the calm control of oneself

47   The water churned and bubbled—*tsaan!* The oni's hideous face appeared in the water.

48   "How did you learn my name?" the oni raged. "Who told you my name?" His face turned crimson and great gusts of steam shot from his nose and mouth. At last, he regained his composure. "Keep your silly eyes," he rumbled. "But never tell my name to anyone else, and do not ever dare come back here again."

49   You may be sure that the master builder never did.

Develop Vocabulary

The vocabulary an author chooses can help you analyze characters in traditional tales and other works of fiction.

My TURN Use words from the Word Bank to complete the paragraph. Use each word only once. Then answer the questions.

Word Bank

astonishment   bargain   composure   deceived   reputation

Della knew that she had been _____. Although her _____ with Laszlo was that they would share everything, he had a _____ for putting his own interests ahead of everything else. So despite her initial _____, she quickly accepted that she should have known he would betray their agreement. Therefore, Della kept her _____ and acted as if nothing was wrong.

1. What do the words *bargain*, *astonishment*, and *composure* tell you about Della's character?

_____

_____

_____

2. What do the words *reputation* and *deceived* tell you about Laszlo?

_____

_____

_____

Check for Understanding

My TURN Look back at the texts to answer the questions.

1. What common elements reveal that these three stories are traditional tales?

2. How is the plot of "How Ijapa the Tortoise Tricked the Hippopotamus" different from the plots of the other two stories? Why might this story have been included with the other two?

3. What gives Titeliture, Isantim, and Oniroku their confidence? Why is that confidence misplaced? Cite evidence to support your response.

4. Based on these tales, conclude whether you think luck or thoughtfulness is more useful for getting out of a difficult situation. Write a short argument to convey your opinion, reasons, and evidence.

Analyze Characters

Traditional tales have characters whose traits are not very complicated. Authors often announce what the traits are.

1. **My TURN** Go to the Close Read notes in the stories and underline text that helps you analyze the characters.

2. **Text Evidence** Summarize the text you underlined in the chart. Then answer the question.

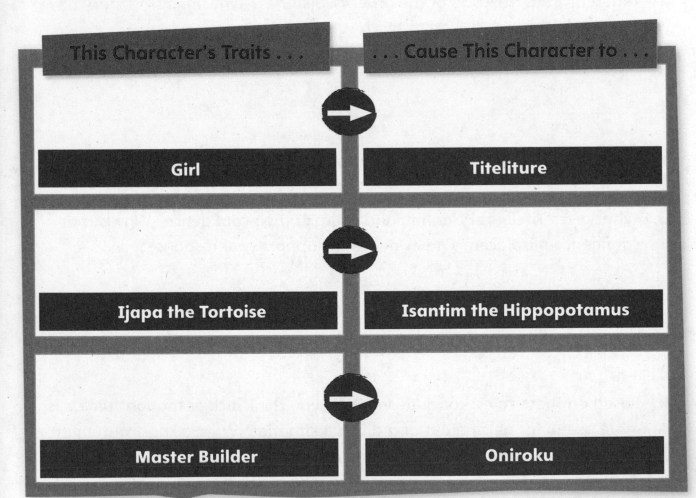

This Character's Traits . . .	. . . Cause This Character to . . .
Girl	Titeliture
Ijapa the Tortoise	Isantim the Hippopotamus
Master Builder	Oniroku

According to your analysis, which character was easiest to trick, and why?

_____

_____

_____

Synthesize Information About Characters

Synthesize, or put together, information from multiple sources to deepen your understanding of traditional tales.

1. **My TURN** Go back to the Close Read notes and highlight text about character interactions in each tale that helps you synthesize evidence to better understand the similarities in the tales.

2. **Text Evidence** Review your annotations and synthesize details to complete the chart.

Question	Synthesis
What action helps the girl and the tortoise remember the secret names?	
How are the bargains of Isantim and Oniroku alike?	
What does the main character do at the end of each story?	
How are the reactions of Titeliture, Isantim, and Oniroku alike at the end of each story?	

New Understanding
What does your synthesis tell you about the stories' shared theme of keeping secrets?

Reflect and Share

Talk About It The characters in *Can You Guess My Name?* face very similar conflicts. Think about all the texts you have read this week. How have characters resolved their conflicts? What did characters do to triumph over evil? Compare and contrast the themes, topics, and patterns of events in the traditional tales and other stories you have read. Use these details to form an opinion about the best way a character achieves his or her goals.

- -

Support an Opinion When you express an opinion, explain your reasons and support them with accurate information. Use these sentence starters to link your statements:

> I think that the best way a character achieves his or her goal is . . .

> I think this because the character . . .

> For example, in the story, I think the theme is . . .

- -

Weekly Question

How can revealing a secret make it lose its power?

Academic Vocabulary

Related words are forms of a word that share roots or word parts. Their meanings are different, but related, and depend on how the words are used in sentences.

My TURN For each vocabulary word,

1. **Read** the Latin origin and meaning.

2. **Consult** a print or digital resource, and write a related word after each arrow.

3. **Use** each related word in a sentence that includes the word's Latin meaning.

Latin *tradere* to hand over	traditional → _____
Latin *praedicere* to foretell	predict → _____
Latin *revelare* to unveil	reveal → _____

1. _____

_____

2. _____

_____

3. _____

_____

Greek and Latin Prefixes

Greek and Latin prefixes add meaning to roots. For example,

- **anti-** is Greek for "against." *Antifreeze* means "against freezing."
- **trans-** is Latin for "across," "through," or "beyond." *Transport* means "carry across."
- **amphi-** is Greek for "on both sides." An *amphibious* vehicle can operate on land and in water.

Sometimes, roots can be added to the front of other roots to change meanings. For example, *auto* is Greek for "self." *Automatic* means "acting on its own."

My TURN In each row, add the prefix to the word. Write the new word and a short definition. If needed, confirm the meaning of the word in a print or online dictionary.

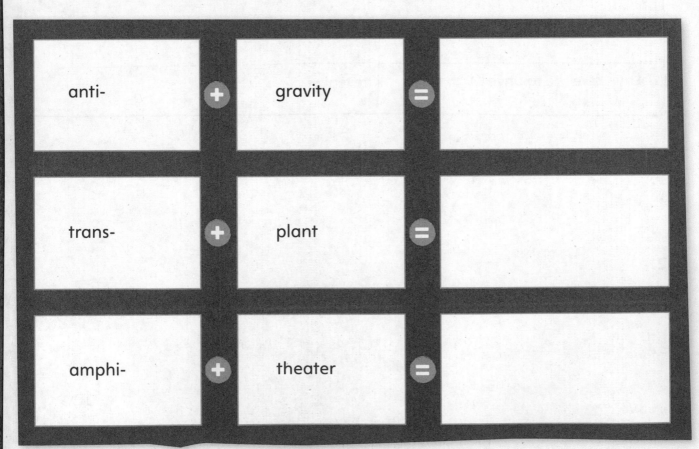

Read Like a Writer

The narrator of a story has a particular **voice** based on a narrative point of view. In traditional texts, narrators are usually all-knowing outsiders. The narrative point of view is called third-person omniscient (all-knowing). An author's use of language contributes to the voice.

Model ! Read the text from "Titeliture."

There was once a poor woman who had an only daughter, and the girl was so lazy that she refused to turn her hand to any work whatsoever. ▶

characters

1. **Identify** In one sentence, Judy Sierra uses the phrases "poor woman," "only daughter," and "so lazy" to introduce two characters.

2. **Question** How do these phrases contribute to the narrator's voice?

3. **Conclude** The phrases show that the third-person narrator knows everything about these characters.

Read the text from "Oniroku."

In a faraway city there lived a man who was rumored to be the finest builder in all of Japan.

My TURN Follow the steps to analyze the author's use of voice.

1. **Identify** In one sentence, Judy Sierra uses the phrases _____ _____ to introduce a character.

2. **Question** How do these phrases contribute to the narrator's voice?

3. **Conclude** The phrases show that _____

Write for a Reader

How much does your narrator know?

A story's narrative point of view helps determine the voice of the narrator. When a narrator knows everything, the author is using third-person omniscient point of view. This means that the narrator's voice will reveal every detail readers need about the characters. An author's use of language contributes to the voice.

My TURN Think about how Judy Sierra's language contributes to the voice in the stories of *Can You Guess My Name?* Now identify how you can choose language to give your narrator a voice.

1. What words and phrases would you use to show that a narrator outside the story knows everything about the character of Ijapa the Tortoise?

_____

_____

2. Write two or three sentences about a character like Titeliture, Isantim, or Oniroku in which the voice reveals the narrator's point of view.

_____

_____

_____

_____

_____

_____

Spell Greek and Latin Word Parts

Understanding Greek and Latin word parts can help you better understand unfamiliar words.

- The word part *anti-* is **Greek** for "against."
- The word part *trans-* is **Latin** for "across," "through," or "beyond."
- The word part *amphi-* is **Greek** for "on both sides."
- The word part *auto-* is **Greek** for "self."

My TURN   Read the words. Spell each one by writing it in the category that corresponds to the meaning of its word part. Use a print or online dictionary to confirm the full meaning of each word.

SPELLING WORDS

automobile	automatic	autopilot	automation
autocracy	transaction	transect	transform
amphibian	amphitheater	autonomous	autoimmune
transparent	transit	transfer	amphibious
antidote	antiseptic	antimatter	antibiotic

Self	Against	Across, Through, Beyond	On Both Sides

Pronouns

Pronouns are words that can replace nouns or groups of nouns.

Subjective	Objective	Possessive	Reflexive
used as the subject of a sentence or clause	used as the object of a verb or a preposition	used to show ownership	used to reflect an action back to the subject
I	me	my, mine	myself
you	you	your, yours	yourself
he	him	his	himself
she	her	her, hers	herself
it	it	its	itself
we	us	our, ours	ourselves
you	you	your, yours	yourselves
they	them	their, theirs	themselves

My TURN Edit this draft by replacing three nouns (and their articles, if present) with pronouns.

Joey let Raj borrow Joey's truck. Later, Raj told Joey the truck had broken. Raj said, "Raj did not break it! Raj's sister broke it."

Joey wasn't so sure, so he said, "Let me ask her herself."

Analyze an Opinion Essay

In an **opinion essay**, a writer expresses a point of view or makes a claim. An opinion essay is an argumentative text that requires three things.

1. The **opinion**, which is the writer's stated preference or point of view about a text or a topic

2. **Reasons** that state why the writer has the opinion

3. **Information** that supports each reason

Swimming is a sport for people of all ability levels. ◄··· The stated point of view

Basic swimming skills will help you enjoy being in the water.

With more skills, you can play and compete in races. ◄··· Two reasons for the point of view

For example, once you know freestyle, you can join the youth

team at the city pool. ◄··· Information that supports the second reason

My TURN Read an opinion essay from your classroom library. Then complete the chart.

Opinion:	Reasons:	Information:

Understand Point of View

An opinion is a stated preference or point of view on a topic. Your point of view is how you think or feel about a topic.

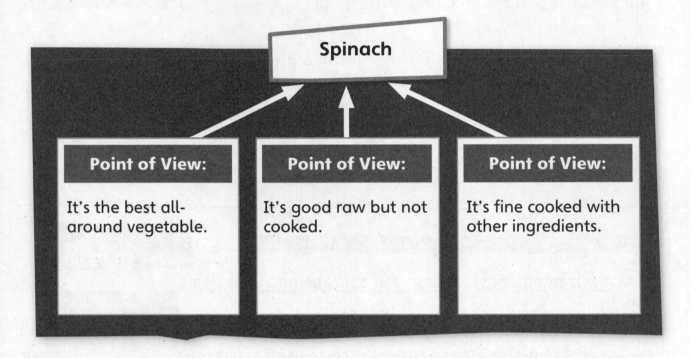

Spinach

Point of View:

It's the best all-around vegetable.

Point of View:

It's good raw but not cooked.

Point of View:

It's fine cooked with other ingredients.

People usually have different points of view about a topic. Your job in an opinion essay is to use strong reasons to support a point of view or a claim.

My TURN Draw an empty copy of the diagram in your writing notebook. Then choose an opinion essay from your classroom library. Find the topic and point of view of the essay, and write them in the diagram. Then write two additional points of view a person might hold about the same topic.

Strong reasons may persuade readers to agree with your point of view.

Understand Reasons and Information

In an opinion essay, give reasons for your opinion. Readers need information that will help them decide how to respond to your opinion. The information you use to support reasons can be any type of detail—facts, definitions, examples, and quotations.

My TURN Read the paragraph. With a partner, highlight the opinion and three reasons the writer gives for the opinion. Find the information the writer gives to support each reason, and underline it. Then discuss each question and write an answer for it together.

Spinach

  Spinach is the best all-around vegetable because it has few calories, it is nutritious, and it is good to eat raw or cooked. Spinach is fat free. One cup of spinach has more than half the vitamin A people need each day. Also, spinach contains a lot of iron. Fresh spinach is crunchy and tasty. Cooked spinach may lose some of its nutrients, but people have cooked spinach for centuries.

1. Does all of the information support a reason? Explain.

_____

_____

_____

2. Are all of the reasons convincing? Explain.

_____

_____

_____

Brainstorm a Topic and Opinion

A **topic** is what you will write about. For an opinion essay, you will need a topic about which you have a point of view or a preference. That point of view or preference will be your opinion.

Writers generate ideas as they begin to plan an opinion essay. One way to generate ideas is **brainstorming**.

My TURN Complete each sentence to brainstorm ideas for an opinion essay. Then highlight the opinion for which you have the strongest reasons.

In my opinion, _____ is the most entertaining sport to watch because

_____

_____ .

In my opinion, _____ is the best book I have read this year because

_____

_____ .

In my opinion, _____ is the best way to spend summer vacation because

_____

_____ .

Make sure you can support strong reasons with information your readers will understand.

Plan Your Opinion Essay

My TURN Complete the checklist to plan your essay. Share your checklist with your Writing Club.

PLANNING AN OPINION ESSAY

☐ I chose a topic about which I have a strong point of view.

☐ I clearly stated my point of view, or my opinion.

☐ I mapped out the reasons I will use to support my opinion.

☐ I mapped out the information I will use to support each reason, using a mapping organizer similar to this one.

Reason 1	Reason 2	Reason 3
Supporting Information	Supporting Information	Supporting Information

☐ I reviewed my plan to make sure it will achieve my purpose.

But
I TRIED OUT
For . . .

Briony whispered before class,
"The cast gets named today!"
The two of us expected roles
in this year's fourth-grade play.

5   Duvall the dancer, that is I.
I'm great at stomps and kicks.
Briony's good at any roles
with singing in the mix.

The tryouts covered everything—
10 dramatics, singing, dance—
we each did well, and so we thought
each had a solid chance.

"Duvall, you'll be lead singer, then.
Briony, you're in charge.
15 You'll lead rehearsals of the songs
because the cast's so large!"

I am surprised, to say the least.
I never knew my voice
was something anybody liked—
20 yet I'm the teacher's choice.

Because it's different, I will try
to pass this startling test.
I guess the teacher trusts that I
will do my very best!

Weekly Question

How can being
different be an
advantage?

TURN and TALK With a partner,
use text evidence to discuss this
question: What specific ideas
about difference is the speaker in
the poem trying to tell readers?
Take notes on your discussion.

Copyright © SAVVAS Learning Company LLC. All Rights Reserved.

Learning Goal

I can learn more about traditional literature by inferring theme.

Spotlight on Genre

Tall Tales

Traditional literature includes many types of stories, such as folktales, fables, and legends. **Tall tales** are a type of traditional tale that is strongly associated with the American frontier. These stories include

- **Humor**
- Impossible **events**
- A **character** or **characters** with superhuman abilities

Establish Purpose The purpose, or reason, for reading tall tales is usually enjoyment. You could also read to find themes that develop in the tales.

A tall tale is an impossible, outrageous story!

TURN and TALK With a partner, discuss different purposes for reading *Thunder Rose*. For example, you may want to discover how the story portrays the American frontier. Set your purpose for reading this text.

My PURPOSE _____

_____

_____

258

Tall Tales Anchor Chart

Purpose

to entertain by contrasting unlikely events with a straightforward style

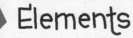

Elements

→ exaggeration for emphasis or humorous effect, also called hyperbole

→ multiple variations as a tale is told and retold

→ usually a particular place and time

→ realistic detail, which highlights the fantastic, exaggerated elements

→ common speech, or conversational style

Text Structure

usually chronological

Kadir Nelson is an artist whose work has appeared on album covers, in museum exhibition halls, and in the collection of the United States House of Representatives. His illustrations for children's books have earned several awards.

Thunder Rose

Preview Vocabulary

As you read *Thunder Rose*, pay attention to these vocabulary words. Notice how they help develop a humorous, casual tone in the tall tale.

> accentuated   obliged
>
> misled   commendable   riled

Read

Active readers of **tall tales** follow these strategies when they read a text the first time.

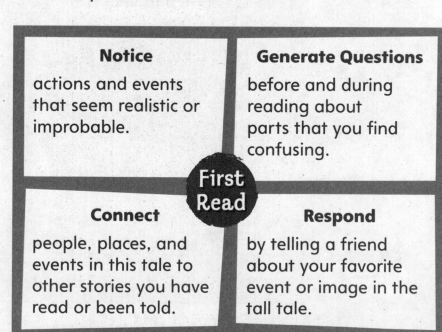

Notice
actions and events that seem realistic or improbable.

Generate Questions
before and during reading about parts that you find confusing.

First Read

Connect
people, places, and events in this tale to other stories you have read or been told.

Respond
by telling a friend about your favorite event or image in the tall tale.

THUNDER ROSE

by JERDINE NOLEN

illustrated by
KADIR NELSON

United States of America

AUDIO

ANNOTATE

CLOSE READ

Make Connections

How do events in this tall tale differ from what you might find in realistic fiction? Highlight text evidence in paragraphs 2–4 that you can connect and contrast with other stories you have read.

accentuated
highlighted; called attention to

1   Rose was the first child born free and easy to Jackson and Millicent MacGruder. I recall most vividly the night she came into this world. Hailing rain, flashing lightning, and booming thunder pounded the door, inviting themselves in for the blessed event.

2   Taking in her first breath of life, the infant did not cry out. Rather, she sat up and looked around. She took hold of that lightning, rolled it into a ball, and set it above her shoulder, while the thunder echoed out over the other. They say this just accentuated the fact that the child had the power of thunder and lightning coursing through her veins.

3   "She's going to grow up to be good and strong, all right," Doc Hollerday said.

4   The child turned to the good doctor with a thoughtful glance and replied, "I reckon I will want to do more than that. Thank you very kindly!"

5   Shifting her gaze to the two loving lights shining on her, which were her ma and pa, she remarked, "Much obliged to you both for this chance to make my way in the world!" Then she announced to no one in particular, "I am right partial to the name Rose."

6   So much in love with this gift of their lives, her ma and pa hovered over her in watchful splendor. Overcome with that love, they lifted their voices in song, an old song and a melody so sweet and true—a lullaby passed down from the ages, echoing since the beginning of time.

7   "There is a music ringing so sweetly in my ears," the newborn exclaimed. "It's giving me a fortunate feeling rumbling deep in the pit of me. I'll register it here at the bull's-eye set in the center of my heart, and see what I can do with it one day!"

8   Rose snored up plenty that first night breathing on her own, rattling the rafters on the roof right along with the booming thunder. There was nothing quiet about her slumber. She seemed determined to be just as forceful as that storm. With the thunder and lightning keeping watch over her the rest of the night, her ma and pa just took to calling her Thunder Rose.

CLOSE READ

Infer Theme

Underline text evidence that helps you understand Rose's character.

obliged grateful; thankful

Vocabulary in Context

Context clues are words and sentences around a word that you can use to determine its meaning.

Use context clues to determine the meaning of *quench*. <u>Underline</u> context clues that support your definition.

misled caused to believe something untrue

9   The next morning, when the sun was high yellow in that billowy blue sky, Rose woke up hungry as a bear in spring, but not the least bit ornery. Minding her manners, she politely thanked her ma for the milk, but it was not enough to quench her hungry thirst. Rose preferred, instead, to drink her milk straight from the cow.

10   Her ma was right grateful to have such a resourceful child. No other newborn had the utter strength to lift a whole cow clear over her head and almost drink it dry. In a moment's time, Rose did, and quite daintily so. She was as pretty as a picture, had the sweetest disposition, but don't let yourself be misled, that child was full of lightning *and* thunder.

11   Out on that paper-bag brown, dusty dry, wide-open space, Rose often was found humming a sweet little tune as she did her chores. And true to her word, Rose did more than grow good and strong.

12   The two-year-old became quite curious about the pile of scrap iron lying next to the barn. Rose took a good-sized piece, stretched it here, bent and twisted it there. She constructed a thunderbolt as black as pitch to punctuate her name. She called it Cole. Wherever she went, Cole was always by her side. Noticing how skilled Rose was with the metal, her pa made sure there was an extra supply of it always around.

13   At the age of five, Rose did a commendable job of staking the fence without a bit of help. During her eighth and ninth years, Rose assembled some iron beams together with the wood blocks she used to play with and constructed a building tall enough to scrape the sky, always humming as she worked.

14   By the time she turned twelve, Rose had perfected her metal-bending practices. She formed delicately shaped alphabet letters to help the young ones learn to read. For his birthday, Rose presented her pa with a branding iron, a circle with a big M-A-C for MacGruder in the middle, just in time, too, because a herd of quick-tempered longhorn steer was stampeding its way up from the Rio Grande. They were plowing a path straight toward her front door.

CLOSE READ

Infer Theme

Underline words and phrases that help you determine how Rose achieves her goals.

commendable worthy of praise

Make Connections

15   Rose performed an eye-catching wonder, the likes of which was something to see. Running lightning-fast toward the herd, using Cole for support, Rose vaulted into the air and landed on the back of the biggest lead steer like he was a merry-go-round pony. Grabbing a horn in each hand, Rose twisted that varmint to a complete halt. It was just enough to restrain that top bull and the rest of the herd.

16   But I believe what touched that critter's heart was when Rose began humming her little tune. That cantankerous ton of beef was restless no more. He became as playful as a kitten and even tried to purr. Rose named him Tater on account of that was his favorite vegetable. Hearing Rose's lullaby put that considerable creature to sleep was the sweetest thing I had witnessed in a long, long time.

17   After the dust had settled, Ma and Pa counted twenty-seven hundred head of cattle, after they added in the five hundred they already had. Using the scrap iron, Rose had to add a new section to the bull pen to hold them all.

18   "What did you do to the wire, Rose?" Ma asked, surprised and pleased at her daughter's latest creation.

19   "Oh, that," she said. "While I was staking the fence, Pa asked me to keep little Barbara Jay company. That little twisty pattern seemed to make the baby laugh. So I like to think of it as Barbara's Wire."

Make Connections

Highlight text that reminds you of another tall tale or traditional tale.

Infer Theme

Underline text evidence that tells you about what Rose values.

20   "That was right clever of you to be so entertaining to the little one like that!" her ma said. Rose just blushed. Over the years, that twisty wire caught on, and folks just called it barbed wire.

21   Rose and her pa spent the whole next day sorting the animals that had not been branded. "One day soon, before the cold weather gets in," she told her pa, "I'll have to get this herd up the Chisholm Trail and to market in Abilene. I suspect Tater is the right kind of horse for the long drive northward."

22   On Rose's first trip to Abilene, while right outside of Caldwell, that irascible, full-of-outrage-and-ire outlaw Jesse Baines and his gang of desperadoes tried to rustle that herd away from Rose.

23   Using the spare metal rods she always carried with her, Rose lassoed those hot-tempered hooligans up good and tight. She dropped them all off to jail, tied up in a nice neat iron bow. "It wasn't any trouble at all," she told Sheriff Weaver. "Somebody had to put a stop to their thieving ways."

24   But that wasn't the only thieving going on. The mighty sun was draining the moisture out of every living thing it touched. Even the rocks were crying out. Those clouds stood by and watched it all happen. They weren't even trying to be helpful.

Copyright © SAVVAS Learning Company LLC. All Rights Reserved.

CLOSE READ

Vocabulary in Context

Look at paragraph 25. Determine the meaning of *parched*.

<u>Underline</u> context clues that support your definition.

25   Why, the air had turned so dry and sour, time seemed to all but stand still. And there was not a drop of water in sight. Steer will not move without water. And that was making those bulls mad, real mad. And when a bull gets angry, it's like a disease that's catching, making the rest of the herd mad, too. Tater was looking parched and mighty thirsty.

26   "I've got to do something about this!" Rose declared.

27   Stretching out several iron rods lasso-fashion, then launching Cole high in the air, Rose hoped she could get the heavens to yield forth. She caught hold of a mass of clouds and squeezed them hard, real hard, all the while humming her song. Gentle rain began to fall. But anyone looking could see there was not enough moisture to refresh two ants, let alone a herd of wild cows.

28   Suddenly a rotating column of air came whirling and swirling around, picking up everything in its path. It sneaked up on Rose. "Whoa, there, now just hold on a minute," Rose called out to the storm. Tater was helpless to do anything about that sort of wind. Those meddlesome clouds caused it. They didn't take kindly to someone telling them what to do. And they were set on creating a riotous rampage all on their own.

29   Oh, this riled Rose so much, she became the only two-legged tempest to walk the western plains. "You don't know who you're fooling with," Rose called out to the storm. Her eyes flashed lightning. She bit down and gnashed thunder from her teeth. I don't know why anyone would want to mess with a pretty young woman who had the power of thunder and lightning coursing through her veins. But, pity for them, the clouds did!

30   Rose reached for her iron rod. But there was only one piece left. She did not know which way to turn. She knew Cole alone was not enough to do the job right. Unarmed against her own growing thirst and the might of the elements, Rose felt weighted down. Then that churning column split, and now there were two. They were coming at her from opposite directions. Rose had some fast thinking to do. Never being one to bow down under pressure, she considered her options, for she was not sure how this would all come out in the end.

CLOSE READ

Infer Theme

Underline events or actions that help you determine a theme of the tall tale.

riled irritated; aggravated

31   "Is this the fork in the road with which I have my final supper? Will this be my first and my last ride of the roundup?" she queried herself in the depths of her heart. Her contemplations brought her little relief as she witnessed the merciless, the cataclysmic efforts of a windstorm bent on her disaster. Then the winds joined hands and cranked and churned a path heading straight toward her! Calmly Rose spoke out loud to the storm as she stood alone to face the wrack and ruin, the multiplying devastation. "I could ride at least one of you out to the end of time! But I've got this fortunate feeling rumbling deep in the pit of me, and I see what I am to do with it this day!" Rose said, smiling.

32   The winds belted at a rumbling pitch. Rose squarely faced that storm. "Come and join me, winds!" She opened her arms wide as if to embrace the torrent. She opened her mouth as if she were planning to take a good long drink. But from deep inside her, she heard a melody so real and sweet and true. And when she lifted her heart, she unleashed her song of thunder. It was a sight to see: Rose making thunder and lightning rise and fall to the ground at her command, at the sound of her song. Oh, how her voice rang out so clear and real and true. It rang from the mountaintops. It filled up the valleys. It flowed like a healing river in the breathing air around her.

33   Those tornadoes, calmed by her song, stopped their churning masses and raged no more. And, gentle as a baby's bath, a soft, drenching-and-soaking rain fell.

34   And Rose realized that by reaching into her own heart to bring forth the music that was there, she had even touched the hearts of the clouds.

CLOSE READ

Make Connections

Highlight a sentence that connects to a previous scene in the tall tale.

Infer Theme

Underline words and phrases that help you determine a theme of this tall tale.

Infer Theme

<u>Underline</u> sentences that
help you infer a theme
of the text.

35   The stories of Rose's amazing abilities spread
like wildfire, far and wide. And as sure as thunder
follows lightning, and sun follows rain, whenever you
see a spark of light flash across a heavy steel gray
sky, listen to the sound of the thunder and think of
Thunder Rose and her song. That mighty, mighty
song pressing on the bull's-eye that was set at the
center of her heart.

Develop Vocabulary

Characters in tall tales set on the frontier often speak in an informal, old-fashioned way. The feelings or associations that their words suggest—the words' **connotations**—give hints to themes in the text.

My TURN Read each excerpt in the chart. Determine if the connotation for each bold word is positive, negative, or neutral. Next, write a sentence for each word that gives it the same connotation. Refer to print or online resources if you wish.

Connotations

Negative ←-- -- -- -- -- -- -- -- Neutral -- -- -- -- -- -- -- --→ Positive

accentuated

Use in *Thunder Rose*	My Sentence
They say this just **accentuated** the fact that the child had the power of thunder and lightning coursing through her veins.	The earrings accentuated her long neck.
"Much **obliged** to you both for this chance to make my way in the world!"	
. . . but don't let yourself be **misled** . . .	
Rose did a **commendable** job of staking the fence without a bit of help.	
Oh, this **riled** Rose so much, she became the only two-legged tempest to walk the western plains.	

Check for Understanding

My TURN Look back at the text to answer the questions.

1. How are characters in a tall tale different from those in realistic fiction? Give two examples from *Thunder Rose* to illustrate the differences.

2. Retell *Thunder Rose*. Remember to maintain the story's meaning and logical order in your retelling.

3. Trace the song Rose has in her heart, starting with the time she first hears it. Observe how she uses it. Based on Rose's actions, what can you conclude about the source and power of the song?

4. Based on what you have read about Thunder Rose, how might being polite, being helpful, and feeling fortunate affect a real person's self-confidence? Cite evidence from the story to support your ideas.

Infer Theme

A **theme** is a main idea or central message. It is an idea that holds
a story together. Often you can infer a theme by thinking about a
character's goals, the actions a character takes to reach them, and
how successful the character is.

1. **My TURN** Go to the Close Read notes in *Thunder Rose* and
   underline text evidence that helps you infer a theme of the story.

2. **Text Evidence** Paraphrase the parts you underlined to fill in the
   web and infer a theme.

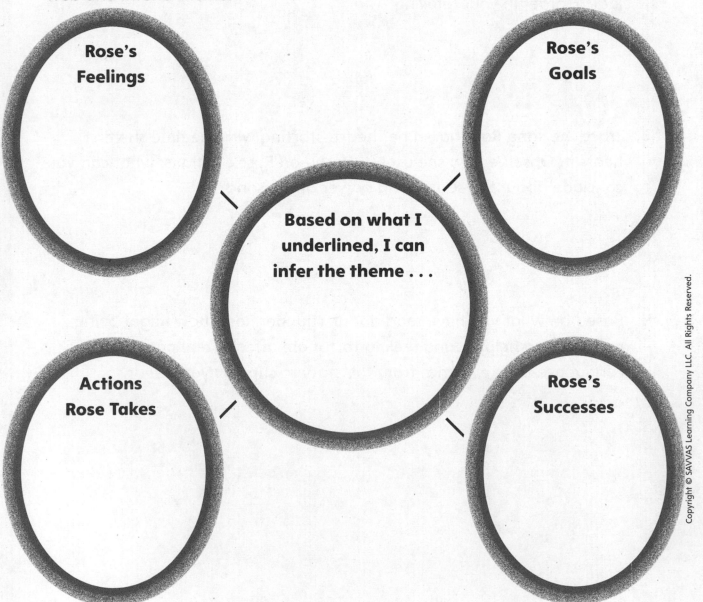

Rose's
Feelings

Rose's
Goals

Based on what I
underlined, I can
infer the theme . . .

Actions
Rose Takes

Rose's
Successes

Make Connections

Readers regularly make connections between ideas in the text they are reading and ideas in other texts. Think about other texts that are like the text you are reading. Think about connections you can make between the texts.

1. **My TURN** Go back to the Close Read notes in *Thunder Rose* and highlight evidence that helps you connect ideas within and across texts.

2. **Text Evidence** Paraphrase your highlighted evidence so that it makes sense and the events are in order. Then answer the question to make connections.

Exaggerated Good Deed	What Motivates the Deed
This Text	**This Text**
Other Texts	**Other Texts**

Make the Connection: How do Thunder Rose's deeds and motivations resemble the motivations and actions of a character in another text you have read?

Reflect and Share

Write to Sources Thunder Rose accomplishes astounding tasks by relying on the song "pressing on the bull's-eye that was set at the center of her heart." Why is the song located there? What makes it press? What strong feelings have you read about or experienced that work in the same way? Follow the process to write about personal connections.

Personal Connections No real person is quite like Thunder Rose. However, like her, real people and characters in other stories have strong feelings that help them achieve their goals.

- Choose two fictional characters who feel something like Thunder Rose's song.

- Describe the characters' and your own thoughts, words, and actions in detail.

- Include a description of what you and the characters have in common that is similar to
  - the song's location
  - the power the song has
- Choose text evidence to support the connections you make.

On a separate sheet of paper, organize your response in two or three paragraphs.

Weekly Question

How can being different be an advantage?

Academic Vocabulary

Learning Goal

I can use language to make connections between reading and writing.

A **synonym** is a word that has the same or nearly the same meaning as another word. An **antonym** is a word that means the opposite of another word. Identifying synonyms and antonyms can help you better understand unfamiliar words.

My TURN For each sentence or pair of sentences,

1. Determine if the sentence or sentences contain a synonym or an antonym for the bold word.

2. Underline the synonyms. **Highlight** the antonyms.

3. Write a short sentence using the synonym or antonym.

1. Bethany hosted the **traditional** family reunion. In keeping with past reunions, she used dishes <u>inherited</u> from her ancestors.
   She inherited her grandmother's silver.

2. Samuel didn't want to **reveal** his feelings. Luckily, he was able to hide his face behind a book.

3. Mr. Martinez asked us to **illustrate** how the machine worked, so we decided to demonstrate it in action.

4. Mariah **interpreted** Joe's messy handwriting, but she completely misunderstood it.

5. We expect that events will transpire as you **predict**.

Suffixes -able, -ible

Suffixes -able and **-ible** are added to nouns or verbs to form adjectives with the meaning "capable of being" or "deserving." For example, the word *irascible* from paragraph 22 of *Thunder Rose* comes from the Latin word *ira* for *anger* and means "capable of being angry." To decode a word with *-able* or *-ible*, look for possible changes to the base word, such as a dropped final e.

My TURN Read each bold word to determine its base word. Then write a definition for the word in the web.

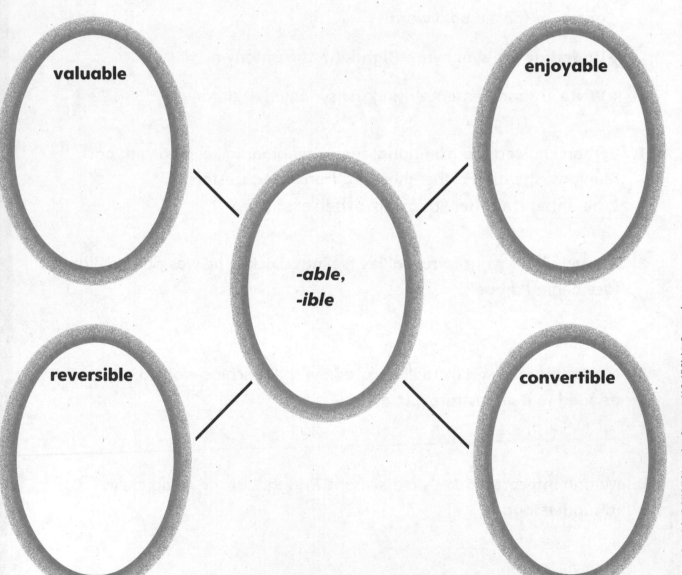

valuable

enjoyable

-able, -ible

reversible

convertible

Read Like a Writer

Authors use exaggeration, a type of figurative language, to emphasize a point or for its comical effect. To exaggerate is to make something greater than it really is.

Model !   Read the text from *Thunder Rose*.

Her ma was right grateful to have such a resourceful child. No other newborn had the utter strength to lift a whole cow clear over her head and almost drink it dry.

exaggeration

1. Identify Jerdine Nolen exaggerates Rose's abilities as a newborn.

2. Question What does this exaggeration emphasize about Rose?

3. Conclude This exaggeration emphasizes Rose's superhuman powers.

Reread paragraph 13.

MyTURN Follow the steps to describe how the author uses exaggeration.

1. Identify Jerdine Nolen exaggerates _____

_____

2. Question What does this exaggeration emphasize about Rose?

3. Conclude Exaggeration of _____

_____

_____

_____

Picture an exaggeration in your mind: does it seem real? intense? humorous?

Write for a Reader

Writers use elements of craft, including figurative language, to call attention to the ideas they want readers to remember. Exaggeration is a tool that writers use for emphasis and for its comical effect.

My TURN Think about how Jerdine Nolen emphasizes Rose's resourcefulness and dedication through exaggeration. Now think of ways you can use exaggeration to emphasize an idea you want readers to remember.

1. To emphasize the features of a setting, what exaggerated descriptions could you use?

_____

_____

_____

_____

2. Write a fictional paragraph that describes the setting of a tall tale. Use exaggeration to emphasize parts of the setting that will strongly affect characters and events.

_____

_____

_____

_____

_____

_____

_____

_____

Spell Words with Suffixes

Suffixes -*able* and **-*ible*** have the same meaning: "capable of being" or "deserving." If the base word ends in *e*, often the *e* is dropped before adding the suffix. For example, the word *sensible* is spelled by dropping the *e* from the base word *sense* and adding *-ible*. Other words, such as *eligible*, do not have English base words. For those words, you must learn their meanings and spellings. Use a print or digital dictionary to determine whether a word uses *-able* or *-ible*.

My TURN Read the words. Then sort and spell the words in alphabetical order.

SPELLING WORDS			
valuable	lovable	reversible	favorable
sensible	collapsible	eligible	audible
comfortable	horrible	divisible	measurable
gullible	tolerable	excusable	understandable
excitable	responsible	plausible	sizable

_____ _____

_____ _____

_____ _____

_____ _____

_____ _____

_____ _____

Adjectives

An **adjective** describes a noun or pronoun. A **comparative adjective** compares two nouns. To make a short adjective comparative, add *-er*: *dark → darker*. To make a long adjective comparative, use the word *more* in front of it: *mysterious → more mysterious*.

A **superlative adjective** compares three or more nouns. To make a short adjective superlative, add *-est*: *bright → brightest*. To make a long adjective superlative, use the word *most* in front of it: *outspoken → most outspoken*.

Adjectives usually come before the word they describe. When you use two or more adjectives to describe one thing, put the adjectives in the correct order. Use the chart to see how adjectives should be listed.

opinion	size	age	shape	color	noun
appetizing	large	fresh	round	yellow	vegetable

My TURN Edit this draft by using correct comparative and superlative adjectives and by placing adjectives in the correct order.

Max turned over the red rectangular box. On the bottom were the stranger markings he had ever seen. He wondered which would be quickest: asking Ms. Huang to translate them or taking a photo and sending it to the new fancy library.

Develop a Topic and Opinion

You develop an opinion—a point of view or a preference about a topic—based on experiences and information you have. Your experiences and information can give strong reasons for your opinion.

Topic: Lace-up shoes versus strap shoes

Experiences and Information

My shoelaces come untied when I run.
Untied shoelaces can cause a runner to fall.
Many shoes close with straps instead of laces.

↓

Strong Reasons

Loose shoelaces are dangerous to runners.
Strap shoes do not come undone when running.

↓

Strong Opinion

I think strap shoes are better for running than lace-up shoes are.

This writer's opinion about running shoes is based on strong reasons that developed from the writer's experiences and information.

My TURN Develop a topic and an opinion as you draft an opinion essay in your writing notebook.

Develop Reasons

You can give reasons for an opinion that will help readers understand it by choosing and developing reasons with an audience in mind.

Topic: Playing on a Basketball Team

Opinion: Players of every level can benefit from playing on a basketball team.

Audience A	Audience B
Students who are choosing which school sports team to try out for	Students who do not plan to join a school sports team
Reasons should answer the question: Why is basketball better than other sports for me?	Reasons should answer the question: How would playing on a basketball team be good for me?

For Audience A, reasons could be that the basketball team outshines other school sports teams and has a winning reputation. For Audience B, reasons could be that team sports benefit everyone and are just as rewarding as non-sports activities.

My TURN Read about the opinion and each audience. Label a reason A if it will appeal *more* to Audience A and B if it will appeal *more* to Audience B.

Opinion: Every classroom should have a pet to care for.

Audience A: teachers who love science

Audience B: teachers who are allergic to cats

_____ 1. Students will learn what animals need to stay healthy.

_____ 2. Students can learn about fish or reptiles.

_____ 3. Students will learn why people choose particular pets.

_____ 4. Students will learn how an animal behaves.

Develop Supporting Details and Facts

A coherent opinion essay includes information that helps readers understand your reasons. The information consists of details such as facts, examples, and quotations. The details are **relevant**, meaning that they are directly related to the topic and focus of the essay.

My TURN The writer's reasons are underlined in the paragraph. Highlight relevant details that support each reason. Cross out details that are not relevant in order to make the paragraph more coherent.

In my opinion, the best thing to do over summer vacation is play outdoors as much as possible. For one thing, the weather is usually the best in summer. Summer is a sunny season. Even if it is hot, it is nicer to be outside than inside. Rain may fall, but it is good for crops. Another reason is that during the school year, there is not much time to play outdoors. Classes start early, by 8 a.m. When classes end, at 3 p.m., most students have to stay in programs until their parents can get them. I have to walk the dog. Then parents want you to eat dinner and do homework. As the year goes by, it gets dark by mid-afternoon. So people should take advantage of the nice weather and the free time during the summer. They should play outside as much as possible.

My TURN Choose relevant supporting details as you compose the draft of an opinion essay in your writing notebook.

Compose a Concluding Statement

The concluding statement in an opinion essay reminds readers of your opinion and reasons. In this example, the writer states a strong opinion and uses *First*, *Second*, and *Third* to make it easy to find reasons for the opinion.

> In conclusion, a four-door car is much more useful than a two-door car for three reasons. First, experience tells us that people can get in and out of a four-door car quickly. Second, the individual doors are not as heavy in a four-door car as they are in a two-door car. Third, passengers in the back seat of a four-door car have their own door handles and window controls to use.

My TURN Read the reasons in the following concluding statement. Then write an opinion the reasons support.

_____

_____

Pandas are native to China, so they belong there. Furthermore, pandas often appear to be unhappy at zoos in countries other than China. In addition, many zoos cannot get enough bamboo to feed pandas.

My TURN Remind readers of your reasons and opinion when you compose the concluding statement for an opinion essay in your writing notebook.

Why should I agree with your opinion?

Compose Using Technology

As you draft an opinion essay, technology can help you find the best structure for your reasons and supporting information. That is because you can experiment with rearranging sentences and paragraphs on a computer.

Type the first draft of your essay on a computer and save it. Learn how to make a copy of the file and rename it, such as adding "experiment" to the filename. Using the copy, learn how to highlight a sentence or paragraph, copy or cut it, and paste it somewhere else.

Think about your readers. Which reason will interest them most? Put it first. For each reason, which supporting detail will mean the most? Put it first.

When you are finished experimenting, save the changes you want to keep, and make this your new draft essay.

My TURN Complete this checklist when you use technology to produce a draft of your opinion essay. Share your completed checklist with your Writing Club.

USING TECHNOLOGY TO PRODUCE WRITING

☐ I made a copy of my draft and renamed it.

☐ I tried to think like one of my readers.

☐ I used technology to put the most interesting reason first.

☐ I used technology to put the most meaningful supporting information first.

☐ I saved the changes I wanted to keep in my new draft essay.

291

INTERACTIVITY

The MYSTERIOUS MASK
A Fairy Tale

Long ago and far away, there lived an angry king. His subjects feared him and would not look at his frightening face. His people's fear made the king even angrier. He ordered his most trusted advisor to find a way to make the people nicer to him.

The advisor created a mask exactly like the king's face with one exception. The mask had a kind expression. The advisor told the king to wear the mask for one hundred days. Now, anyone who looked at the angry king would see a gentle smile.

Word spread that the king had become kinder. Soon the people smiled at him and even began to greet him without fear.

As time went on, the king got to know his people. As he learned about their difficulties, he started to make arrangements. Soon each family had everything they needed. In return, the people held festivals honoring their king.

Why should we do good deeds without expecting anything in return?

The king began to feel that he must stop wearing the mask. Even though the one hundred days had not yet passed, he removed the mask.

When he looked in the mirror, he saw that the smile on the mask had become his own, and that kindness showed in his eyes.

Act It Out With a small group, act out the fairy tale. Then watch other groups perform their versions of the fairy tale. Discuss as a class how reading a story is different from hearing it performed. How do details change when the story is spoken aloud?

Drama

A **drama**, or play, is a story that is written for actors to perform on a stage. A drama includes

- A **cast** of characters
- **Dialogue** between characters
- **Character tags** to identify which character is speaking
- **Stage directions** to tell performers how to speak or what to do
- A **conflict** between characters and its **resolution**
- A **theme**, or central meaning, that guides the action

Some dramas also include **acts** and **scenes**. **Acts** are major divisions of the overall action of the drama. **Scenes** are smaller divisions of action within an act. Authors can use both types of divisions or choose not to use them depending on how the author wants the audience to experience the story.

The structure of a drama helps performers know what to say and how to act.

TURN and TALK   To compare two genres, describe how they are similar. To contrast, explain how the purposes, elements, or structures of the genres are different. With a partner, use the anchor chart to compare and contrast dramas and traditional stories. Take notes on your discussion.

My NOTES _____

_____

_____

Drama
Anchor Chart

Purpose:

To entertain an audience

Elements:

Cast of characters—played by actors on a stage

Setting—a description of the time and place the action occurs

Dialogue—the characters' speech and character tags

Stage directions—instructions for the actors, setting description

Structure—action can be organized into acts and scenes

Point of View:

Third-person objective

Pamela Gerke loves drama. She has been a drama and music teacher for more than twenty-five years. She has also written books about drama and even founded a theater group for children! Pamela Gerke enjoys folktale dramas because they help us "learn about other groups of people" and spread "awareness and understanding."

La Culebra (The Snake)

Preview Vocabulary

As you read the drama "La Culebra," pay attention to these vocabulary words. Notice how they help you understand the characters and connect the drama to the unit theme, *Impacts*.

sensitive	exchange
deed insisted	satisfied

Read

Remember to establish your purpose before you begin reading. Then follow these strategies as you read the **drama** for the first time.

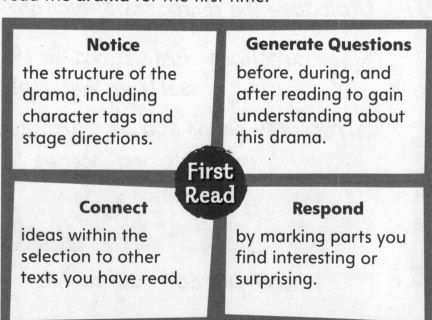

Notice the structure of the drama, including character tags and stage directions.

Generate Questions before, during, and after reading to gain understanding about this drama.

First Read

Connect ideas within the selection to other texts you have read.

Respond by marking parts you find interesting or surprising.

LA CULEBRA

(THE SNAKE)

from *Multicultural Plays for Children*
by *Pamela Gerke*

Teacher Notes

This script includes a large Spanish vocabulary which is useful for integrating Spanish language studies with reading and social studies. Because this play is fairly simple to rehearse and produce, it's a good one for when you don't have a lot of preparation time, or can be used simply as a reading activity. There are very few characters but all characters can be played as small groups. See Appendix A for plural endings to the Spanish words.

In this tale, *Coyote* plays the sly "Trickster," a figure well-known as well in some North American Native traditions. In the Pacific Northwest, "Raven" plays a like figure, as does "Anansi the Spider" in tales from Ghana and Liberia.

AUDIO

ANNOTATE

Explain Elements of a Drama

The script of a drama, or play, contains elements not found in prose.

<u>Underline</u> text evidence that shows how a drama is different from other forms of literature.

RUNNING TIME OF SHOW *(approximate)*:
15 minutes

REHEARSAL TIME NEEDED:
6–8 hours

OTHER PRODUCTION TIME NEEDED:
2–4 hours

CAST SIZE:
Minimum: 5, plus ABUELA/NARRATOR (actors playing NIETO, ESPOSA and PERROS can play other characters)
Maximum: 20–25 (all characters can be played as small groups — see Appendix A to change word endings to plural)

GENDER OF CHARACTERS:
CAMPESINO is a male farmer and ESPOSA is his wife. GALLINA is a hen. All other characters can be played as either female or male — see Appendix A to change gender of words.

CHARACTERS:
ABUELA / ABUELO (NARRATOR),
     grandmother / grandfather
NIETO / NIETA, grandson / granddaughter
BURRO, donkey
GALLINA, chicken, hen
PERROS, dogs
CULEBRA, snake
CAMPESINO, farmer
COYOTE
ESPOSA, wife of the farmer

Setting: A small farm in Mexico. There need not be a set but there will need to be places where CAMPESINO *can escape* COYOTE. *A couple of sturdy tables can serve as house and barn, with cloth hanging down the front, and* CAMPESINO *can escape to the rooftops. A backdrop of a Mexican farm is optional.* LIGHTS UP. BURRO, GALLINA & PERROS *enter and stand around the barnyard.* ABUELA *enters and stands to one side, watching.* NIETO *enters and goes up to* BURRO.

CLOSE READ

Explain Elements of a Drama

<u>Underline</u> text evidence that tells you where the drama takes place.

1 **NIETO.** *¡Hola, Señor Burro! ¿Habla español?*

2 **BURRO.** Hee haw! Hee haw!

3 **NIETO.** *¡Hola, Señorita Gallina! ¿Habla español?*

4 **GALLINA.** Plock-plock-plock-plock-plu-PLOCK!

5 **NIETO.** *¡Hola, Perros! ¿Hablan español?*

6 **PERROS.** Woof! Woof!

7 **NIETO.** (*Frustrated.*) Doesn't anyone around here speak Spanish?!!

Explain Elements of a Drama

Underline words that tell you which character says each line of dialogue.

sensitive capable of responding to stimulation; easily affected

exchange return

(*ABUELA comes over to her.*)

8   ABUELA. I do! *¡Hola, Nieto!* Hello, grandson!

9   NIETO. *¡Hola, Abuela!* Hello, Grandmother!

10 ABUELA. *Nieto*, did you know there was a time when nobody in Mexico spoke Spanish? When the Aztecs lived here they spoke a language called *Náhuatl*. And before that, there was a time when humans and *los animales* spoke the same language. Would you like to talk with *los animales, Nieto*?

11 NIETO. *¡Sí! ¡Sí!*

12 ABUELA. You can learn a lot from *los animales*. When *los animales* were able to talk with the children, *los niños*, the children were a lot smarter. And more sensitive. Back then, *los niños* didn't ask for money in exchange for a favor. They were not demanding and did not throw tantrums. The snake, *La Culebra*, taught them these things. I will tell you a story about *La Culebra*. This happened a long time ago.

(*ANIMALES exit. ABUELA stands to one side while NIETO either stands with her throughout the play or goes backstage in order to play another character.*)

13 **ABUELA.** In a small town in *México* called *San Miguel Tejocote*, there once was a terrible windstorm.

(*SOUND EFFECTS: WINDSTORM. CULEBRA enters and lies down, center, and a large tree trunk is placed over her. SOUND EFFECTS END.*)

14 **ABUELA.** Later that day, *El Campesino*, the farmer, was working on his land when he heard someone screaming.

(*CAMPESINO enters, with hoe.*)

15 **CULEBRA.** (*Screaming.*) ¡Ay, socorro! ¡Ay, socorro!

16 **ABUELA.** *La Culebra* was trapped under a tree trunk and would surely die if she was not released!

CLOSE READ

Explain Elements of a Drama

In a drama, the characters move around and sometimes come onto or leave the stage.

Underline words and phrases that tell you about the movements of the characters.

Explain Elements of a Drama

This drama contains one character who tells a story. The story is about the actions of other characters in the drama.

Underline text evidence that shows the relationship between Abuela's words and the other characters.

deed something that is done; an action taken

insisted demanded or required something forcefully

(CAMPESINO *goes over to* CULEBRA *and lifts tree off of her.* CULEBRA *shakes off the splinters.*)

17   CULEBRA. *¡Gracias!* . . . Now I'm going to eat you!! *¡Te voy a comer!*

(CULEBRA *chases* CAMPESINO)

18   CAMPESINO. *¡Ay, socorro! ¡Ay, socorro!*

(CAMPESINO *finds a safe place, such as on a rooftop.*)

19   CAMPESINO. But I saved your life!

20   CULEBRA. *Sí*, but remember the old proverb: If you do a good deed, in return something bad will happen to you!

21   ABUELA. *El Campesino* tried to explain that *La Culebra* had it all wrong, that if you do good, then good will come back to you in return. But *La Culebra* would not agree and insisted on eating *El Campesino* in return for saving her life. They argued for some time, until finally they agreed to ask *tres animales*, three animals, for their opinions on this matter. If all agreed with *La Culebra*, then she would eat *El Campesino*. They walked around the farm until they found *un burro*, a donkey.

(BURRO enters and CAMPESINO & CULEBRA walk over to him.)

22 **CAMPESINO & CULEBRA.** *¡Hola, Señor Burro!*

23 **BURRO.** *¡Hola, Campesino! ¡Hola, Culebra!*

24 **CAMPESINO & CULEBRA.** Is it true that if you do a good deed, in return something bad will happen to you?

25 **BURRO.** *(Thinks a moment.)* . . . *¡Sí!* I've worked hard all my life but when I get old they will surely kill me for my skin. So, if you do a good deed, in return something bad will happen to you! At least that's so for burros.

26 **CULEBRA.** *¡Te voy a comer!*

27 **CAMPESINO.** *¡Ay, socorro! ¡Ay, socorro!*

(CULEBRA chases CAMPESINO and BURRO joins in the chase until CAMPESINO finds a safe place.)

28 **CAMPESINO.** But we still have two more *animales* to ask—that was the deal!

Vocabulary in Context

Context clues can help you determine a term's meaning.

Where does "*¡Ay, socorro!*" appear in the dialogue of the drama? Use context clues to come up with a translation of the term. <u>Underline</u> text evidence that supports your translation.

29   **CULEBRA.** *Sí.*

30   **ABUELA.** They continued on their way and after awhile they met *una gallina*, a chicken.

        (*GALLINA enters and the others walk over to her.*)

31   **CAMPESINO, CULEBRA & BURRO.** *¡Hola, Señorita Gallina!*

32   **GALLINA.** *¡Hola, Campesino! ¡Hola, Culebra! ¡Hola, Burro!*

33   **CAMPESINO, CULEBRA & BURRO.** Is it true that if you do a good deed, in return something bad will happen to you?

34   **GALLINA.** (*Thinks a moment.*) . . . *¡Sí!* I lay eggs every day for people to eat. But when I get old they will surely kill me and make me into chicken soup! So if you do a good deed, in return something bad will happen to you. At least that's so for *gallinas*.

35   **CULEBRA.** *¡Te voy a comer!*

36   **CAMPESINO.** *¡Ay, socorro! ¡Ay, socorro!*

        (*CULEBRA chases CAMPESINO and BURRO & GALLINA join in the chase until CAMPESINO finds a safe place.*)

37   **CAMPESINO.** But we still have one more *animale* to ask— that was the deal!

38   **CULEBRA.** *Sí.*

39   **ABUELA.** After a while they met *un coyote*, a coyote.

     (COYOTE *enters and the others walk up to him.*)

40   **CAMPESINO, CULEBRA, BURRO & GALLINA.** ¡Hola, Coyote!

41   **COYOTE.** *¡Hola, Campesino! ¡Hola, Culebra! ¡Hola, Burro! ¡Hola, Gallina!*

42   **CAMPESINO, CULEBRA, BURRO & GALLINA.** Is it true that if you do a good deed, in return something bad will happen to you?

43   **COYOTE.** How would I know? Everyone knows *Coyote* never does a good deed!

44   **ALL.** But you have to decide! You're the last *animal!*

45   **CULEBRA.** Besides, I'm getting very hungry!

46   **COYOTE.** *(Thinks a moment.)* . . . You must show me exactly how it was.

47   **ABUELA.** And so they went back and put the tree trunk on top of *La Culebra* just like it was before.

     (*They do so.*)

48   **COYOTE.** *(To CULEBRA:)*
     Can you move now?

Summarize Literary Text

Summaries include the most important events and details, retold in order.

Highlight words and phrases that you would include in a summary of the drama.

Explain Elements of a Drama

Underline words and phrases in paragraphs 55–58 that tell the reader what a character is thinking or what a character's personality is like.

satisfied pleased or happy with something

49 CULEBRA. No!

50 COYOTE. Are you sure?

51 CULEBRA. Of course I'm sure! I can't move!

52 COYOTE. Not even *un poco*, a little?

53 CULEBRA. No, not even *un poco*!

54 COYOTE. So now you're just like at the beginning—the good deed is undone. Therefore, you cannot eat him! *¿Sí?*

55 CULEBRA. (*Sighs, outsmarted.*) *Sí.*

56 ABUELA. Satisfied that the matter was solved, everyone went back to their business about the farm.

(*BURRO & GALLINA exit.*)

57   CAMPESINO. *(To* COYOTE:*)* ¡*Gracias, Coyote!* You saved my life!

58   COYOTE. *(With false sweetness.)* Well, I believe we should all help each other in this world. Just look at me: I'm sick! I'm soooo sick and faint with hunger. . . . But you can help me.

59   CAMPESINO. How?

60   COYOTE. Bring me *dos borregos,* two of your best sheep. When I eat them, I will feel better!

61   CAMPESINO. ¡*Sí!*

(COYOTE *exits while* CAMPESINO *goes to his house as* ESPOSA *enters. Meanwhile,* CULEBRA *can either exit or stay in place under the log until the end of the play.)*

Summarize Literary Text

What does the audience of the drama know that the characters in the drama do not know?

Highlight an event that you would include in a summary of the drama.

62 **ABUELA.** *El Campesino* went home and told his *esposa*, his wife, the whole story.

63 **ESPOSA.** You're crazy! *¡Estás loco!*

64 **CAMPESINO.** Just give *Coyote dos borregos!*

(*CAMPESINO exits.*)

65 **ESPOSA.** Those coyotes are tricky but I know how to deal with them! (*Calls out:*) *¡Perros! ¡Perros!*

(*PERROS enter, barking.*)

66 **PERROS.** *¿Sí, Señora?*

67 **ESPOSA.** Get in this sack, *por favor.*

68 **PERROS.** *Sí, Señora.*

(*PERROS get into the sack. CAMPESINO enters.*)

69 **ESPOSA.** Here they are, *dos borregos!*

70 **CAMPESINO.** *¡Gracias!*

(*ESPOSA exits but watches the following scene from a hiding place. COYOTE enters.*)

71 **CAMPESINO.** Here they are, *dos borregos!*

72 **COYOTE.** *¡Gracias!*

(*COYOTE opens the sack. PERROS jump out, barking and snapping and chase COYOTE.*)

73 **COYOTE.** *¡Ay, socorro! ¡Ay, socorro!*

(*COYOTE finds a safe place temporarily.*)

74   **COYOTE.** *La Culebra* was right! I did a good deed for *El Campesino* and in return something bad happened to me!

     (*PERROS* chase COYOTE *offstage.* ALL *exit.*)

75   **ABUELA.** And that, *Nieto,* is the end of the story of *La Culebra.*

76   **NIETO.** Is it true? If so, I will never do any good deeds!

77   **ABUELA.** No, no, that's not the way it works! You should always do good deeds—but you should never expect something in return. If you only do good in order to get something back, then you will be tricked like *El Coyote. ¿Comprendes?*

78   **NIETO.** *¡Sí! ¡Sí!*

     (*MUSIC BEGINS: "La Bamba" or other Mexican folksongs.* ALL *enter and sing / dance. MUSIC ENDS.*)

79   **ALL.** *¡El fin!* The end!

     (*LIGHTS DOWN.*)

CLOSE READ

Summarize Literary Text

Summaries should include the theme or message of a text.

Highlight text evidence that helps you determine a theme.

Summarize Literary Text

Highlight words that you would use to summarize or retell the drama in a meaningful way.

APPENDIX A:
Vocabulary List of Foreign Language

SPANISH	ENGLISH	PRONUNCIATION
abuela / abuelo	grandmother / grandfather	ah-booeh'-la / ah-booeh'-lo
animales	animals	ah-nee-mah'- lehs
¡Ay, socorro!	Help!	eye' suh-ko'-ro! *
borregos	sheep	bo-ray'-goes * (soft "s")
burro, el (plural: los burros)	donkey	boo'-ro *
campesino, el (plural: los campesinos)	farmer	kahm-pah-see'-no
coyote, el (plural: los coyotes)	coyote	ko-jo'-tay
culebra, la (plural: las culebras)	snake	koo-lay'-brah
el fin	the end	el feen'
esposa, la (plural: las esposas)	wife	eh-spo'-sah
estás loco	you're crazy	eh-stahs' lo'-ko
gallina, la (plural: las gallinas)	chicken, hen	gah-djee'-nah
gracias	thank you	grah'-see-ahs * (soft "s")
¿Habla español?	Do you speak Spanish?	ahb'-lah es-pah-nyol'?

SPANISH	ENGLISH	PRONUNCIATION
hola	hello	oh'-lah
la / el / las / los	the (feminine / masculine / feminine-plural / masculine-plural)	lah / el / lahs / lohs
México	Mexico	meh'-hee-ko
Náhuatl	(language of the Aztecs)	naw'-tl
nieto / nieta	grandson / granddaughter	nee-eh'-toe / nee-eh'-tah
perros, los	dogs	pair'-ros * (soft "s")
por favor	please	pour fah-vohr'
señor	Mr. or sir	see-nyor'
señora / señorita	Mrs. or madame / Miss	see-nyor'-ah / see-nyor-ee'-tah
sí	yes	see
San Miguel Tejocote	(name of a town)	sahn mee-gel' tah-ho-ko'-tay (hard "g")
una / un	a	oo'-nah / oon
un poco	a little	oon po'-ko
"La Bamba" (song)		
Para bailar la bamba	In order to dance "La Bamba"	pah'-rah bye'-yah lah bahn' bah
Se necesita	You need to have	say neh-seh-see'-tah
una poca de gracia;	a little gracefulness	oo'-nah poh'-kah day grah'-see-yah
Y otra cosita,	And something else:	ee oh'-trah ko-see'-ta
ay arriba y arriba!	UPBEAT! Yahoo!	yah-ree'-bah, yah-ree'-bah
por ti seré	it's for you to be	por tee seh-rey'

* NOTE: roll the "r's"

Develop Vocabulary

The events in a drama are revealed by dialogue and actions. To understand what is happening, the audience must interpret what characters say and do.

My TURN Each section of dialogue contains an underlined synonym of a word in the Word Bank. Identify which Word Bank word goes with each synonym. Then write that word on the line.

Word Bank
deed   insisted   sensitive   exchange   satisfied

DEREK: We must find a way to calm down the prince. He is so <u>emotional</u> about his shoes!

_____

PAOLO: I know, I know. I never meant to make a <u>trade</u> with his slippers. I thought they were yours!

_____

DEREK: I should not have <u>demanded</u> that you get the golden apple at all costs. Now we just have to solve our problem.

_____

PAOLO: Still, I wish I could undo my <u>action</u>. But you are right. Our job now is to settle him down.

_____

DEREK: So we agree. He will never be <u>content</u> with an apology. We must find an even better pair of slippers.

_____

Check for Understanding

My TURN Look back at the text to answer the questions.

1. Imagine that you are in charge of sharing "La Culebra" with another class. Which elements of the text would help you?

2. What evidence supports the conclusion that this drama resembles traditional literature, such as legends, tall tales, and myths?

3. How do Esposa's actions affect the other characters, including Abuela and Nieto? Do these characters undergo any changes?

4. What does the drama "La Culebra" imply about why animals might be given human words and actions in a drama?

Explain Elements of a Drama

The script of a drama tells how the stage should look, how characters should move, what characters should say, and the emotions characters should express. Explaining these elements will help you understand a drama and how it compares to other types of literary writing.

1. **My TURN** Go to the Close Read notes in "La Culebra" and underline elements of the drama.

2. **Text Evidence** Complete the diagram by explaining what you underlined and giving quotations as examples.

Elements of a drama the audience sees and hears	Elements of this drama that are like elements of a story
Examples	Examples

Explain how the structure of "La Culebra" is similar to and different from the structure of a story and a poem you have read.

Summarize Literary Text

When you summarize a drama, use your own words to describe the characters and the setting and tell the main events in order.

1. **My TURN** Go back to the Close Read notes in "La Culebra" and highlight parts you would use in a summary of the drama.

2. **Text Evidence** Use your highlighted text to complete the diagram and answer the question.

Title

Characters	Setting

Events

1. First

2. Next

3. Then

4. Last

Question: What theme, or message, does the end of "La Culebra" have for all people, not just for Abuela's grandson?

Reflect and Share

Write to Sources This week you read a drama in which people and animals taught a lesson about doing good deeds. What other texts have you read that teach about doing good deeds? Think about characters' thoughts, words, and actions. In your opinion, should people consider risks and rewards before they do good deeds? Use the following process to gather evidence for an opinion paragraph.

- -

Use Text Evidence Support the opinion you express with examples from texts you have read. Write a sentence that states your opinion. Then gather evidence:

> Review texts that have taught you about the risks and rewards of doing good deeds. →

> Describe how characters are affected by good deeds. ↓

> Paraphrase examples that support your opinion. Cite each source. Write your opinion paragraph on a separate sheet of paper.

- -

Weekly Question

Why should we do good deeds without expecting anything in return?

Academic Vocabulary

Learning Goal

I can use language to make connections between reading and writing.

Context Clues The context in which a word is used gives you clues to its meaning. Context clues include definitions, examples, synonyms, and antonyms.

My TURN Using the Word Bank,

1. **Identify** pairs of words with similar meanings.

2. **Write** a sentence for each pair of words, using one as a context clue to the meaning of the other. Underline the word pair in each sentence.

Word Bank				
customary	forecast	show	traditional	reveal
illustrate	interpret	clarify	predict	uncover

1. After you <u>interpret</u> the signals, please <u>clarify</u> their meaning for me.

2. _____

3. _____

4. _____

5. _____

Syllable Pattern VV

Syllable pattern VV occurs when two vowels are next to each other but in different syllables. For example, a syllable breaks between *e* and *a* in mal/le/a/ble, and between *o* and *i* in so/lo/ist.

MyTURN Read each word by saying it aloud to yourself. Then rewrite it with a slash (/) between any vowels that are in separate syllables.

continuing _____

violet _____

dialogue _____

continuation _____

pianist _____

dietician _____

High-Frequency Words

High-frequency words are words that you will see over and over again in texts. Sometimes they do not follow regular sound-spelling patterns. Read these high-frequency words: *instead, type, temperature, everyone, method, iron*. Try to identify them in your independent reading.

Read Like a Writer

One way authors draw attention to their messages is to write something that contradicts the expectations of readers.

Model !   Read the text from "La Culebra."

> CULEBRA: Si, but remember the old proverb: If you do a good deed, in return something bad will happen to you!
>
> ABUELA: *El Campesino* tried to explain that *La Culebra* had it all wrong, that if you do good, then good will come back to you in return. . . .

contradiction

1. Identify Pamela Gerke shows a contradiction between the snake's belief and that of the man.

2. Question Why does she include this contradiction?

3. Conclude Pamela Gerke includes this contradiction to make readers think about which message is correct.

Reread paragraph 77.

My TURN Follow the steps to analyze the passage. Describe how the author uses a contradiction to call attention to a message.

1. Identify Pamela Gerke shows a contradiction between _____

_____

2. Question Why does she include this contradiction?

3. Conclude Pamela Gerke includes this contradiction to _____

_____

_____

Write for a Reader

Hold readers' attention by making them think about the unexpected!

Writers may put surprising or contradictory ideas together to encourage readers to analyze the message of a text.

My TURN Think about how Pamela Gerke contrasted proverbs about doing good deeds so that readers would have to think about her message. Now imagine how you could use the same strategy to communicate a message to your readers.

1. If you wanted readers to remember an idea about the benefit of attending an orchestra concert, what contrast or contradiction could you use to get their attention?

_____

_____

_____

2. Write a fictional passage with a contradiction that will encourage readers to think about your message.

_____

_____

_____

_____

_____

_____

_____

Spell Words with Syllable Patterns

Syllable patterns can help you identify vowels you need to spell words. For example, when you pronounce words with the VV syllable pattern, you can hear the vowels in each syllable.

My TURN Read each word aloud to hear its sound spelling. Then sort and spell the words by the VV syllable pattern.

SPELLING WORDS

trial	violet	pioneer	fluid
client	dialogue	reality	pliable
reliable	diagonal	poetry	triumph
create	diagram	gradual	quiet
denial	immediate	duality	variety

Vowels in the VV Syllable Pattern

ia

trial

iu

io

ui

ea

ie

oe

ua

Adverbs

Use adverbs to make your writing vivid by modifying verbs, adjectives, and other adverbs.

Adverbs of frequency—such as *always, never, occasionally,* and *sometimes*—describe a verb by telling how frequently the action happens.

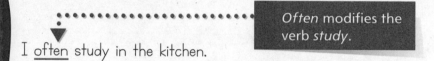

I <u>often</u> study in the kitchen.

> *Often* modifies the verb *study*.

Adverbs of degree—such as *very, quite, somewhat,* and *slightly*—describe an adjective or an adverb by telling how strongly it applies to a situation.

Our takeout order is <u>somewhat</u> late.

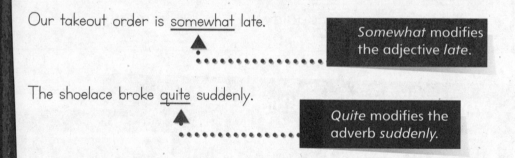

> *Somewhat* modifies the adjective *late*.

The shoelace broke <u>quite</u> suddenly.

> *Quite* modifies the adverb *suddenly*.

My TURN Edit this draft to change its meaning slightly by replacing at least four adverbs.

Luna often takes her scooter to the store. She frequently leaves it next to a parking meter while she shops. In contrast, Hiram is careful and rarely lets his scooter out of his sight. Whenever he sees Luna's scooter at the store, he is slightly tempted to hide it and teach her a lesson!

Compose the Introduction and Conclusion

Learning Goal

I can use elements of opinion writing to write an essay.

To write an opinion essay, state an opinion in the introduction. After presenting reasons and supporting information in the body of the essay, conclude by restating your opinion and summarizing your reasons.

My TURN Write a conclusion that reflects the introduction in the chart.

Introduction	Reasons	Conclusion
"The Circuit" by Francisco Jiménez is the best story we read this year.	• The story shows how people overcome problems. • They adjust to new places over and over. • Concrete details make the characters and settings easy to imagine.	

My TURN Include an introduction and conclusion when you develop and compose an opinion essay.

Organize Reasons

Organize reasons to best support the purpose of an opinion essay. Often the reason that will interest readers most is mentioned first.

Topic: Science Class
Audience: Students who will be voting for the class they enjoy most
Opinion: Science class is the most fun of all the classes in school.
Reasons should answer the question readers will have: Why do I have more fun in science class than in any other class?

Read these sample reasons and explanations.

Reasons	Explanations
With appropriate safety measures in place, students have fun trying out their own ideas in science class. The science classroom has models of plants and animals.	This reason goes first because it directly answers the readers' question. This reason does not directly answer the readers' question, so it should go second.

My TURN Read the opinion and notice the audience. Then number the reasons to show the best order.

Opinion: The perfect lunch is a salad.
Audience: Fifth-grade students

_____ Reason: Eating salad gives energy for the afternoon.

_____ Reason: Two cups of raw leafy greens count as about half of a person's daily vegetable requirement.

_____ Reason: Fresh vegetables taste great with added protein, such as eggs or cheese.

My TURN To appeal to your audience, organize your reasons logically when you draft an opinion essay. Use a paragraph for each reason. State the reason in a topic sentence. Follow that with information that relates to the reason.

Organize Supporting Details

Readers are most likely to agree with your opinion when you give them convincing reasons to agree. Supporting details such as facts, definitions, examples, and quotations from experts help make your reasons convincing.

Facts are true statements that can be proved with evidence. Make it easy for readers to find the relevant facts that support your reasons. As you read the paragraph, notice that a reader could use resources to prove that the **facts** are true.

Topic Sentence: A meal built around beans can be very nutritious. For example, **Fact:** Beans are excellent sources of protein, iron, and zinc. **Fact:** Serving-for-serving, they have as much protein as many kinds of meat or fish. **Fact:** Like many vegetables, beans are also good sources of fiber.

My TURN Read all of the sentences below. Then number each example sentence to show the best order of supporting details.

Topic Sentence: One reason to see a dentist regularly is to make sure your teeth stay healthy.

_____ If you wait until you have a problem to see the dentist, you might need to have teeth repaired.

_____ For example, if you don't fix cavities right away, the cavities will be bigger next time.

_____ Even if your teeth are cavity free, a dentist can clean them more thoroughly than you can at home.

_____ A dentist can evaluate your teeth, fix problems, and prevent new problems from starting.

My TURN Include relevant supporting details when you compose an opinion essay in your writing notebook.

Use Transition Words and Phrases

Use as many **transitions** as possible to make the connections between ideas completely clear and coherent. These words and phrases link reasons to opinions and link supporting details to reasons.

Opinion: The country should set aside grazing lands for bison.

Reason: Bison were once plentiful, and without them the prairies suffer. **For instance**, bison make the prairie healthier when they graze. **This became clear** when one bison herd kept tall grasses from taking too many nutrients from the soil. This allowed shorter grasses to grow. **Therefore**, setting aside a habitat for bison will protect the prairie as well as the animals.

My TURN Use each term from the Transitions Bank just once to coherently connect reasons to the opinion in the paragraph.

Transitions Bank

In addition   In order to   For instance   Finally

Beads are great for making all kinds of jewelry. _____, you can string beads together to make a necklace or a bracelet or dangling earrings. _____, you can find beads in a huge range of shapes and colors. _____ make jewelry with beads, you only need creativity and a needle and thread. _____, by working with beads, you learn an artistic skill that jewelers have practiced for centuries.

Make the connection between your ideas!

Use Technology to Collaborate

Work with a group to analyze model opinion essays and begin composing your own opinion essays.

My TURN Choose one of the following options for interacting and collaborating with a group.

- Choose an opinion essay from your classroom library. Use a scanner to provide an electronic copy for each member of your group. Have individuals add notes to the scan that identify the writer's opinion, reasons, and supporting information. Then print, exchange, and discuss your annotated scans.

- Keyboard a brainstorming document with five topics for an opinion essay. List an opinion and reasons for each topic. Print and exchange documents in your group and ask the person who receives yours to mark his or her two favorite ideas. Retrieve your brainstorming document. Use the other person's choices to better understand the audience that will read your essay.

- Have your group choose one of the topics below. With adult assistance, search the Internet for an opinion essay about the topic. Read the essay and then work with a partner to type a response to it.

  Whether or not students benefit from tests

  Whether or not boys and girls should play on the same teams

My TURN Identify a topic, purpose, and audience. Then select any genre, and plan a draft by mapping your ideas.

StoryCorps

StoryCorps is an organization that creates opportunities for people from all walks of life to make high-quality audio recordings of their one-on-one conversations and interviews.

Stories come from all fifty states, and interviews are conducted by young children, elderly adults, and everyone in between. The talks offer insight into important themes in life: relationships, growing up, recognizing and overcoming challenges, and more. These oral histories are preserved in a section of the Library of Congress whose mission is to document folklife, or the culture and everyday life of a particular community or group.

How can what we learn from stories guide our actions?

Quick Write How are your actions in the present connected to stories from your family's or community's past?

Library of Congress to House the StoryCorps Archive

StoryCorps is a national initiative to instruct and inspire Americans to record one another's stories in sound. . . . It has the potential to become one of the largest documentary oral history projects ever donated to the Library of Congress, and it will be one of the first "born-digital" collections to come to the American Folklife Center. . . .

The American Folklife Center was created by Congress in 1976 and placed at the Library of Congress to "preserve and present American folklife" . . . .

The Archive of Folk Culture will be the repository for the StoryCorps collection. . . . In this way, the StoryCorps collection will be available to future generations of researchers and family descendants.

Historical Fiction

Historical fiction is **set**, or takes place, in the past. The author combines facts with imagined details, events, and characters. Historical fiction includes

- Believable **characters**
- Reasonable **events** and responses
- Details based on historical **fact**

TURN and TALK What setting details tell you that you are reading fiction that takes place in the past? With a partner, discuss clues you have found in texts that helped you understand the setting and genre.

What connects us to the past?

Be a Fluent Reader Practice reading both silently and aloud. Be aware of what you are reading. Reading at the right speed and with accuracy will help you and others understand what you read. When you read aloud,

- ◎ Preview the text for new vocabulary.
- ◎ Listen to yourself and adjust your rate so that all the words make sense.
- ◎ Monitor and correct your pronunciation as you read.
- ◎ Keep practicing until you can read smoothly.
- ◎ Take time to use spelling patterns to read words as needed.

HISTORICAL FICTION
ANCHOR CHART

Setting

* has a **MAJOR INFLUENCE** on story events
* details based on **HISTORICAL FACT**
* may include true historical events

Characters

* may be entirely fictional
* may include real figures from history
* may be a combination of **FACTUAL** and **IMAGINED**

Purpose, Text Structure, Plot, and Theme = same as Realistic Fiction

Jacqueline Guest has written nineteen novels for readers of all ages. While on the job as a writer, she has stood on an iceberg, flown a kite in a hurricane, and dodged a pride of hungry lions! Jacqueline lives in a log cabin in the foothills of the Rocky Mountains of Alberta, Canada.

The Secret of the Winter Count

Preview Vocabulary

As you read *The Secret of the Winter Count*, pay attention to these vocabulary words. Notice how they help you understand the characters and events in the text.

> **drought**   **intricate**
>
> **wavering**   **unbidden**   **snoozing**

Read

Before you begin, establish a purpose for reading. Active readers of **historical fiction** follow these strategies when they read a text the first time.

Notice

the importance of time and place to the story events.

Generate Questions

before and during reading to deepen your understanding.

First Read

Connect

details about the characters and events to facts from other texts.

Respond

by taking notes about a character you think is interesting or important.

The Secret of the Winter Count

by Jacqueline Guest

 AUDIO

 ANNOTATE

Make Connections

What are some difficulties that communities can face together?

Highlight text evidence that tells about a challenge.

drought a long time of low or no rainfall

CHAPTER 1 NEW FRIENDS

1   Emma looked at the shriveled huckleberry bushes. Not a berry clung to the withered branches. She'd wanted to gather a bucketful to cheer her parents, who were worried about the shortage of water. Her father said that 1886 would be the worst drought in Montana's history, and now their well was already dry and the small stream near their cabin had to provide water for both the family and the cattle.

2   In the distance, she spied the soaring canyon wall that reminded Emma of a curtain dropping from the sky, and though she'd never been there, she knew that was where the Blackfoot Indian village was.

3   Emma thought for a moment. Her mother had said the people of the tribe knew where to find food on the land, and weren't huckleberries food? She'd ask the villagers where to find the tasty treats.

4   As Emma walked into the Blackfoot village, she stared at all the strikingly decorated tipis. She was greeted by a dozen children along with a tall man wearing a beautifully beaded vest and a hat with a black feather stuck in the band. His warm smile put her at ease.

5   "Hello," she said politely. "My name is Emma Arcand, and I live on the farm down in the valley. Do you know where I can find some huckleberries?"

6   The children began running around her like playful foxes, and the man chuckled. "Nice to meet you, Emma Arcand. I am Star Walker, storyteller of my tribe, and I'm sorry, but there are no berries. There has been no rain, and without rain, the berries do not grow. There is little food of any kind this year."

7   One of the younger children ran up to Emma and stared at her. Star Walker shooed the little boy away, saying, "He does not mean to be rude, but with your dark skin and hair, you do not look like the other white people from this area, and he is curious."

8   "That's because I'm Métis; my ancestry is mixed," Emma laughed. "My grandpa is French Canadian and my grandma is Cree, and on my next birthday, when I'm twelve, we're going to visit them in Canada."

9   Star Walker nodded. "I have many friends among the Cree people."

10   She swung her empty bucket. "What does a storyteller do, Mr. Star Walker?" Emma couldn't imagine someone having the job of telling stories all day long.

CLOSE READ

Vocabulary in Context

Context clues are words and phrases that help readers understand new vocabulary. In paragraph 8, underline context clues that help you understand the meaning of *ancestry*.

CLOSE READ

Make Connections

Think of ways you know of for a society to pass down history and wisdom from older people to younger people.

Highlight evidence that tells how Star Walker does that.

intricate complicated; very detailed

11 "I speak the legends and history of our tribe to the young people," he replied, "which is how children learn the wisdom of the elders."

12 Emma loved stories. "Could you tell me some of your stories?"

13 "You are in luck," Star Walker said, "I am about to share the history of our tribe with the children, and you are welcome to join us."

14 Emma brightened. "I'd like that."

15 Star Walker showed Emma and the children an animal hide covered with drawings in an intricate spiral pattern.

16 "This is called a Winter Count. Each of these pictures shows the most important event that happened to our tribe that year." He pointed to a drawing of tiny human figures circling a buffalo with a string of ten horses extending outward in a line and ending at a small circle. "This was many years ago when a terrible drought came and our tribe was saved by the Little People."

17   Star Walker pointed to another buffalo image, but this one showed twenty horses ending at the little circle. "And here was a second time we were saved from a drought."

18   "The legend tells of the Little People, nature spirits not much bigger than you, Emma, who told one of our children that he should go to the rock shaped like the sacred buffalo and walk ten horse lengths from it to find water. The boy did as the Little People instructed, found a pool of water waiting, and all our people were saved. During the next drought, another child was told to walk the same path from the Buffalo Rock, but this time ten more horse lengths, twenty horse lengths total, and sure enough, there was the water."

19   "Could the Little People help with *this* drought?" Emma asked hopefully.

20   Star Walker shook his head sadly. "None of our children has seen the Little People."

CLOSE READ

Infer Theme

You can combine information you already know with details from a story to infer a theme.

Underline text evidence in paragraph 16 that you can add to the title of the story to make an inference.

Infer Theme

Underline text evidence that tells you of the importance that mathematics plays in developing a theme of this story.

21 When Emma arrived home, her parents were down by the stream where they were digging a big pit, and, watching her parents work, Emma told the story of the Winter Count and how the Little People saved the tribe.

22 "Old stories won't save us from a drought, but this dugout will," her father said as he swung the heavy pick, hitting the ground with a thunk.

23 "Fingers crossed!" Her mother said as she shoveled the loosened dirt out of the wide hole.

24 Finally, they laid their tools on the top edge of the pit, climbed out of the hole, and walked to the stream.

25 "Once I unblock this trench, the stream will be diverted into the dugout and it will fill to the brim. Then we'll have a mighty fine reserve of water." Her father moved some rocks and used his shovel to reroute the water.

26 As they watched, a trickle ran from the stream into the dugout.

27 "This is going to take all night to fill," her mother said, watching the thin thread of water. "Let's have supper and hear more about Emma's day." She put an arm around her daughter. "I hope you weren't bothering our neighbors, Em."

28 "No, Ma. I was good. Can I go back tomorrow?" She wanted to hear more of Mr. Star Walker's stories.

29 "All of your arithmetic must be done. School work is important."

30   With no schoolhouse near their farm, it was up to Emma's mother to teach her all about reading, writing, and arithmetic.

31   "After I finish all the questions, then can I go?" she sighed.

32   "They must not only be finished," her mother replied, laughing, "but they must also be correct."

33   That night, Emma worked very hard on her arithmetic, but the right answers didn't come easily. Addition was one thing—not so hard—but the multiplication tables seemed particularly tricky to her.

34   The wavering light from the coal oil lamp made the numbers on her slate tablet jump and wiggle, and, frustrated with the work, Emma found herself doodling pictures she'd seen on the Winter Count.

35   First she drew ten horses in a row, and then added another group of ten onto the line to get twenty. That's what the two pictures on the Winter Count had shown—the second chosen child had to walk ten more horse lengths to find water in the second drought.

36   "Ten horses for the first drought, plus ten horses for the second drought," she said to herself. "It's like an arithmetic problem!"

37   **10 + 10 = 20**

38   She wrote the equation below the drawings. It *was* arithmetic, but more fun because it used horses, and Emma liked horses.

Make Connections

Think about the ways that groups or societies approach and solve problems.

Highlight text that you can connect to a problem-solving method or approach that your community uses.

wavering changing

Infer Theme

What message does Emma think she is receiving in her dream?

<u>Underline</u> text evidence in paragraphs 40–48 that helps you determine the story's theme.

39 She was tired, too tired for more arithmetic, and, excusing herself, Emma kissed her parents goodnight and went to bed.

40 *They galloped into her dream on silent hooves, beautiful horses with the same markings painted on them as she'd seen on the village tipis. Emma sat astride an impossibly tall buffalo as tiny humanlike dancers circled the huge animal. The horses stood by the buffalo, but instead of staying in one big group like the horses she knew, the dream horses formed two groups of ten, then stepped out in single file to form one line. At the end of the line was a pool of cool, clear water. The horses were beautiful, with flowing manes and gentle brown eyes that seemed to know a secret . . .*

41 Emma woke with a start. The Little People had come to her. There was something about the horses and the number ten. She fumbled in the dark as she made her way to the table, lit the lamp, and finding her slate, began to sketch her dream.

42 She drew the buffalo and the horses.

43 "The water was ten horse lengths from the Buffalo Rock for the first drought. Then ten more horse lengths for the second. Could it be . . ."

44 There was clearly a pattern in the drawing.

45 *"One drought—ten horses. A second drought—ten more horses. So this is the third drought—just add ten more horses!"* she whispered, jotting down a new equation.

46 **10 + 10 + 10 = 30**

47 They would find water thirty horse lengths from the Buffalo Rock!

48 Tomorrow she would ask Mr. Star Walker to take her to the special rock. Maybe dreams could come true.

49 The next morning, Emma tried to explain her dream and the pattern of horse lengths from the Winter Count to her parents, but they were too preoccupied.

Vocabulary in Context

Reread paragraph 25. In that paragraph, *brim* means "the top edge."

Read paragraph 54. What does *brim* mean here? Underline a context clue in the text to support your definition.

50   "My, you're finding some imaginative ways to do your arithmetic!" said her mother, taking her bonnet from the peg by the door. "But with our dugout full, we'll have no water worries!"

51   Emma followed her parents as they hurried down to the dugout, but when they arrived, all they could do was stand and stare.

52   The dugout was completely empty!

53   "Where did the water go?" Emma asked, confused.

54   Her father took off his hat and slapped his thigh with the brim. His disappointment was clear to Emma.

55   "Sometimes there are cracks under the soil, and the water drains back into the ground to underground rivers. The level of the underground river has sunk farther than I'd thought."

56   His face looked so tired that it made Emma sad, but then she saw that something else had happened.

57   "Pa, the stream stopped flowing!" Emma ran to the streambed, but there was no water.

58   Emma looked from her mother's stricken face to her father's. She wanted to repeat the whole story of her dream, but now wasn't the time. Her father seemed to be holding something in, like a volcano just bubbling with hot lava and ready to explode. Emma and Ma had read about volcanoes in one of the few schoolbooks they had—a geography book.

59   "I'll be back later," she whispered, and walked away.

60   Now Mr. Star Walker *had* to take her to the Buffalo Rock.

CHAPTER 3   WATER WALKING

61   When Emma got to the village, the storyteller was sitting cross-legged on the ground outside his tipi studying the Winter Count. "Excuse me, Mr. Star Walker, will you show me the Buffalo Rock?"

62   He looked up from the hide with its spiral of drawings.

63   "Good morning, Emma. The Buffalo Rock is not something we share with outsiders."

64   "But you let me listen to your stories yesterday," she protested. "And I *am* part Cree. Am I still an outsider? Please, Mr. Star Walker, it's important."

65   He seemed to weigh this in his mind, and then his eyes twinkled, and he smiled. "I'm sure your Cree grandmother would want me to show you."

66   Together Emma and Star Walker hiked high into the canyon and finally stopped in a clearing that opened out to a wide valley.

67   Emma gasped. Standing before her was a gigantic buffalo!

68   When she looked closer, she realized this was the Buffalo Rock. It looked so real!

Make Connections

What are some things or ideas that people in your community or society do not like to share outside the group?

Highlight text that tells how Emma and Star Walker come to an agreement.

Infer Theme

<u>Underline</u> details in paragraphs 76–80 that you can add to what you know about the characters in the story to help you determine a theme.

69 "How long is a horse?" she asked, trying to figure out the distance from the rock to the first water hole.

70 Star Walker took three slightly big steps. The distance looked to Emma to be about eight feet, and she scrunched up her nose as she calculated how far from the Buffalo Rock ten horses would be.

71 $$8 + 8 + 8 + 8 + 8 + 8 + 8 + 8 + 8 + 8 = 80$$

72 "The first water was found eighty feet from here," she said.

73 "It was in this direction," said Star Walker, moving away from the big boulder and down the hill into the valley.

74 When they'd gone eighty feet, Emma stopped. There was a shallow depression in the ground. "This matches the Winter Count. I can see where the water was. Now we need to walk another ten horse lengths, another eighty feet, to the second pool."

75 They paced off eighty more feet down into the valley and sure enough, there was an irregular pattern in the earth there, too. "I think this drought's water will be found down there," Emma pointed down the hill. "It's the pattern in the Winter Count. Every drought, the Little People came to tell about ten more horses. So, it will be exactly ten more horse lengths from here!"

76 Star Walker seemed about to say something, but instead, followed Emma, who was taking big steps, the same size as Star Walker's, and carefully counting. "One . . . two . . . three . . . that's one horse."

77 " . . . . One, two, three—that's the tenth horse!" She smiled, then looked around and frowned.

78   There was no pool of fresh, clear water waiting—
only dry grass, seared brown by the scorching summer
sun.

79   Star Walker shook his head knowingly. "The secrets
of the Winter Count are sometimes hard to understand,
but I thank you for trying. The answer will only be
found when the Little People speak."

80   But the Little People *had* been in her dream, and her
addition *had* been correct. The water should have been
here. Dejected, Emma wracked her brain, examining
each detail from her dream. She wanted to go home
and talk it through with her parents, but she knew they
had their own worries.

Vocabulary in Context

Synonyms, or words with similar meanings, can act as context clues and help you determine word meaning.

Use context clues in paragraph 81 to determine the meaning of *whirled.* Underline a word that supports your definition.

81   *Emma again sat on the huge buffalo while the tiny dancers whirled around her, and in her dream, she smiled at the Little People, who laughed and waved back. A long line of horses ran in single file from the buffalo to the edge of the giant Winter Count hide they were all standing on, and the dream horses seemed to multiply as they galloped off the edge and up into a starry sky that swirled and pulsed with light. There were so many horses dancing in the stars!*

82   Emma sat up in her bed, the early dawn light making the walls of her room glow pink. The dream was so real. She'd seen the horses again, but many more than in her previous dream. *They'd multiplied in front of her eyes.*

83   "Of course!" Emma blurted out. "The Little People weren't wrong, but I was! It's a pattern, but it's not the one I thought it was."

84   Earlier that day, she and Star Walker had paced off the horse lengths—first, ten horse lengths from the Buffalo Rock to the first pool location, and then another ten horse lengths to the second location. It had made sense that the water for this drought would be ten more horse lengths farther down the hill—just add ten more.

85    $10 + 10 + 10 = 30$

86   So, why hadn't they found a third pool?

87   Her mother always told her that the wonderful thing about numbers was that they never changed—two plus two was always four; four divided by two was always two and . . . two *times* two was always four.

88   Emma thought of her dream and remembered thinking that the horses had *multiplied* right in front of her eyes. Then it came to her.

89   The Winter Count horses weren't increasing by *adding* ten plus ten to get twenty. They were doubling, and that was multiplication—*multiplying* ten times two to get twenty. It was a multiplication pattern!

90   She threw back the covers and ran to her parents' room.

CLOSE READ

Infer Theme
What does Emma's mother consider important?

Underline text evidence to support your ideas.

Infer Theme

How do Emma's experiences and Star Walker's traditions combine to help you infer the story's theme?

Underline text evidence that supports your inference.

91 "I know where the water is!" she exclaimed excitedly.

92 Her father rubbed the sleep from his eyes. "Honey, the well is dry, the creek is dry, and the dugout is dry."

93 "I know how to find the water! I thought the pattern had to do with addition, but it is multiplication! One drought—ten horse lengths. Two droughts—twice the horse lengths of the first drought, so ten times two."

94 10 x 2 = 20

95 "Now, the third drought—twice that many horse lengths again—twenty times two. The water will be found twenty times two for a total of *forty* horse lengths this time!"

96 20 x 2 = 40

97 "With a 'horse length' being eight feet, that means the water is eight times forty…" she scrunched up her nose as she did the calculation.

98 8 x 40 = 320

99 *"Three hundred twenty feet from the Buffalo Rock!* The Little People in my dream were right. We have to tell Mr. Star Walker!"

100 Before her parents could say no, Emma continued pleading. "I know I was wrong before, but I'm right this time, and it will mean water for the tribe, and if there is enough, we could have some, too." It was a big gamble, but she was sure she was right.

101 At the village, Emma told Star Walker of her dream and how by her calculations, the water was three hundred twenty feet from the Buffalo Rock.

102 Together, her parents and Star Walker went to the ancient, weathered stone.

103 "I'm right, you'll see!" Laughing, Emma ran down the hill, sure she would find water.

104 When her parents and Star Walker caught up, they found Emma shaking her head in disbelief.

105 There was no water.

106 She knelt and scooped up the dry dirt. "This can't be."

107 Her mother rested a hand on her shoulder. "Let's go home, Em."

108 "No, Ma. It's here! Why would I have had that second dream?" She threw the dirt down, making a cloud of fine, powdery dust.

109 "For heaven's sake, Emma," her mother spoke with a stern voice, "this is like the boy who cried wolf, except instead of false wolves, you keep crying that there is water. There is no water!"

110 Emma wiped unbidden tears from her face. "But at the end of that story, there really were wolves." She stood, and then looked around as though seeing the valley for the first time.

CLOSE READ

Make Connections

Many groups have shared stories that warn against telling falsehoods to get attention.

Highlight words and phrases on this page that connect to such a shared story in your society.

unbidden not asked for

Infer Theme

What message about "a dream come true" can you find in this story?

Underline text evidence you can use to make an inference about a theme of the story.

snoozing dozing; sleeping lightly

Fluency

Read paragraphs 116–122 aloud to a small group. Practice reading the paragraphs so that you can read them with accuracy and so that you don't read too fast or too slowly. Use what you know about spelling patterns to read words that are new to you.

111   "Pa . . . remember the dugout? You said the ground was cracked, and the water drained down to an underground river. Maybe we just have to dig . . ." Hope sprang up as it became clear to her. "Don't you see? The water *is* here, beneath our feet in a river under the ground. We're farther down the hill, lower than where the water was found before. It's here, we just have to dig for it!"

112   Emma's father started to smile. "Emma, your confidence is making me think it's worth a try! I can go fetch my tools from home—buckets, picks, and shovels. We have nothing to lose and a whole lot to gain!"

113   Star Walker stepped forward. "I will help. I do not know about underground rivers, but I, too, see Emma's confidence."

114   Emma and her mother sat down under a nearby tree to wait. They were actually snoozing when the clank of tools announced that the men had returned.

115   The hot afternoon sun beat down on them mercilessly as Emma, her parents, and Star Walker worked, the men digging, while Emma and her mother hauled the dirt away in wooden buckets.

116   When they reached six feet, Emma noticed something odd.

117   "Look! The ground is different there!" She pointed to one side of the hole.

118   The pale, dry dirt did look different. It was darker. Her father and Star Walker dug furiously at that spot and soon, the dirt wasn't just darker, it was damp.

119   "I know what this needs." Emma's father winked at her, then took up his big pick and gave it a mighty swing.

120 *Ker-thunk!*

121 It struck deep into the earth and suddenly, a jet of water gushed out of the ground. The water swirled and bubbled, filling the pit so quickly that Emma's father and Star Walker had to climb out or become wet.

122 Emma's mother hugged her, and shouted, "You did it! My wonderful daughter did it!"

123 Star Walker reached down and scooped up a handful of water, offering it to Emma's father. "I am grateful, my people are grateful, and we are happy to share the water with your family. We will make another pool, and you can pasture your cattle by the pool, where they will have all the water they need."

124 Emma's father stuck out his hand, and shaking the storyteller's hand, said, "And we will share our cattle with your people."

125 Star Walker then turned to Emma, and spoke, "It was the Little People all along. They came to you in your dream, Emma, and you were clever enough to understand their message. You are the chosen child for this drought, and you have saved us all."

126 Emma beamed. "I'll be happy to do my arithmetic from now on, because it turns out those tricky numbers are actually pretty darn useful!"

CLOSE READ

Infer Theme

What inference can you make about how the words of elders shape Emma's actions?

Underline text evidence that supports your inference.

Develop Vocabulary

In historical fiction, authors use precise words to help readers visualize characters and scenes.

My TURN Answer each question with a complete sentence that demonstrates your understanding of the bold vocabulary word.

1. If there is **wavering** light in a room, how well could you see what is in the room?

   _____

   _____

2. If a pattern is **intricate**, describe how you would copy it.

   _____

   _____

   _____

3. If someone joins a game **unbidden**, how might the other players react?

   _____

   _____

   _____

4. If there is a **drought**, how does it affect plants and animals?

   _____

   _____

   _____

5. What time of day are you most likely to be **snoozing**?

   _____

   _____

   _____

Check for Understanding

My TURN Look back at the text to answer the questions.

1. Which parts of *The Secret of the Winter Count* are historical, and which are fictional?

2. How does the historical setting influence the events in *The Secret of the Winter Count*?

3. Each group—Emma's family and the Blackfoot tribe—has an approach to finding water that the other group does not. What are those different techniques, and what leads the groups to share information?

4. What is the secret of the title, and how is it revealed?

Infer Theme

A **symbol** is something that has its own meaning and also suggests other meanings. When you infer a theme, you put together text evidence, such as symbols, and what you already know to understand the text's big idea.

1. **My TURN** Go to the Close Read notes in *The Secret of the Winter Count* and underline text that helps you infer a theme.

2. **Text Evidence** Use your evidence to complete the diagram. Then infer a theme of the story.

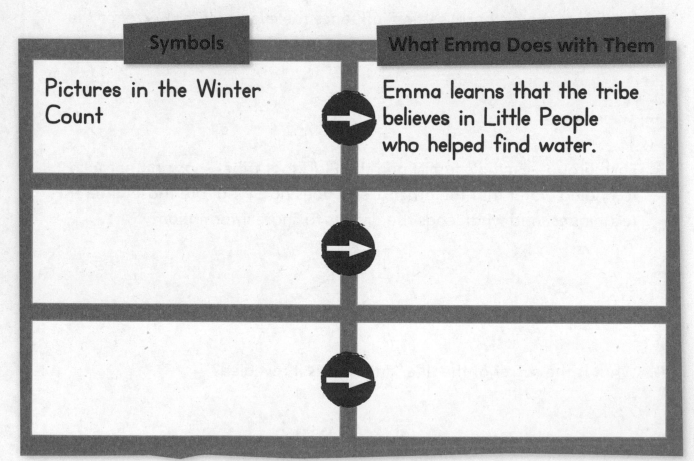

Symbols		What Emma Does with Them
Pictures in the Winter Count	→	Emma learns that the tribe believes in Little People who helped find water.
	→	
	→	

The Theme I Infer:

_____

_____

Make Connections

One theme in this story is that we should keep thinking about a problem even if it seems impossible to solve. When you read, considering real world problems faced by people, or societies, can help you uncover real world issues.

1. **My TURN** Go back to the Close Read notes and highlight evidence that you can use to make connections between the story and society.

2. **Text Evidence** To complete the chart, paraphrase how societies face challenges, solve problems, and share wisdom.

Societies

Face difficulties by

Solve problems by

Share wisdom by

Connect to Theme

In *The Secret of the Winter Count* and in my community, people solve problems and overcome challenges by _____

_____

Reflect and Share

Write to Sources Early in *The Secret of the Winter Count*, Emma's father says, "Old stories won't save us from a drought, but this dugout will." Later, the dugout fails to fill with water. How does this failure affect Emma's father? What other stories have you read in which an old way of doing something did not work? Use the following process to write and support a response.

- -

Take Notes Writing a response to literature requires taking notes to support ideas with text evidence. To write your response, begin by choosing two texts with characters who must learn a new way to solve a problem. Have paper and pen or pencil ready. Reread each text and take notes as follows:

- ◎ State the problem.
- ◎ Describe how a character expected to solve the problem.
- ◎ Explain why the solution did not work.
- ◎ Describe what the character said, felt, or thought and what he or she had to do to solve the problem in a new way.
- ◎ Summarize how the experience affected the character.

Review your notes, and then use them to write your response.

- -

Weekly Question

How can what we learn from stories guide our actions?

Academic Vocabulary

Figurative language is language that expresses a meaning that goes beyond dictionary definitions. One type of figurative language is an idiom.

- "Her new approach *breaks the mold*," meaning that she is making a big change from tradition.
- "He *let the cat out of the bag*," meaning that he revealed a secret.
- "I *have a funny feeling*," meaning that you can make a prediction.

My TURN Write each idiom from the Idiom Bank in the circle to which it belongs.

Idiom Bank

spill the beans	go out on a limb
a new broom sweeps clean	take the lid off
see the handwriting on the wall	make a clean break

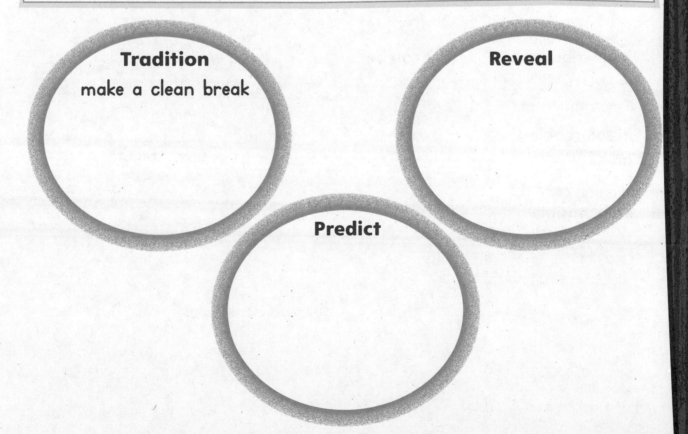

Tradition
make a clean break

Reveal

Predict

Prefixes *im-*, *in-*, *ir-*

The **prefixes** *im-*, *in-*, and *ir-* all add the meaning "opposite of" to a base word. Adding these prefixes to a base word changes its meaning, but does not change how you read the base word. For example, the base word *possible* and the word *impossible* are read the same way.

My TURN Read each word with a prefix. Highlight the base word. Then complete each sentence using both the word and its base.

1. improper _Shaking hands_ is _proper_ , while _ignoring someone_ is _improper_ .

2. impersonal _____ are _____, while _____ are _____.

3. insignificant _____ is _____, while _____ is _____.

4. indescribable _____ can be _____, while _____ is _____.

5. irreplaceable _____ are _____, while _____ are _____.

6. irresponsible _____ is _____, while _____ is _____.

Read Like a Writer

An author uses figurative language to achieve specific purposes, such as establishing a mood. The **mood** of a text is the feeling a reader gets while reading it, such as serious, happy, or anxious. Similes are a type of figurative language. They compare two unlike things using the words *like* or *as*.

Model !   Reread paragraph 58 from *The Secret of the Winter Count*.

1. **Identify** Jacqueline Guest has the narrator use the simile "like a volcano" to compare a volcano and Emma's father.

2. **Question** What mood does the simile create? How does it work?

3. **Conclude** The simile creates a suspenseful, slightly frightening mood by showing that Emma's father is struggling to control himself.

Reread paragraph 36.

My TURN   Follow the steps to analyze how the author uses a simile to help establish a mood.

1. **Identify** Jacqueline Guest has the character use the simile _____ to compare _____

_____

2. **Question** What mood does the simile create? How does it work?

3. **Conclude** The simile creates _____ by showing that _____

_____

Write for a Reader

Writers use figurative language for specific purposes, such as to help create the mood, or feeling, a reader gets from their work. Similes are a type of figurative language.

Make an image memorable by comparing things that are not really alike.

My TURN Think about how Jacqueline Guest uses similes to create a mood in *The Secret of the Winter Count*. Now identify how you can use similes to create a mood in your own writing.

1. To create an excited mood with a simile, what could you compare to a bubbling pot of soup?

   _____

   _____

2. To create a mood of peace and security, what simile could you create?

   _____

   _____

3. Write a fictional passage about the last day of school that creates a mood using at least one simile.

   _____

   _____

   _____

   _____

   _____

   _____

Spell Words with Prefixes

The **prefixes** *im-*, *in-*, and *ir-* all mean "opposite of." Adding these prefixes does not change the spelling of the base word.

My TURN   Read the words. Spell the words by writing each base word. Then write the new word formed by the prefix added to the base. An example has been done for you.

SPELLING WORDS

irresistible	mature	practical	complete
impractical	incapable	imprecise	patient
immature	irregular	relevant	injustice
irrelevant	precise	justice	incomplete
capable	regular	impatient	resistible

mature

immature

Comparative Adjectives

Comparative adjectives compare two people, places, things, or groups of items. For many adjectives, adding -er creates the comparative form. If an adjective ends with a y, the y changes to an i before -er is added.

full → fuller   *heavy → heavier*

Adding -er to longer adjectives is awkward. Therefore, use the word *more* in front of longer adjectives to make them comparative.

Adjective	Awkward	Comparative
generous	generouser	more generous
understandable	understandabler	more understandable

A few adjectives have irregular comparative forms. It is useful to learn the comparative forms of such words.

good → better   *much → more*   *little → less*

My TURN Edit this draft by replacing four incorrect comparative adjectives with correct ones.

After Liam's solo, Felicia said, "That was a more good performance than last time! You put mucher feeling into your music this week." Liam replied, "I did intenser practices this week than last so that I could give a more great performance than the time before."

Rearrange Ideas for Coherence and Clarity

Rearrange ideas in sentences and paragraphs to improve structure and word choice.

Original Paragraph	Rearranged Paragraph
Oklahoma is another place where Texas's most memorable animal, the nine-banded armadillo, lives. If surprised, an armadillo might jump straight up in the air! The armadillo is quite a surprising animal to see. Along the road at night in Texas, you may catch a glimpse of one walking swiftly into the grass.	Texas's most memorable animal, the nine-banded armadillo, may surprise you when you see it along a road. But you are more likely to be a surprise to it. A startled armadillo might jump straight up into the air! Wherever armadillos live, most people simply see them trotting into the grass at dusk.

Explanation The focus of the paragraph is seeing armadillos, so that idea comes first. The writer incorporates Oklahoma into the phrase "Wherever armadillos live" and revises word choice to help readers clearly visualize the animal's behavior.

My TURN Rearrange the ideas to clarify the sentence.

In November and December the number of crawfish skyrockets, and their bodies start getting bigger, so people begin to fish for crawfish in February or March.

_____

_____

My TURN Rearrange ideas for clarity when you revise the draft of an opinion essay in your writing notebook.

Combine Ideas for Coherence and Clarity

You can improve sentence structure and write more clearly by combining ideas.

Separate Ideas	Combined Ideas
To make a paste, add water to flour and then stir the water and the flour together.	Make a paste by mixing flour and water.
It is important to understand the rules because when you don't know them no one knows what to do when the game starts.	When they know the rules, players can begin the game.

Often as a writer you can choose words that combine ideas. Make the choice about whether to combine ideas or not based on the feeling and reading experience you want your audience to have.

Three Words	Two Words	One Word
lumpy all over	bumpy texture	nubby
polite to others	showing respect	respectful
get the giggles	laugh uncontrollably	chortle
wild prairie habitat	grassy plain	grassland

My TURN Combine ideas for clarity as you revise the draft of an opinion essay in your writing notebook.

Peer Edit

Writers can help each other improve their opinion essays. When you edit another writer's work, follow these guidelines.

- Give the writer feedback about the strongest and weakest reasons in the essay.
- Provide positive feedback with statements such as, "This is very convincing evidence" and "This reason has very strong support."
- Tell the writer where you think the essay needs more supporting details.
- Point out where the essay lacks clarity or seems disorganized.
- Make comments the writer can do something about, such as "repeats earlier information" instead of "boring" and "needs supporting facts" instead of "unbelievable!"

My TURN When you edit a peer's opinion essay, complete this checklist before you give the essay back.

HELPFUL PEER EDITING

☐ I told the writer about the essay's strengths.

☐ I clearly marked parts that were hard for me to follow.

☐ I showed the writer how to make a sentence or paragraph better.

☐ I made comments that the writer can change in the next draft.

Edit for Complete Sentences

A complete **simple sentence** is a complete thought and has a subject and a predicate. The subject is a **noun** or a **pronoun**. The predicate is a **verb**.

Subject	Predicate
Felicia	**snuggled** in her grandmother's arms.
The **kittens**	**ate** greedily.
They	just **left** for the store.

In a complete sentence, the subject and the verb must agree in number. A singular subject must have a singular verb (as in *she walks*), and a plural subject must have a plural verb (as in *they walk*).

Sometimes writers want to combine two simple sentences to make a **compound sentence.** Follow the first sentence with a comma and a coordinating conjunction (*and*, *but*, or *or*). Then start the second sentence with a lowercase letter. Each part of a compound sentence must have subject-verb agreement.

First Sentence	Conjunction	Second Sentence
The **sun rises,**	and	**birds begin singing.**
We saw two herons,	but	**we missed** the storks.

My TURN Edit for complete sentences and for subject-verb agreement when you draft an opinion essay in your writing notebook.

Edit Nouns

A **noun** names a person, place, or thing. A **common noun,** such as *president*, names any person, place, or thing. Common nouns begin with lowercase letters unless they are at the beginning of a sentence.

A **proper noun,** such as *President Lyndon B. Johnson*, names a particular person, place, or thing. Proper nouns begin with capital letters. When a proper noun has more than one word, the first letter of each important word is capitalized, as in *Gulf of Mexico*.

Nouns that name *one* person, place, or thing are **singular:** *child, hallway, bench.* Nouns that name *more than one* person, place, or thing are **plural:** *children, hallways, benches.*

My TURN Edit the paragraph to correct nouns. Cross out nouns that are incorrectly capitalized, nouns that should be capitalized, and nouns that should be made either singular or plural. Write the correct noun to replace each noun you cross out.

In the 1960s, Lady Bird Johnson launched a campaigns to beautify america. The effort started in the Nation's Capital city, washington, D.C. Some Efforts focused on Tourist Areas, and other focused on the Neighborhoods where most people lived.

My TURN Edit for nouns when you draft an opinion essay on your own paper. Discuss editing tips with your Writing Club.

Should you capitalize? Check a dictionary!

Texts That GUIDE OUR ACTIONS

Rules for behavior and advice for life can be woven into common stories. Traditional literature often communicates the values of a community. Many communities value rules and obedience.

FAIRY TALE

LITTLE RED RIDING HOOD

Instead of listening to her mother's advice to always stay on the path, Little Red Riding Hood takes a shortcut and meets a mean wolf.

ICARUS

To escape from a high tower prison, Daedalus makes mechanical wings. He tells his son Icarus that they must fly low, but instead Icarus flies so high that his wings melt and he falls.

MYTH

FABLE

WOLF!

THE BOY WHO CRIED WOLF

A shepherd boy always lies when he tells everyone that a wolf is nearby, waiting to eat his sheep. When a real wolf shows up, no one believes the boy when he cries for help.

Weekly Question

How can being disobedient cause problems?

TURN and TALK With a partner, discuss a time when a person or character in a story did not do as he or she was told. What was the result? Give specific details from the stories you discuss.

Spotlight on Genre

Myths

Myths are a form of traditional literature that often answer the question "Why?" Some myths explain aspects of nature, such as the changing seasons.

Myths

- are based on the folk **beliefs** of a particular group.
- feature **characters** with few traits.
- have simple **plots**.
- can be brief retellings about important **themes**.

TURN and TALK With a partner, make a list of stories that answer "Why?" Use the anchor chart to explain why each story is or is not a myth.

My NOTES _____

_____

_____

_____

_____

_____

_____

Tell me why!

Myths Anchor Chart

Myths reflect human beliefs about **WHY** and **HOW** the world is.

  CHARACTERS

- ⊙ may personify, or represent, a natural force (thunder)
- ⊙ may personify an abstract idea (fate)

SETTING

- ⊙ may indicate the people from whom the myth comes
- ⊙ often influences the characters and events

STYLE

- ⊙ simple, direct, limited description
- ⊙ may change slightly as the myth is retold over time

Cynthia Rylant, author and illustrator, has "always loved cats and dogs" and often includes her pets in her books. She has written award-winning books for many audiences, from toddlers up to middle grade students.

Pandora

Preview Vocabulary

As you read "Pandora," pay attention to these vocabulary words. Notice how they help you identify and analyze elements of myth.

shrewd   ornate

Read

Before you read "Pandora," establish a purpose for reading. Active readers of **myths** follow these strategies when they read a text the first time.

Notice

big ideas that the myth explains.

Generate Questions

before and during reading by skimming, scanning, and noting new information.

First Read

Connect

events in this story with events you have heard about or read in other texts.

Respond

by writing a question you would like to ask one of the characters in the myth.

PANDORA

from THE BEAUTIFUL STORIES OF LIFE

BY CYNTHIA RYLANT

Greece

BACKGROUND

The Greek pantheon, or gods and goddesses featured in myths and stories, is very well known today. You may have read other tales about Zeus, the god who ruled over all the other deities that lived with him on Mount Olympus. The tale of how Prometheus stole fire and gave it to mankind is so common that his name has become synonymous with boldness and creativity. This myth tells about what happened after that daring act.

 AUDIO

 ANNOTATE

Analyze Myths

Underline text evidence that tells you what this myth is about.

1   Zeus was ruler of the universe, and if there were only one thing to remember about him, it was this: Never cross him. But someone did.

2   Zeus had always controlled fire. Men could have all the water, all the air, all the earth they wanted. But fire would remain with the gods, for it was the source of all creation. Without it, men would never find their genius, their passion, their own gods within. This was precisely what Zeus intended.

3   But a heroic—and some say foolhardy—man named Prometheus tricked Zeus. He stole fire from the god of gods, and as always happens in the stories of life, action creates consequences.

4   Prometheus not only drew the vengeance of the most powerful god in the universe upon his head. He also set in motion a story that would change the hearts of men forever.

5   When Zeus discovered he had been tricked by a mere mortal—a *man*—the god's anger was so searing, it might have destroyed Earth had Zeus allowed its release.

6　But Zeus was not only powerful. He was shrewd. He understood that true vengeance takes place quietly, intelligently, and with a plan. He swallowed his rage and made one.

7　Zeus took a good long look at men. He was searching for their greatest weakness, for that would be the target of his revenge.

8　Zeus found man's greatest weakness by first finding man's greatest strength: It was Love.

9　Those who get what they want—both gods and men—rarely attempt taking it outright. A blatant grab for power is not nearly as effective as a subtle one.

10　Prometheus, thief of fire, had a brother named Epimetheus. Epimetheus was not as cunning as his sibling. In fact, Epimetheus was naive, gullible beyond belief.

11　He was also lonely—but for what or whom, he did not know. There was simply a hunger in him, which had never been fulfilled.

CLOSE READ

Evaluate Details

Closely examine the illustration. Highlight details in paragraphs 1–11 that describe the characters in the myth.

shrewd clever; showing good judgment

Evaluate Details

What element or feature of human nature does this part of the myth help to explain? Highlight words and phrases that support a key idea.

12   The god of gods knew what that hunger was. It was what most men on Earth hungered for without knowing so.

13   What Epimetheus wanted was the love of a woman.

14   Up until this time in the universe, only men had lived on the earth. There were female goddesses in the heavens, but Earth was deprived of the feminine. Zeus had seen no reason to create woman. Men were both useful and uninteresting to Zeus. Why stir them up with women?

15   But when fire was suddenly in men's hands, and it was inevitable that they would use it to create, to grow beyond their animal natures, the question of stirring them up became moot. With fire, the stirring had begun.

16   Zeus loathed this situation. But he had a plan.

17   Zeus would create a mortal woman. He put a great deal of thought into what she would be like, and he asked the other gods and goddesses to assist in her making. Zeus invited them to contribute their best qualities to the molding of this first woman so that she would be magnificent. Naturally they all accepted the invitation. Vanity has never been in short supply among the gods.

18   Aphrodite gave her beauty. Apollo gave her intelligence. Hermes gave her cleverness. And so it went, god by goddess, until finally the first mortal woman was complete and she took her first breath of life.

19   Her name was Pandora.

20   Pandora would be a gift from Zeus to Epimetheus, brother of Prometheus, thief of fire. Zeus would send Pandora with all her beauty, intelligence, cleverness, and rare femininity to Epimetheus, who was both innocent and desperate enough to accept an unearned gift from the most powerful god in the universe. Epimetheus would accept that gift in spite of the warnings from his brother, who was certain Zeus was up to something.

Evaluate Details

Details in the text and illustration tell what traits were given to Pandora by the gods. Highlight those details in the text.

CLOSE READ

Evaluate Details

Analyze the illustration. Highlight information in paragraphs 21–29 that helps you understand the gift Zeus gave to Pandora.

ornate highly decorated; complex and fancy

21   Pandora did not arrive empty-handed. She was delivered to Epimetheus along with a beautiful, ornate box, which came with a specific instruction from Zeus: The box was not to be opened.

22   Epimetheus accepted this condition without question. He did not care what was in the box. He had what he wanted and was lost in his love for her. He had Pandora.

23   And beautiful Pandora loved Epimetheus in return. Of course she would. She was the essence of femininity, and she instinctively gave her heart and soul to her husband. With her beauty, she pleased him. With her intelligence, she understood him. With her cleverness, she delighted him.

24   Pandora was everything Epimetheus had ever wanted, and he no longer hungered for anything in the world.

25   Pandora, as well, was deeply satisfied with her lot. She loved being a woman and wanted nothing more than to give her husband anything that might make him happy.

26   This is why she could not stop thinking about the box.

27   Surely, thought Pandora, whatever was inside the box was meant for Epimetheus, just as she was meant for him. Surely something wonderful was in there, a wedding gift from Zeus, perhaps, meant to tease them awhile until the time came to lift up the lid.

28   Pandora waited for word from Zeus, but it did not come. Her husband was not troubled. He was too content. Epimetheus was a man of small mind and not one to care about finding answers to mysteries.

29   But Pandora was made of the gods, and she cared. She cared about why things were as they were and what might be found inside a forbidden box.

30   Being made of the gods, Pandora was perfect in every way, perfect in all ways, except one. She lacked one quality that none of the gods ever needed and so could not have given her.

31   Pandora lacked patience.

32   Waiting for something requires a strength unknown to the gods, for they have their own magic and they concoct their own stories.

33   Patience is a purely human strength, sustained by hope. And if it is inspired by deep love, patience can be in its own way invincible.

34   Beautiful Pandora could not even imagine such a quality.

CLOSE READ

Analyze Myths
What does this myth tell you about patience? Underline details in paragraphs 29–33 that refer to the benefits of patience.

Evaluate Details

Read the text closely and examine the illustration. <mark>Highlight</mark> specific descriptions that connect to what you see in the image.

Vocabulary in Context

Skilled readers use **context clues** to determine the meaning of unknown phrases.

Read paragraph 39 to determine the meaning of *human anguish*. <u>Underline</u> clues that support your definition.

35   So one day she grew tired of waiting. And she opened the box.

36   Pandora first thought they were butterflies, the dozens of winged creatures that flew from inside. She reached for them.

37   Then she caught her breath. Horrified.

38   Each winged creature had the face of a demon. Pandora was paralyzed with disbelief as they flew from the box, hovered a moment so she might look into their empty eyes, then disappeared through the window, out into the world.

39   Pandora began to weep. She now knew what Zeus had done. She knew what she had done. Together they had unleashed a multitude of sufferings upon mankind: disease, war, starvation, depravity, insanity. Whatever might create human anguish.

40   Pandora wept. But then, impulsively, as the last winged creature exited the box, this woman created of the gods reached out her hand, caught the creature, and put it back inside.

41   And with that one small act, Pandora changed the fate of mankind. For what she caught and returned to the box was Hope.

42   Zeus had put hope in the box, along with the pestilence and the cruelty, believing that hope would not survive in a world so filled with suffering. And he knew mankind could not survive without hope.

43   But Pandora reached out and she captured it and did not let it go. Because she did so, and placed it back inside the box, hope is alive today. It lives in darkness.

44   And in darkness man finds it.

CLOSE READ

Analyze Myths

How does this myth connect to the topic of "conflict between opposites"? <u>Underline</u> text evidence that supports your answer.

London author **Geraldine McCaughrean** has written well over one hundred books, including multiple volumes of mythology for young readers. Her novel *Peter Pan in Scarlet*, a New York Times bestseller, is the official sequel to J. M. Barrie's classic book.

Race to the Top

Preview Vocabulary

As you read "Race to the Top," pay attention to these vocabulary words. Notice how they help you identify and analyze elements of myth.

temperaments	parapet	infernal

Read and Compare

Before you read "Race to the Top," establish a purpose for reading. Active readers of **myths** follow these strategies when they read a text the first time.

Notice
how the myth answers the question "Why?"

Generate Questions
before and during reading to increase your comprehension.

First Read

Connect
ideas in this myth to important ideas in society.

Respond
by noting parts of this myth that are similar to or different from other myths you know.

Race to the Top

from The Crystal Pool: Myths and Legends of the World

A Maori Myth

by Geraldine McCaughrean

BACKGROUND

It is not uncommon for mythological figures to go by many names. As stories are told over time, or different parts of a person or supernatural being are emphasized, the names in the tales can shift. Io, the all-powerful figure in this tale, is also known as Io Matua. Tane, associated with light and the sun, is sometimes called Tane-Mahuta and at other times known as Tane-te-Wananga.

AUDIO

ANNOTATE

Evaluate Details

Look closely at the image. Highlight text that is closely connected to what you see.

Analyze Myths

How does this myth connect to the topic of "conflict between opposites"? Underline text evidence in paragraphs 1–3 that supports your answer.

temperaments personalities; usual attitudes or behaviors

parapet a low wall at the edge of a structure, such as a bridge

1   In the very Highest Heaven, Papa Io prepared three presents for the Human Race. He took three baskets and into one put Peace and Love. Into the second he put Songs and Spells. Into the third he put Help and Understanding. The people of Earth would need all these if they were to get along with one another successfully. And Papa Io knew all about the importance of getting along. He had two sons, Tane and Whiro, who could no more agree than fire and water. He had put Tane in charge of light, Whiro in charge of darkness. The jobs suited their temperaments perfectly, he thought. For Tane was all brightness, kindness, and goodness, while Whiro (although Io wept to admit it) was gloomy, evil, and dangerous.

2   Naturally, when the three baskets were ready, it was easy to choose which son should deliver them. Io stuck his head out over Heaven's parapet and called through his speaking trumpet, "Tane! Come up here! I need you to take these gifts to Humankind!"

3   Now Whiro knew full well that whoever delivered such fine presents to the people of Earth would win them, heart and mind. They would never stop thanking or praising the messenger. The thought of praise appealed to Whiro. So, while Tane climbed the Great Tower of Overworlds, story by story, up the ladders that led from one floor to the next, Whiro set off to climb the outside of the Tower. Like ivy, like a fat black spider creeping silently up a wall, he raced his brother skyward, determined to reach the top first. In his pockets were all the tools of his trade, all the tricks that would give him the advantage. . . .

CLOSE READ

Analyze Myths

The repetition of similar actions, often building to a climax, is a typical element of myths and traditional tales.

Underline words and phrases in paragraphs 4–8 that establish a pattern of events.

4   It was slow going. But by the time he reached the second story, Whiro found Tane was already on the third. So, out of his pocket he pulled handfuls of mosquitoes, sand flies, and bats. "Kiss my brother for me, my dearios," he said, and flung them in the air.

5   Unsteadily balanced on the ladder between worlds, Tane was suddenly engulfed in a cloud of flying black particles. They flew in his eyes, his ears, his mouth, and up his nose. He bent his head down against the swarm, clinging to the ladder with one hand while, with the other, he fumbled in his pocket. At last he tugged out a twist of North Wind as big as a towel, and waved it around his head. The insects and bats were swept by a frosty gusting gale miles out to sea.

6   So, when Whiro, climbing the outside of the Tower, reached the third story, Tane was already well on his way to the fourth. Whiro put his hand in his other pocket and drew out, like a fisherman's maggots, a handful of ants, centipedes, hornets, spiders, and scorpions. "Say hello to my brother from me, sweetlings," he said, and threw them in the air.

7   Halfway up the next tall ladder, Tane heard a crackling, and was suddenly, vilely beset by creepy-crawlies. They swarmed through his hair, infested his clothing; they stung his bare arms and cheeks and calves. Feeling in his pocket, he found no rags of wind, nothing at all to swat them away. There was nothing he could do but shut tight his eyes and mouth and go on climbing — higher and higher — from the eighth to the ninth to the tenth story.

8   Gradually, the air became thinner, purer. The holiness emanating from the magic realms above filled the upper stories with a glorious perfume. The disgusting crawling creatures began to fall away, overcome, like mountaineers succumbing to altitude sickness.

CLOSE READ

Evaluate Details

Reread paragraphs 4–8. How are descriptions of characters and events reflected in the image? Highlight text that supports your answer.

Vocabulary in Context

Look at paragraph 9. *Flag* is commonly used as a noun, but here it is a verb. Determine the meaning of the word as it is used here.

<u>Underline</u> context clues that support your definition.

infernal unpleasant; related to the underworld

9   Outside, on the wall of the Great Tower of Overworlds, even Whiro began to flag. His arms and legs ached. His fingers could barely grip. When he looked down, his head swam at the dizzying drop. He would never make it as far as the eleventh story before Tane.

10   Spotting a small window in the side of the Tower, Whiro slipped through it, feetfirst, and found himself on the ninth floor. Very well. If he could not catch Tane on the way up, he would ambush him on the way down. Hiding himself in the shadows behind the ladder, he settled down to wait. . . .

11   In the uppermost Overworld, welcoming hands helped Tane from the ladder and led him before Papa Io. And there, while pink evening clouds drifted between the white pillars of Highest Heaven, Io entrusted his three precious presents into Tane's keeping. "Give them to Humankind with my love and blessing," said Io. "And tell them to watch out for that infernal brother of yours. He's a tricky one, that Whiro, though I weep to say it about my own son."

12   Carefully, carefully, Tane started back down, the baskets balanced neatly on top of one another. The perfumes of Highest Heaven were heady, and he was feeling a little light-headed as he stepped onto the ladder from tenth to ninth Overworld. He had only one hand free to grasp the rungs now, and he could not properly see where to place his feet.

13   Suddenly a hand grabbed his ankle and wrenched him off the ladder. He fell, the baskets tumbling on top of him, on top of Whiro, who was just then sinking his teeth deep into Tane's thigh.

14   There in the darkness they fought, good and evil, sparks and foulness spilling from the folds of their clothing. Their panting breaths sped the clouds across the evening sky. Against a blood-red sunset, the Tower of Overworlds trembled and rocked, while the birds screamed around its shaken frame: "Help! Murder! Ambush!"

CLOSE READ

Analyze Myths

How does this myth connect to the topic of "conflict between opposites"? <u>Underline</u> text evidence that supports your answer.

Analyze Myths

What is a possible theme of this myth? <u>Underline</u> text evidence in paragraph 15 that tells you about a message of this myth.

15   Whiro was rested. He liked a fight, liked to inflict pain, whereas his brother was naturally a gentle soul. But Tane knew, as his brother's hands closed around his throat to throttle him, that if Whiro once got hold of the baskets, he would either spill them or use them to take control of Earth and its people. He slapped feebly at his brother's chest, but there was no pushing him away. He reached out a hand across the creaking floor; his fingers brushed a fallen basket; the lid came off and rolled away into the darkness. A wordless song and a single magic spell spilled into Tane's open palm.

16   Suddenly a sacred, magic warmth crept up his wrist and arm, into his aching muscles, inspiring him to one last effort. Pushing Whiro backward, Tane toppled him over the edge of the hatchway and — *thud* — down into Overworld Eight; *crash* — down into Overworld Seven; *bang* — down into Six . . . and Five and Four and so, by painful stages, all the way down to the stony Earth.

17   He was not killed: immortals don't die. And the whole episode did not serve to sweeten his nasty temper. Picking himself up, Whiro snarled, "Not deliver the baskets? Well, then, I shall make Humankind some presents of my own! Sickness for one! Crime for another! DEATH for a third!" And he slouched away to find baskets big enough for all the miseries he had in store.

18   Tane delivered the three baskets safely to the people of Earth. So after that, they were armed against anything Whiro could hurl at them. The only lasting damage was to the Tower. Shaken and rocked by the titanic struggle on the ninth floor, its rickety structure teeters now, condemned, on the world's edge. It would not carry the weight of the smallest child, let alone the great bulk of Papa Io climbing down from the sky. So Humankind are on their own now. They will have to make do as best they can with what the gods gave them.

CLOSE READ

Analyze Myths

How does this myth address the question of "why good things and suffering are part of life"? Underline text evidence that supports your answer.

Develop Vocabulary

The individuals in myths often stand for recognizable types of people. In addition, myths often contain vocabulary that expresses strong contrasts and emotions. These features help listeners and readers relate to the lesson of the myth.

My TURN Find a word in the Word Bank that could be used in each example sentence. Then write your own sentence using the same word.

Word Bank				
shrewd	ornate	temperaments	parapet	infernal

Example Sentence	Word	My Sentence
The stork stands guard on the highest rim of the castle roof.	parapet	The queen looked down at the crowds from the parapet.
A duck waits until the fox is asleep to lead her ducklings to the pond.		
The unpleasant storm raged with rain, sleet, and even hail.		
The twins look alike, but one always smiles and the other smirks.		
The palace was filled with richly detailed, delicate artwork.		

Check for Understanding

My TURN Look back at the texts to answer the questions.

1. What characteristics of myths do the stories share?

2. Compare and contrast Zeus and Papa Io based on their personalities, how they treat people, and what they want for people.

3. Which brother in "Race to the Top" is more like Pandora? Use text evidence to support your opinion.

4. When someone today says that a person or event has "opened a Pandora's box," what does the phrase mean? If Whiro from "Race to the Top" said this, what would he be talking about? Cite text evidence to support your responses.

Analyze Myths

Analyzing means studying the parts of something to understand how it works. When you analyze myths, you study their patterns of events and infer their themes.

1. **My TURN** Go to the Close Read notes in the stories and underline the parts that help you analyze patterns of events and the theme of good versus evil.

2. **Text Evidence** Use the parts you underlined to paraphrase in logical order three events from each myth. Demonstrate your knowledge about myths by comparing the patterns of events. Then write a theme that both patterns imply.

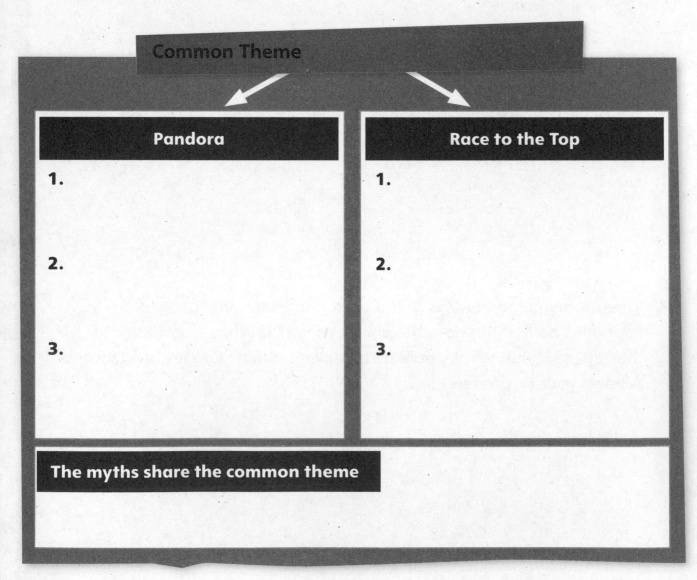

Common Theme

Pandora	Race to the Top
1.	1.
2.	2.
3.	3.

The myths share the common theme

Evaluate Details

Readers can determine key ideas in a text by noticing details. They evaluate the details to decide which are important to meaning and to figure out what the author is telling them about a character, setting, or topic.

1. **My TURN** Go back to the Close Read notes and highlight details about Zeus, Papa Io, evil, and good.

2. **Text Evidence** Use the details you highlighted to fill in the chart. Then evaluate the details to help you answer the question that follows.

Zeus and Papa Io	Evil	Good

Question: What key idea do the authors communicate by using winged creatures to represent evil and suffering?

_____

_____

_____

_____

_____

Reflect and Share

Talk About It Think about the myths you read this week. Which character in each story determines the fate of all the others? What does the character do? Is the character a god or a human being? What other stories or drama have you read with similar characters? Use examples from the texts to discuss why authors include such characters in traditional literature.

- -

Use Accurate Information During a discussion, especially one in which people have different opinions, make sure to use accurate information to support your views. You can prepare for this discussion by reviewing what characters actually do in the stories and drama. Use these steps:

1. Decide which characters you want to discuss.
2. Reread the stories and drama, and take notes to make sure you know what the characters really do.
3. Based on your notes, record accurate information about how each character determines the fate of others.
4. Use paragraph, act, scene, or line numbers to show where you found your evidence.

At the end of the discussion, consider whether your classmates' points of view changed your own opinions. Explain how your thinking changed.

- -

Weekly Question

How can being disobedient cause problems?

Academic Vocabulary

Learning Goal

I can use language to make connections between reading and writing.

Parts of speech are categories of words. They include nouns, verbs, adjectives, adverbs, and prepositions.

- **Nouns** name people, places, and things.
- **Verbs** name actions and states of being.
- **Adjectives** describe nouns and pronouns.
- **Adverbs** describe verbs, adjectives, and other adverbs.
- **Prepositions** relate nouns to other words.

Flowers in gardens look very pretty.

With changes in spelling, many words can be used as different parts of speech.

My TURN For each bold word,

1. **Find** the entry in an online or print dictionary.

2. **Locate** other parts of speech the word can become.

3. **Write** the forms of the word as other parts of speech in the chart.

Noun	Verb	Adjective	Adverb
	reveal		
	illustrate		
	interpret		
	predict		
		traditional	

Homophones

Homophones are words that sound the same but are spelled differently and have different meanings. For example, *one* and *won* sound the same. However, their spelling and context reveal that *one* means a single thing, and *won* is a past-tense verb for being first in a competition.

My TURN Underline the correct homophone in each sentence. Then explain the meaning of each underlined word. On a separate sheet of paper, write 2–3 sentences using pairs of homophones.

He was (too, two, to) content.

The jobs suited (there, their) temperaments perfectly, he thought.

In the uppermost Overworld, welcoming hands helped Tane from the ladder and (lead, led) him before Papa Io.

Amazingly, people survived the floods caused by the (rain, reign) that fell because of the god's anger.

His anger does not (affect/effect) me.

1. _____

2. _____

3. _____

4. _____

5. _____

Read Like a Writer

Authors include **allusions,** or references to well-known stories, myths, or history, in their stories. For example, the phrase *that was a Herculean effort* is an allusion to the Greek myth of Hercules, who had to complete twelve difficult tasks.

Model ! Read the text.   allusion

In a display of Promethean cunning, the baby escaped her crib so she could play with her favorite toy.

1. Identify The author includes an allusion to Prometheus.

2. Question What does the allusion to Prometheus tell me about the story?

3. Conclude Because I know that Prometheus was well-known for his bravery and slyness, I know that the baby must be sneaky and clever to have escaped the crib.

Read the text.

"I just wanted to see what would happen!" Luce said as she tried to scrub permanent marker off of the couch.

Mom sighed. "You just had to open that Pandora's box, huh? Our living room may never look the same!"

My TURN Follow the steps to analyze the text.

1. Identify The author includes an allusion to _____

2. Question What does the allusion tell me about the story?

3. Conclude Because I know _____
I understand that _____

Write for a Reader

Allusions are references to well-known stories or myths. Authors who use allusions show their understanding of history and literature. They add depth to their stories through these references.

Allusions add more levels of meaning to your writing.

My TURN Think of the mythological characters you read about in *Pandora*. Choose one character, conduct more research if needed, and identify how you could use an allusion to his or her story in your own writing.

1. What mythological figure did you choose? What aspect of his or her story will you allude to in your own writing?

_____

_____

_____

2. Now write a short story that features the allusion you chose.

_____

_____

_____

_____

_____

_____

_____

_____

_____

Spell Homophones

Homophones are words that sound exactly the same, but they are spelled differently and have different meanings. Learn the different spellings and meanings of homophones so you can spell them correctly in your writing.

My TURN Read the words. Sort and spell each pair of homophones.

SPELLING WORDS			
stare	peek	break	counsel
thrown	idol	pair	passed
sole	stair	peak	council
idle	steal	pear	steel
soul	throne	past	brake

stare

_____

_____

_____

_____

_____

_____

_____

stair

_____

_____

_____

_____

_____

_____

_____

Superlative Adjectives

Superlative adjectives compare three or more people, places, things, or groups of items. For many adjectives, adding *-est* creates the superlative form. If an adjective ends with *y*, the *y* changes to an *i* before *-est* is added.

tall → tallest   curly → curliest

Adding *-est* to longer adjectives is awkward. Therefore, writers use the word *most* in front of longer adjectives to make them superlative.

Adjective	Awkward	Superlative
thoughtful	thoughtfullest	most thoughtful
circular	circularest	most circular

A few adjectives have irregular superlative forms. It is useful to learn the superlative forms of such words.

good → best   much → most   little → least

My TURN Edit this draft by replacing four incorrect superlative adjectives with correct ones.

Duffy is the goodest dog ever. He was the most small puppy in the litter, but that made him the bravest creature of all. At our house he gets up and does the entertainingest little dance by the most high bunk beds to make us laugh and get up.

Incorporate Peer and Teacher Suggestions

Learning Goal

I can use elements of opinion writing to write an essay.

The purpose of an opinion essay is to provide readers with the writer's perspective on a topic. Your classmates and your teacher can tell you whether your essay supports your point of view with strong reasons. When you receive their suggestions, follow these steps.

Remember that your readers are your audience. Does your audience think you have supported your opinion with strong reasons? Whether yes or no, make sure you understand why.

If your audience **does not think** you have provided strong reasons, ask for written notes that explain why a reason is weak. Ask for help with planning or revising, if needed.

If your audience **does think** you have provided strong reasons, make sure to learn why so that you can use this knowledge when you write your next opinion essay.

Discuss with your peers and your teacher any questions you have about their suggestions. Ask if they would be willing to read your essay again when you have revised it.

My TURN Follow these steps to incorporate suggestions from people who read your opinion essay.

Publish a Final Draft

When you are satisfied with your opinion essay, publish it in two ways.

- Write a legible copy of your essay in cursive.
- Type your essay on a tablet or a computer. Type at least one full page before taking a break. When you have typed your entire essay, print out your electronic file.

My TURN Read the questions below, and then read your opinion essay aloud to yourself. Afterward, answer the questions.

1. Who is my audience?

_____

_____

2. How well will my audience understand my opinion?

_____

3. How can I strengthen my reasons to help my audience understand my point of view?

_____

_____

_____

Proofread your essay to make sure readers will have no trouble following your reasoning.

Publish and Celebrate

My TURN Complete these sentences about your writing experience.

You can tell that I thought about the audience for my opinion essay because

_____

_____

_____

_____

The way I organized the reasons for my opinion was

_____

_____

_____

_____

I am pleased with my introduction and my conclusion because

_____

_____

_____

_____

The next time I write an opinion essay, I want to

_____

_____

_____

_____

Prepare for Assessment

MyTURN Follow a plan as you prepare to write an opinion essay in response to a prompt. Use your own paper.

1. Study the prompt.

You will receive an assignment called a writing prompt. Carefully read the practice prompt. Highlight the type of writing you must do. Underline the topic you must write about.

Prompt: Write an opinion essay about a recent event that you think should cause people to see the world differently.

2. Brainstorm.

List three news stories you have read and about which you have an opinion. Then highlight your favorite idea.

3. Assemble your reasons and information.

Always keep your audience in mind.

4. Outline your essay.

Decide what you will put in the introduction and the conclusion. When you plan your body paragraphs, put the strongest reason first. List information under the reason it supports.

5. Write your draft.

Follow your outline. Use technology to rearrange and combine sentences and paragraphs as necessary.

6. Revise and edit your opinion essay.

Revise your essay for coherence, clarity, and correctness. Remember to edit to apply the rules you have learned to polish your writing.

Assessment

My TURN Before you write an opinion essay for your
assessment, rate how well you understand the skills you have
learned in this unit. Go back and review any skills you mark "No."

		Yes!	No
Ideas and Organization	☺ I can recognize a writer's opinion, point of view, reasons, and supporting information.	☐	☐
	☺ I can brainstorm a topic and opinion and plan an opinion essay.	☐	☐
	☺ I can develop my topic and opinion.	☐	☐
	☺ I can develop reasons and supporting details.	☐	☐
Craft	☺ I can develop a concluding statement.	☐	☐
	☺ I can write an effective introduction and conclusion.	☐	☐
	☺ I can organize my reasons.	☐	☐
	☺ I can organize my supporting details.	☐	☐
	☺ I can use linking words and phrases to connect ideas.	☐	☐
	☺ I can use appropriate technology to present my writing.	☐	☐
	☺ I can use technology to interact and collaborate.	☐	☐
	☺ I can rearrange and combine ideas for coherence and clarity.	☐	☐
	☺ I can participate in peer editing and incorporate editors' suggestions.	☐	☐
Conventions	☺ I can edit for subject-verb agreement.	☐	☐
	☺ I can capitalize and use nouns correctly.	☐	☐

UNIT THEME
Impacts

TURNand**TALK**

Question the Answers

Read the sentence under each selection title. Then, with a partner, review the selection and write a question for each "answer" sentence. Finally, talk to your partner about how the answer relates to the theme *Impacts*.

"La Culebra"

If you do a good deed, this will happen.

_____

BOOK CLUB

WEEK 2

Thunder Rose

Thunder Rose was unique because she had this power coursing through her veins.

_____

BOOK CLUB

WEEK 1

from Can You Guess My Name?

In the tales, the names are discovered because it is hard for people to keep these.

_____

BOOK CLUB

The Secret of the Winter Count

Emma understood this from the Little People.

WEEK 4

BOOK CLUB

WEEK 5

"Pandora" and "Race to the Top"

Pandora lacked this "purely human strength."

Essential Question

My TURN

In your notebook, answer the Essential Question: How do our stories shape our world?

BOOK CLUB

Project

WEEK 6

Now it is time to apply what you learned about impacts in your WEEK 6 PROJECT — The Tale Behind the Tale!

The TALE Behind the TALE

Activity

The origin of a story is where it all began. Choose an American tall tale, folktale, or legend, such as one about Paul Bunyan, John Henry, Johnny Appleseed, Calamity Jane, or Pecos Bill. Research and explain the origin of the tale to create a post for a class blog.

Research Articles

With your partner, read "The Truth Behind the Legend" to generate questions you have about traditional tales. Then make a research plan for creating your blog post.

1 The Truth Behind the Legend

2 The Library of Congress

3 Who's Your Hero?

Generate Questions

COLLABORATE After reading "The Truth Behind the Legend," generate questions about the article. Write the three most important questions you have to share with the class.

1. _____

2. _____

3. _____

Use Academic Words

COLLABORATE In this unit, you learned many words related to the theme *Impacts*. Review the chart, and work with your partner to add more academic vocabulary words to each category. If appropriate, use some of these words when you create your blog post.

Academic Vocabulary	Word Forms	Synonyms	Antonyms
reveal	reveals revealing revealed	show tell uncover	hide conceal mask
traditional	traditions traditionally nontraditional	customary normal established	modern strange unusual
illustrate	illustrator illustrating illustration	show prove explain	hide conceal confuse
interpret	interpreter interpreting interpretation	understand explain clarify	misunderstand misjudge confuse
predict	predicts prediction predictable	forecast guess foresee	surprise shock know

Building a Better Blog

I can share different kinds of **information**—including facts, definitions, quotations, and illustrations—when I create a blog post.

People write **informative texts** to look at a topic closely and explain it to readers. The information should be accurate, complete, and clear. When reading informational text, look for

- a clearly identified topic,
- a main idea,
- supporting details based on facts and research,
- a logical organization, and
- precise language that describes and links ideas.

RESEARCH

COLLABORATE With your partner, read "The Library of Congress." Then answer the following questions about the text.

1. What are the topic and main idea of the article?

_____

_____

_____

2. What are two specific details the writer shares to support the main idea?

_____

_____

_____

3. Who is the audience for this article? How do you know?

_____

_____

_____

Plan Your Research

COLLABORATE Before you begin researching story origins, you will need to come up with a research plan. Use this activity to help write a main idea and plan how you will look for supporting details.

Definition	Examples
MAIN IDEA A main idea is the author's main point about a topic. A main idea • addresses the topic, • is specific, and • is supported with details, such as facts and examples. Read the two examples in the right column. Then, with your partner, write a main idea for your blog post about a traditional tale.	• This blog is about a popular song related to baseball. No • The biggest hit in baseball is the song "Take Me Out to the Ball Game." Yes! My main idea: _____ _____ _____
EVIDENCE You can support your main idea with details, such as • facts • statistics • quotations • examples	**Fact:** A composer named Albert von Tilzer wrote the music to "Take Me Out to the Ball Game." **Statistic:** The song has been recorded more than 400 times. **Quote:** "Today you can't go to a game without hearing the song," noted Fred Arms, a devoted Cubs fan. **Example:** Song ideas can come from many places, even a subway poster.

With your partner, use your writing notebook to list some possible options for finding evidence for your blog post.

Question and Answer

The Library of Congress is a research library that includes more than 38 million books as well as photographs, films, and digital files. Anyone can use the information in the Library of Congress. You can visit the Web site (www.loc.gov) and conduct your own search. The site offers two features to help you find the facts you are looking for by starting an online chat or submitting an e-mail.

EXAMPLE Afshin wants to write a blog post about the stories behind famous American songs. He knows that the topic is too big for one blog post. He uses the Library of Congress to compose correspondence requesting information about one great song.

You can talk live to a Library of Congress librarian any weekday during special hours.

You can generate and clarify formal inquiry questions any time you are at a computer, and a librarian will respond by e-mail within five business days. You must fill out every field in the form that has an asterisk (*).

LIBRARY OF CONGRESS (ASK A LIBRARIAN) (DIGITAL COLLECTIONS) (CATALOGS) | SEARCH [GO]

Name*

Afshin Parsi

Question*
Please add as much detail as you can

Where can I look in the Library of Congress for information about the stories behind American sports songs? I would like to find out more about famous baseball songs. I have looked for information about baseball songs in our middle school library and online using two different search engines.

Be specific: when you ask your question, include details about your project, your goal, and resources you have already consulted.

Country*

United States

ZIP/Postal code*

59105

[CLEAR]   [ASK YOUR QUESTION]

Click here to send your completed form.

Click here to clear the form and start over.

COLLABORATE With your partner, generate and clarify formal questions you will ask a librarian at the Library of Congress. Compose your correspondence in a live web chat or through the Ask a Librarian form on the Web site.

Information About Our Project

Sources We Have Already Used

Specific Questions We Want to Ask

Discuss the response you receive during the online chat or by e-mail. How did the librarian help you decide the next step for your research project?

POST with the MOST!

A blog is a Web site that is updated regularly. The noun is a short form of the word *weblog*. Bloggers (people who write blogs) also use the word as a verb: "I just blogged about a great book I read last week."

Each new blog update is called a **post**. Many blog posts share information the writers learned through research. Posts usually

- focus on one clear main idea,
- combine text with media elements, such as illustrations, photographs, and audio or video clips,
- begin with a title that will grab readers' interest, and
- use informal language.

> **COLLABORATE** Read the Student Model. Work with your partner to recognize the characteristics of informative texts.

Now You Try It!

Discuss the checklist with your partner. Work together to follow the steps to create your blog post.

Make sure your blog post

- ☐ identifies a clear main idea.
- ☐ shares accurate details from your research.
- ☐ presents ideas in a clear and logically organized way.
- ☐ uses precise language to describe and link ideas.

Student Model

about   contact   faq   search 🔍

Baseball's Biggest Hit

The biggest hit in baseball isn't a home run—it's a song! "Take Me Out to the Ball Game" is one of the most popular songs ever. It's been recorded more than 400 times. The song has also been heard in more than 1,200 movies, TV shows, and commercials.

◄······ **Underline** the sentence that names the main idea of the post.

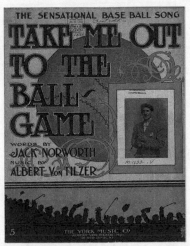

A composer named Albert von Tilzer wrote the music. Jack Norworth wrote the ◄······ lyrics. The song tells about a young woman who really loves baseball. She begs her date to take her to a ballgame instead of a play. The song was written in 1908.

Highlight three specific details the writer shares.

The songwriters must have been huge baseball fans, right? Nope! In fact, they had never seen a live baseball game when they wrote the song. Norworth saw a poster. He got the idea when he was riding the New York subway. The poster said "Baseball Today: Polo Grounds."

That poster had a big effect on baseball history. ◄····· Today, baseball fans love to sing the song together. It's almost as big a part of the game as the ball and bat!

Underline the most important idea in the conclusion.

Image Citation: Norworth, Jack, and Albert Von Tilzer. *Take Me Out to the Ball Game.* The New York Music Co., New York, monographic, 1908. Notated Music. Retrieved from the Library of Congress, https://www.loc.gov/item/ihas.200033481/. (Accessed May 02, 2017.)

Creating a Bibliography

A **bibliography** is a list of the sources you used when researching a topic. It gives readers the information they need to find and check your sources. This chart shows how to cite different kinds of sources.

Books and Magazines

Madison, Emily. *All-American Heroes*. Philadelphia. Power Press, 2017.

- Author (last name first)
- *Title of Book* (in italics or underlined)
- City of Publication
- Publisher, Year of Publication

Encyclopedias

"Heroes." *New Times Encyclopedia*. 2014. ◄••••••••••••

In this example, the article did not list an author.

- Author (if available)
- "Title of Article."
- *Title of Book* (in italics or underlined)
- Date of Edition

Web Sites

Singh, Denyse. "Heroes Are Here." *Center for Student Studies*. Nov. 28, 2017. www.url.here

You can usually find the name of the Web site on the home page, or first page, of the site.

- Author (if available)
- "Title of Page."
- *Name of Site* (in italics or underlined)
- Date of your visit
- <URL—Web site address> in brackets

RESEARCH

COLLABORATE Read the web article "Who's Your Hero?" Then, on a separate sheet of paper or in your writing notebook, work with a partner to create a bibliography entry for the article.

COLLABORATE Read this bibliography for a blog post. Then answer the questions.

"Baseball's Greatest Hits: The Music of Our National Game." Library of Congress. May 3, 2017. <https://www.loc.gov/exhibits/baseballs-greatest-hits/index.html>

Editors of *Sports Illustrated Kids*, "Baseball: Then and WOW!" New York. Liberty Street. 2016.

Klingheim, Trey. "Baseball History." *New Encyclopedia of America.* 2012.

Panchyk, Richard. *Baseball History for Kids: America at Bat from 1900 to Today.* Chicago. Chicago Review Press Inc. 2016.

1. What is the oldest source listed in this bibliography? How can you tell?

_____

_____

2. What is unusual about the authors listed for the book *Baseball: Then to Wow!*?

_____

_____

3. How are the entries in the bibliography organized?

_____

_____

_____

Create a STRONG Media Message

The purpose of a blog can be to share a message or information with a specific audience. Online media communicates messages by combining language, images, and sounds.

The **language** in a blog post includes the blog name, the titles of each blog post, writers' names, dates of each post, and the posts themselves.

THE BIG BLAST: The P.S. 42 Blog

Images are visual elements in a blog. Images that do not move are called still images.

 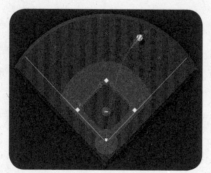 

Blogs also use moving images, such as **videos** or **animation**. These are often indicated by a triangle that points to the right. When you click the triangle, the movie begins to play.

Blogs can include **sounds** in movie clips or audio files. An audio file might play songs, interviews, or sound effects.

COLLABORATE With your partner, think about how adding media elements to your blog post will help you share information with your audience.

Language

What words might you add to make your blog post more informative?

Images	
What still images might you add? Where will you find them?	What moving image could you add? Where will you find it?

Sounds

What sounds could you add? Will you record your own sounds, or include prerecorded songs, interviews, or sound effects?

Revise

Revise Main Idea and Details Reread your blog post with your partner. Have you

☐ clearly stated the main idea of your post?

☐ included enough information to explain your topic?

☐ used the information you discovered during research?

☐ presented ideas in a logical order?

Revise Order of Ideas

The writers of the model blog post in this lesson changed the order of some ideas. Notice how they combined some sentences and moved ideas so that the information is easier to follow.

In 1908, a   , and
   ᐱA composer named Albert von Tilzer wrote the music: ᐱ
Jack Norworth wrote the lyrics. The song tells about a young woman who really loves baseball. She begs her date to take her to a ballgame instead of a play. ~~The song was written in 1908.~~

The songwriters must have been huge baseball fans, right? Nope! In fact, they had never seen a live baseball game when they wrote the song. Norworth ~~saw a poster. He~~ got the idea when he was riding the New York subway. ~~The poster~~ said "Baseball Today: Polo Grounds."   and saw a poster that
                                                              ᐱ

Edit

Conventions Read your blog post again. Have you used correct conventions?

- [ ] spelling
- [ ] punctuation
- [ ] capitalization of names and places
- [ ] quotation marks around ideas quoted directly from sources
- [ ] a complete and accurately formatted bibliography

Peer Review

COLLABORATE Exchange blog posts with another group. Take notes to review the post. Identify and underline the topic. Highlight interesting and important details. Then review your notes and discuss how well the blog post explains the topic.

Time to Celebrate!

COLLABORATE If possible, submit your blog post to a classroom blog, and ask for comments from readers. You can also decide to read your blog post aloud and share any media elements you plan to include. Consider how formal or informal your language should be when you present your blog post. How did your audience react? Write their responses here.

_____

_____

_____

_____

Reflect on Your Project

My TURN Think about your blog post. What parts do you think are strongest? What parts need improvement? Write your thoughts here.

Strengths

_____

_____

_____

Areas of Improvement

_____

_____

_____

Reflect on Your Goals

Look back at your unit goals.
Use a different color to rate yourself again.

Reflect on Your Reading

When you read a biography or autobiography it is important to put yourself in the situation or in the shoes of the character or subject to understand the experience.

Share a personal connection you made while reading one of your independent reading texts.

_____

_____

_____

_____

_____

_____

_____

Reflect on Your Writing

Review the writing you did for this unit. How did writing help you understand the unit theme?

_____

_____

_____

Features

Essential Question

Why is it important to understand our planet?

 Watch

"Our Planet"

 TURN and TALK

Why do we study our planet's features?

SAVVAS
realize™
Go ONLINE for
all lessons.

 VIDEO

 AUDIO

 INTERACTIVITY

 GAME

 ANNOTATE

BOOK

RESEARCH

READING WORKSHOP

READING-WRITING BRIDGE

- Academic Vocabulary • Word Study
- **Read Like a Writer • Write for a Reader**
- Spelling • Language and Conventions

WRITING WORKSHOP

- Introduce and Immerse • Develop Elements   **Poetry**
- Develop Structure • Writer's Craft
- Publish, Celebrate, and Assess

PROJECT-BASED INQUIRY

- Inquire • Research • Collaborate

Independent Reading

In this unit, you will read assigned texts with your teacher. You will also choose texts to read on your own. Before you read, follow these steps to select and to respond to texts you read on your own.

- -

Step 1 Ask questions like these to help you select a book to read on your own.

◎ Is the level of the text right for me—challenging but not too difficult?

◎ What do I know about this genre?

◎ Is the author's purpose to inform me, entertain me, or persuade me?

◎ Will this book hold my attention?

- -

Step 2 Select a text you think you will enjoy. As you read, continue to ask and answer questions about the text. Record your responses.

- -

Step 3 After reading, you might respond by writing a summary or a book review. Share your response with a classmate. Include details in your response that will help your classmate decide whether or not to read the same text.

Independent Reading Log

Date	Book	Genre	Pages Read	Minutes Read	My Ratings
					☆☆☆☆☆

Unit Goals

Shade in the circle to rate how well you meet each goal now.

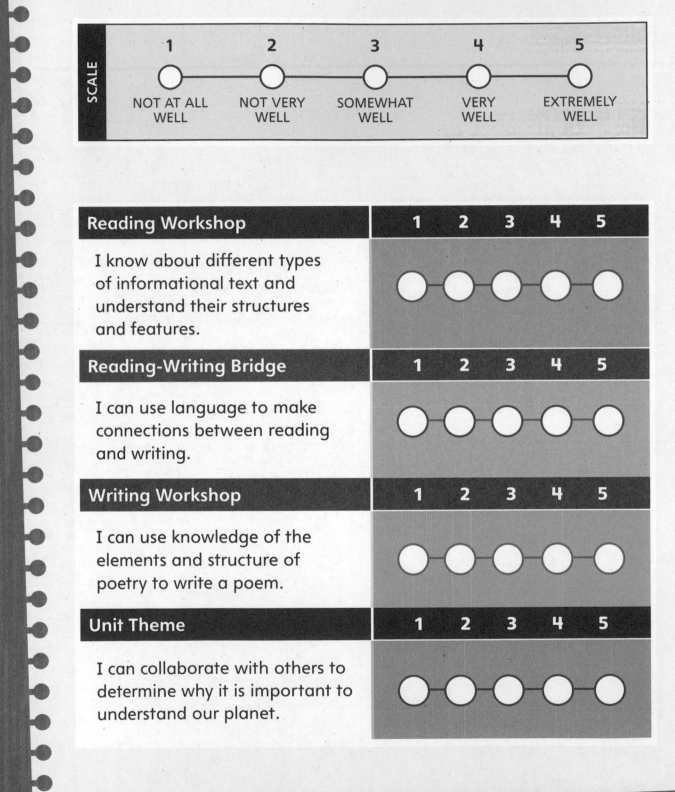

SCALE

1	2	3	4	5
NOT AT ALL WELL	NOT VERY WELL	SOMEWHAT WELL	VERY WELL	EXTREMELY WELL

Reading Workshop — 1 2 3 4 5

I know about different types of informational text and understand their structures and features.

Reading-Writing Bridge — 1 2 3 4 5

I can use language to make connections between reading and writing.

Writing Workshop — 1 2 3 4 5

I can use knowledge of the elements and structure of poetry to write a poem.

Unit Theme — 1 2 3 4 5

I can collaborate with others to determine why it is important to understand our planet.

Academic Vocabulary

Use these words to talk and write about this unit's theme, *Features*: *amazed, border, consequences, label,* and *preserve*.

TURN and TALK Read the words and definitions in the chart. Check the boxes to show in which subject the word might be used. Use each newly acquired word to explain to a partner how the word relates to the subject area.

Academic Vocabulary	Definition	Math	Phys. Ed.	Reading	Science	Social Studies
amazed	awed; impressed; struck					
border	line or boundary; to form a separating edge					
consequences	results; effects					
label	identification tag; to categorize, name, or describe					
preserve	a protected area for plants or animals; to maintain; to keep or save					

INTERACTIVITY

The Surface of
EARTH

LANDFORMS A landform is a natural formation of soil and rock. Earth's landforms include valleys, hills, plateaus, and glaciers. Tundra is the coldest land on Earth. Arctic tundra is found in the Northern Hemisphere and has frozen subsoil called permafrost.

Soil

Sandstone

Artesian aquifer

Rock

EARTH'S WATER About 71% of Earth's surface is covered with water.

We get 51% of our drinking water from GROUNDWATER. This fresh water flows slowly through soil and through cracks in rocks.

DESERTS AND FORESTS

Deserts, very dry areas with little rainfall, cover about 33% of Earth's landmass. Forests account for some 31% of Earth's land surface. Rain forests cover 6% of the planet's surface. Yet more than half of all plant and animal species are found there—approximately 30 million species.

Weekly Question

What do we know about Earth's features and processes?

Quick Write How does learning about Earth's features and processes help you to understand our planet?

North American plate
Juan de Fuca plate
Caribbean plate
Cocos plate
Pacific plate
Easter plate
Nazca plate
Juan Fernandez plate
South American plate
Scotia plate
Eurasian plate
Arabian plate
Indian plate
African plate
Australian plate
Antarctic plate

EARTH'S CRUST

Earth's crust is made up of individual sections called **tectonic plates.** When tectonic plates slowly shift, there is continental drift, or the gradual movement of continents.

CONTINENTAL SHELF

There are seven continents on our planet. Each has a **continental shelf,** which is the edge of the continent that is under the ocean.

433

Spotlight on Genre

Informational Text

Informational texts explain topics using facts and details. In addition, authors often use visual cues, such as formatting and text features, to organize and support their explanations.

- Information is grouped into **sections**.
- **Headings** orient the reader and organize information.
- Relationships between ideas and details are explained in the text or visually through graphic text features.

How do authors help readers understand facts and important ideas?

TURN and TALK Recall an informational text that you read with your class or independently. Use the anchor chart to tell a partner how text features helped you understand a topic. Take notes comparing and contrasting the text features you and your partner noticed.

My NOTES

_____

_____

_____

_____

_____

INFORMATIONAL TEXT ANCHOR CHART

Types of Text Features

Headings and Subheadings

❋ Use type SIZE and color as clues to text organization

 Diagrams

❋ Present information visually
❋ Can explain or add to details from the text

 Photographs

❋ Support text by showing visual examples

 Maps

❋ Show relationships between locations
❋ Put places into context

 Tables and Charts

❋ Make numerical data easier to understand
❋ Show trends

Christine Taylor-Butler has written children's books in a variety of genres. She enjoys learning new facts by doing research to write informational texts. She encourages young people to become writers themselves. She knows that writers are "ordinary people with extraordinary passion."

from
Planet Earth

Preview Vocabulary

As you read *Planet Earth*, pay attention to these vocabulary words. Notice how they help you understand ideas about Earth revealed in the text.

mantle	circulates

adopted	abundant	molten

Read

This **informational text** explains how our planet is structured. Ask yourself what you already know about Earth's features. Preview the text by scanning the text features. Make predictions about what you might learn.

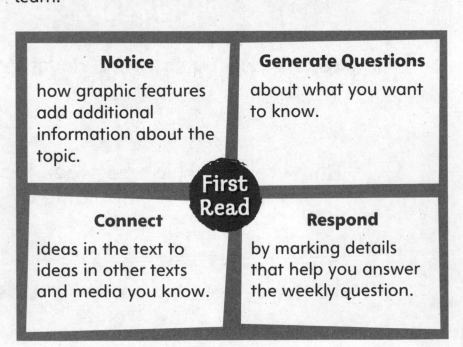

Notice how graphic features add additional information about the topic.

Generate Questions about what you want to know.

First Read

Connect ideas in the text to ideas in other texts and media you know.

Respond by marking details that help you answer the weekly question.

from Planet Earth

by Christine Taylor-Butler

AUDIO

ANNOTATE

BACKGROUND

How do scientists find out about Earth's structure and surface? The study of Earth is known as *geology*. In this excerpt, you will read about the composition of our planet and the methods scientists use to study it.

Analyze Text Features

<u>Underline</u> details in the text that are clarified by text features.

mantle the layer of Earth between the crust and the core

Above and Below

1   Below us, our planet is composed of four main layers. The outer surface is called the crust. Beneath that are the mantle, outer core, and inner core. Circling overhead is a layer of gases that forms our atmosphere. Each layer plays an important part in Earth's ability to sustain life. For example, plants and animals depend on liquid water on Earth's surface to drink. As a gas, water can travel on winds to fall on places around the world as rain, snow, or hail.

Earth is the only planet in our solar system where water exists as a solid, liquid, and gas at its surface.

Crust

Mantle

Outer core

Inner core

Earth has seven major plates and many smaller ones.

Tectonic plates sliding against each other can cause mountains to rise along Earth's surface.

The Crust

2   Earth's outermost layer includes the continental crust and oceanic crust. The crust and the uppermost layer of the mantle are broken into sections called tectonic plates. The plates rest on top of a more fluid layer of mantle and are constantly moving. Scientists believe Earth's continents were once joined as a single landmass called Pangaea. Over millions of years, the tectonic plates shifted. This caused Pangaea to break into sections. The sections drifted apart and formed the continents we know today.

3   When tectonic plates slide over or past each other, an earthquake can occur. Sometimes the pressure causes shifts in the oceans. If the ocean earthquake is strong enough, waves can develop into a deadly tsunami.

4   The collision or constant pressure of tectonic plates can create mountain ranges. For example, the Himalayan mountains in Asia grow taller each year.

CLOSE READ

Make Inferences

Look at the diagram. Highlight evidence in both the caption and the text that supports an inference about one result of sliding tectonic plates.

The movement of water is shown in blue arrows in this diagram.

Analyze Text Features

Underline text details in paragraph 5 that are illustrated by the diagram.

circulates moves through a system

5   Water on Earth circulates constantly through the water, or hydrologic, cycle. Liquid water on the planet's surface is heated by the sun and turns into a gas. This gas, called water vapor, rises into the atmosphere. It gathers into clouds and falls back to the ground as precipitation, such as rain or snow. It collects in bodies of water or soaks into the soil. Then it starts the process over again.

The Mantle

6   Earth's mantle is a semisolid and movable layer of rock. It is composed of silicon, oxygen, iron, magnesium, and aluminum. Sometimes this substance rises through the crust above. It surfaces as a volcanic eruption of molten rock.

Islands such as the Hawaiian Islands were created as molten rock rose up from the mantle through the crust beneath the ocean.

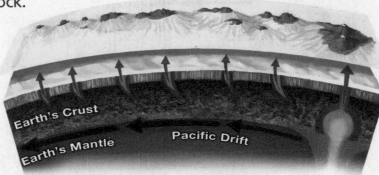

7   Scientists believe the mantle is about 1,860 miles (2,993 km) deep. This calculation is an estimate. No one has ever drilled deeper than 1.4 miles (2.3 km) beneath the ocean or 8 miles (13 km) on land.

The Core

8   Earth's core has two layers. The liquid outer core is composed mostly of iron and nickel, and is about 1,400 miles (2,250 km) thick. It is constantly flowing. Its movement around the inner core creates Earth's magnetic field. Enormous pressure and radiation keep this layer hot. The inner core is solid iron. It may spin faster than Earth's other layers. The whole core is estimated to be 11,000 degrees Fahrenheit (6,000 degrees Celsius).

CLOSE READ

Make Inferences

Highlight a sentence that you can combine with the caption to make an inference about the sun.

Earth's core may be as hot as the surface of the sun.

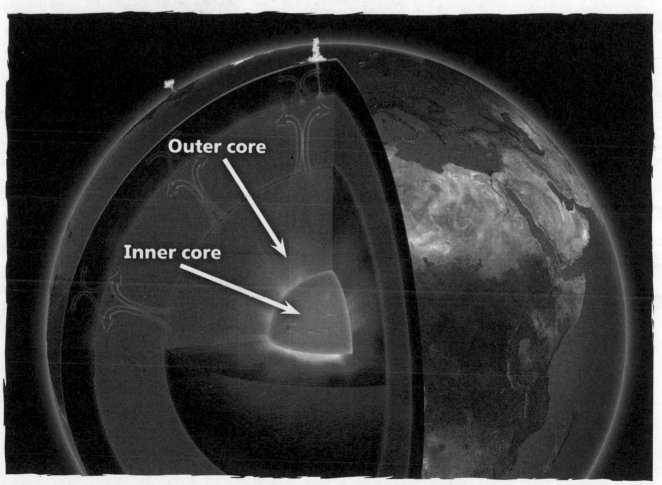

Outer core

Inner core

Analyze Text Features

Look at the heading and the images on this page and at the top of the next page. What topic do the text features help you understand? <u>Underline</u> a sentence about that topic.

A Layer of Protection

This illustration shows the five layers of Earth's atmosphere.

9 Earth's atmosphere wraps the planet like a blanket of insulation. Its two lowest layers are the troposphere and the stratosphere. More layers of thinner and thinner air are above the stratosphere. The troposphere is about 7 miles (11 km) high. It contains the air we breathe. It is 78 percent nitrogen, 21 percent oxygen, and 1 percent other gases. Nearly all of the weather we experience on Earth occurs in the troposphere.

10 The stratosphere is about 30 miles (48 km) high. It contains less water and more ozone than the troposphere. Ozone blocks harmful rays from the sun. The stratosphere and the layers above it also help protect us from objects in space, such as meteoroids. These objects sometimes threaten to crash into Earth. However, a meteoroid creates friction as it moves rapidly through the atmosphere. This usually causes the object to burn up.

Falling stars are actually meteoroids burning up in the upper atmosphere.

Meteoroids rarely make it to Earth's surface. If they do, the chance of them causing harm is very low.

Which Way Is North?

11   A compass needle points to Earth's magnetic north pole. But did you know that the magnetic north pole is not located at the geographic North Pole? The magnetic pole drifts about 6 to 25 miles (10 to 40 km) each year. The north and south magnetic poles sometimes switch places. When this happens, Earth's magnetic field temporarily becomes twisted and scrambled. But this has only happened 170 times in the last 80 million years. After the next switch, a compass needle that would have pointed north will point south.

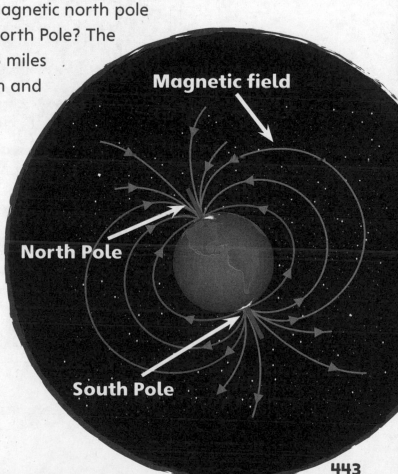

Magnetic field

North Pole

South Pole

Dividing Time

12 Earth is divided into 24 standard time zones. Each time zone is one hour ahead of the zone to the west of it. For example, say it is 12 p.m. in Anchorage, Alaska. At that same moment, it is 1 p.m. in Los Angeles, California.

CLOSE READ

Make Inferences

Use the map and the list of map locations to make an inference about who sets time zones. Highlight details in the text that you include in your inference.

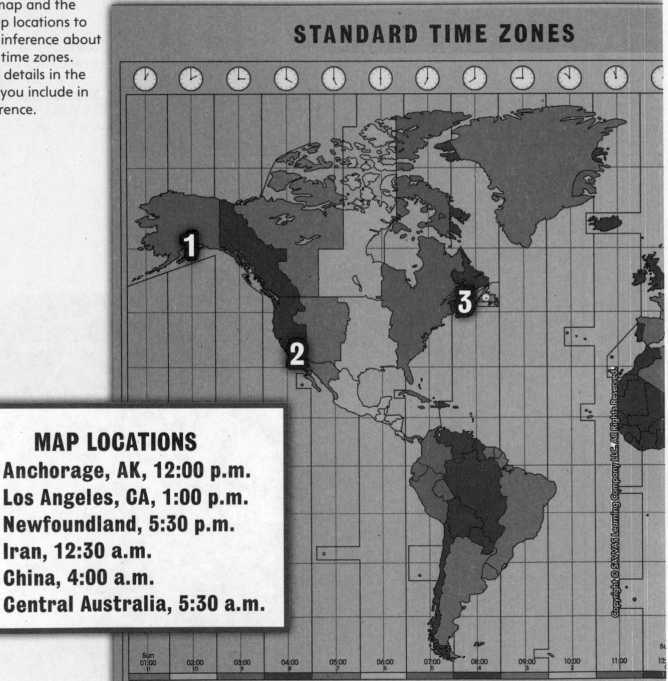

STANDARD TIME ZONES

MAP LOCATIONS
1. **Anchorage, AK, 12:00 p.m.**
2. **Los Angeles, CA, 1:00 p.m.**
3. **Newfoundland, 5:30 p.m.**
4. **Iran, 12:30 a.m.**
5. **China, 4:00 a.m.**
6. **Central Australia, 5:30 a.m.**

13　Most areas have adopted these standard time zones. But there are some exceptions. China crosses three standard time zones. But the country decided to have only one time zone. Some regions divide time zones by half hours. Iran, Newfoundland in Canada, and parts of Australia are examples.

CLOSE READ

adopted started to use a selected idea or method

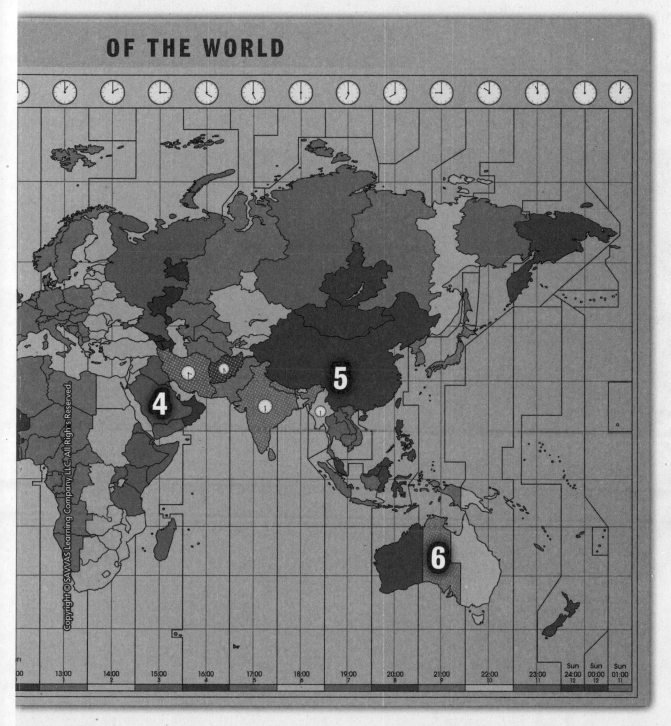

OF THE WORLD

| 13:00 | 14:00 | 15:00 | 16:00 | 17:00 | 18:00 | 19:00 | 20:00 | 21:00 | 22:00 | 23:00 | Sun 24:00 | Sun 00:00 | Sun 01:00 |
| 1 | 2 | 3 | 4 | 5 | 6 | 7 | 8 | 9 | 10 | 11 | 12 | 12 | 11 |

Vocabulary in Context

Context clues are words and sentences around a word that help readers understand the meaning of the word.

Use context clues to determine the meaning of *devastation*.

<u>Underline</u> the context clues that support your definition.

Mission Earth

14   Technology has come a long way since the days of ancient astronomy. Satellites create detailed images of Earth from space. Probes deep inside the earth and in the ocean monitor the health of the planet. Global Positioning System (GPS) satellites allow us to navigate the planet without having to study the stars. Now scientists can spot problems and react quickly to natural disasters. This helps reduce the devastation the events could cause.

A GPS satellite completes one orbit around Earth every 12 hours.

The Japanese vessel Chikyu holds the world's record for deep-ocean drilling.

The Undiscovered Deep

15   Oceans are one of Earth's most abundant resources. But only 5 percent of the ocean floor has been explored. That is changing. The National Oceanic and Atmospheric Administration is studying deepwater canyons off the coast of Virginia. There, they use remote operated vehicles (ROVs) and sonar. Woods Hole Oceanographic Institution uses a human-occupied vehicle and other underwater machines to explore and map even deeper waters. These missions help explain Earth's geologic processes.

To the Center of the Earth

16   The exact nature of Earth's mantle is still unknown. To solve this mystery, scientists are hoping to drill directly into the mantle and take samples. Geologists plan to drill through a section of the Pacific Ocean floor estimated to be less than 4 miles (6.4 km) thick. Special drills are being designed to handle the stress of boring through the hard oceanic crust. This $1 billion project is planned to start drilling in 2020.

CLOSE READ

Analyze Text Features

How does special equipment help us learn about Earth's mantle? Underline details in the text that clarify information in the photo.

abundant plentiful; commonly occurring

A scientist uses specialized equipment to study the crater at Mount Erebus.

Mount Erebus is so popular it has its own Facebook page.

CLOSE READ

Analyze Text Features

<u>Underline</u> details in the text feature that help you understand how scientists study Earth.

molten melted; hot enough to be in liquid form

Exploring Earth's Mantle Through Volcanoes

17   Antarctica's Mount Erebus is one of Earth's most unusual volcanoes. It is largely covered in ice. But it contains a lake of molten hot lava deep inside its crater. Scientists at the McMurdo Station research facility analyze the gas and lava produced by Mount Erebus. The data helps explain how and why volcanoes erupt. It can also tell us a lot about the mantle's chemical composition.

Destination Space

18   Human-made satellites also help us study Earth. The *Aqua* satellite was launched in 2002. *Aqua* uses microwave technology to see through clouds and monitor Earth's water cycle. For example, water and ice from melting polar caps could shift ocean currents. Weather would change, and Earth's temperatures could plunge. Other satellites look for activity signaling earthquakes, tsunamis, or other natural disasters. Satellites can track storms or changes in Earth's climate.

The *Aqua* satellite is a joint project between the U.S. National Aeronautics and Space Administration and Japan's National Space Development Agency.

ISS orbits 240 miles (386 km) above Earth.

19   To learn how things work in a weightless environment, world scientists designed the International Space Station (ISS). ISS welcomed its first astronauts on November 2, 2000. Since then, more than 200 scientists and engineers have visited the station. They have conducted more than 400 experiments. As of 2013, ISS completed more than 57,000 orbits around Earth.

20   Exploration continues to expand. People once thought Earth was the center of the universe. What will we discover next?

Where on Earth Are You?

21   Do you use GPS to navigate? If so, you're receiving information from the 29 GPS satellites orbiting Earth. The U.S. Air Force maintains these satellites. Twenty-four satellites are active. The other five are backups. The satellites transmit radio signals to a GPS receiver in your phone or car. Signals from four or more satellites are needed to accurately determine your position. Digital maps are built into the receiver. They use the satellites' information to help you navigate.

CLOSE READ

Make Inferences

Highlight details in the text that you can combine with facts from paragraph 14 to make an inference about navigation.

Develop Vocabulary

Words develop new meanings as authors use them in different contexts. The original meaning of the word is the same, but a new meaning may become more familiar. For example, the original meaning of *mantle* is "cloak" or "outer covering." When scientists needed a name for the layer of Earth between the core and the crust, they began using *mantle*. Today, when people hear the word *mantle*, many of them think of Earth's crust instead of thinking of a piece of clothing.

My TURN Define each word as it is used in the text. Then complete the sentence to use the word in a different context.

Word	Text Definition	Sentence
mantle	layer of Earth between the crust and the core	The troposphere <u>covers the planet like</u> a mantle.
circulates		The air circulates _____ _____ _____.
adopted		Deng adopted the cook's procedure for _____ _____.
abundant		Orson collected abundant _____ _____ _____.
molten		Greta _____ into the molten cheese.

Check for Understanding

My TURN Look back at the text to answer the questions.

1. What clues tell you that *Planet Earth* is an informational text?

2. Scientists use tools, such as ROVs, drills, and satellites, that are specially designed for studying the planet. Choose one area of the planet that scientists study, and explain the tool or tools that scientists use there.

3. Why do people want to know about the structure of Earth? How is this knowledge helpful? Use a quotation from the text to support your answer.

4. How does heat affect natural systems on Earth? Write a short paragraph about the role that heat plays in the water cycle and inside Earth. Support your paragraph with evidence from the text.

Analyze Text Features

A text's **graphic features** include photographs and diagrams. **Print features,** such as captions and labels, clearly identify what to note in graphic features.

1. **My TURN** Go to the Close Read notes in *Planet Earth* and underline links between text details and information in graphic features.

2. **Text Evidence** Use the parts you underlined to complete the chart. Tell whether the purpose of each feature is to explain a *structure* or a *process* on Earth. Then answer the question.

Graphic Feature	My Annotations	Purpose of Feature
Diagram of Earth near paragraph 1	"crust," "mantle, outer core, and inner core"	to explain a <u>structure</u>
Diagram of Water Movement near paragraph 5		to explain a _____
Photograph of *Chikyu* near paragraph 15		to explain a _____

Choose one graphic feature from the chart to analyze. How does the graphic feature help achieve the author's purpose?

Make Inferences

To make an inference, combine text evidence with what you already know to reach a new understanding about a topic.

1. **My TURN** Go back to the Close Read notes and highlight evidence in diagrams, captions, and the text that will help you make inferences.

2. **Text Evidence** Record your evidence in this chart. Then use what you already know to make an inference about information in *Planet Earth*.

Text Evidence	What I Already Know About This Topic	My Inference
"Tectonic plates sliding against each other can cause mountains to rise along Earth's surface."	I know that mountains can change over time.	Tectonic plates are the reason mountains such as the Himalayas get taller.

Reflect and Share

Talk About It What interests or concerns you most about planet Earth? What more do you want to know about it? Based on what you've read this week, which kind of scientist would be able to give you that information? Discuss with a partner. Use examples from the texts to support your ideas.

- -

Listen Actively and Ask Questions During your discussion with a partner, remember that how you listen is as important as what you say.

- ◎ Listen quietly while your partner speaks. Don't interrupt.
- ◎ Focus on what your partner is saying so that you can ask questions about what is being said.
- ◎ Briefly paraphrase, or restate, what your partner said before you ask for clarification or examples.

Use questions like these to ask for clarification and examples.

Would you tell me more about what that kind of scientist does?

You said _____. Could you give me an example of what you mean?

- -

Weekly Question

What do we know about Earth's features and processes?

Academic Vocabulary

Related words share roots and have similar meanings. Adding prefixes and suffixes to a base word creates related words. For example, the base word *preserve* is related to the words *preservative*, *preserving*, and *preservation*. Related words function as different parts of speech.

My TURN For each pair of related words,

1. **Identify** each word's part of speech.

2. **Tell** what both words are about.

3. **Write** the related word that best completes the sentence.

Related Words	Parts of Speech	Both Words Are About . . .	Sentence Completion
mislabeled labeling	verb verb	naming something	Because she was in a hurry, she __mislabeled__ the hot sauce.
amaze amazement			We looked at the miniature horse in _____.
borderless bordered			He walked to the fence that _____ the pasture.
consequently inconsequential			_____, they returned home without any souvenirs.

Latin Roots

The **Latin roots** *gener, port, dur,* and *ject* form many English base words. The meaning of each root influences the meaning of the word in which it appears.

Root	Latin Meaning	Sample Base Word	Sample Related Words
gener	to produce	generate	generation regenerate
port	to carry	port	import report
dur	to harden	endure	enduring during
ject	to throw	project	projected projecting

My TURN Complete the sentences to explain how each bold word is related to the meaning of its Latin root. Refer to print or digital resources for ideas.

1. If I am **generating** ideas, it means I am _in the process of producing ideas._

2. A **porter** is _____

3. A stone's **durability** usually relates to how _____ the stone is.

4. When I **reject** an idea, I _____

5. The regeneration of the garden meant that it was _____

_____

Read Like a Writer

An author uses an overall text structure, or pattern of organization, to achieve his or her purpose for writing. To inform readers about a topic, authors use a chronological, compare-and-contrast, cause-and-effect, problem-and-solution, or descriptive text structure. Headings provide clues to a text's structure.

Model ! Reread the first heading and paragraph 1 of *Planet Earth*.

1. **Identify** Christine Taylor-Butler introduces text about the planet with the heading **Above and Below.**

2. **Question** What clue does the heading provide about text structure?

3. **Conclude** The heading is a clue that the text structure will be descriptive, organizing facts about the planet according to its parts.

Reread paragraph 14 of *Planet Earth* and the heading above it.

My TURN Follow the steps to explain a text structure.

1. **Identify** Christine Taylor-Butler introduces text about _____
_____ with the heading **Mission Earth.**

2. **Question** What clue does the heading provide about text structure?

3. **Conclude** The heading is a clue that

_____

_____

_____

_____

Write for a Reader

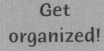

Get organized!

To inform readers, authors decide which text structure will be best for a topic: chronological, compare-and-contrast, cause-and-effect, problem-and-solution, or descriptive. They then use text features, such as headings, to help readers follow the text structure.

My TURN Recall how Christine Taylor-Butler uses headings and a descriptive text structure to inform readers in *Planet Earth*. Now think of how you can use a text structure to help inform your readers.

1. For an informational essay about the benefits of eating fruits and vegetables, which text structure would you use? Why?

_____

_____

_____

2. Write a passage about eating fruits and vegetables that follows the text structure you chose. Then add a heading that will give readers a clue about the structure.

Heading _____

Passage _____

_____

_____

_____

_____

_____

Spell Words with Latin Roots

Some English words have been built with one of the **Latin roots** *gener, port, dur,* or *ject* plus a prefix, suffix, or both. These words usually have a meaning related to the root. Use a dictionary to confirm the meaning. In general, adding a prefix or a suffix does not change the spelling of the root.

My TURN Read the words. Then spell the words in the correct columns. Note that the silent *e* in *endure* is not a suffix.

SPELLING WORDS

generous	generic	degenerated	general	generalization
portable	transport	comport	passport	rapport
duration	durable	endure	endurable	endurance
projector	eject	ejection	interjection	objection

Prefix + Root	Root + Suffix	Prefix + Root + Suffix

Relative Adverbs

To convey complete information, use the **relative adverbs** *where*, *when*, and *why* to connect two clauses that are related. Each **clause** has a subject and a verb. The second clause tells the place of (*where*), the time of (*when*), or the reason for (*why*) an event or statement in the first clause.

Clause 1	Relative Adverb	Clause 2
I must find out	where	the cat is hiding.
I will tell Vanessa	when	I find the cat.
She will ask	why	the cat ran away.

My TURN Use relative adverbs to complete the paragraph.

Hela opened the door _____ she heard Dirsu's knock. She

asked him _____ he had come back so soon. "I forgot to tell

you _____ I put the birthday candles," Dirsu said. "You'll

need them _____ it's time for the cake," he added.

Understand Poetry

Poetry is a form of literature that arranges words into lines and expresses ideas or feelings. Writers of poetry, called poets, use figurative language, concrete details, and sensory language to create images in a reader's mind. Poets also use sound devices such as rhythm, rhyme, and repeated sounds.

There are many kinds of poems. A poem may tell a story, express an emotion, or paint a picture in words. It may be serious, funny, sweet, or challenging. It can also take a specific form, such as a sonnet, lyric poem, or free verse poem.

My TURN Think about poems you have read, and answer the questions.

1. What topics do poets write about?

_____

_____

_____

2. What do you notice about the words poets choose?

_____

_____

_____

3. What patterns of lines and sounds do you remember from poems you have read?

_____

_____

_____

Explore What Poetry Sounds Like

A poem has memorable sounds. One sound is the **rhythm**, which is a regular pattern of stressed and unstressed syllables. The easiest way to understand the term *stressed syllable* is to say a word aloud. Read these sentences aloud to yourself:

I gave her a present.	*The first syllable of* present *is stressed.*
I will present my speech next week.	*The second syllable of* present *is stressed.*

The easiest way to hear a poem's rhythm is to read the poem aloud. For example, in the following lines, every other syllable is stressed. Each line has five stressed syllables. This is a regular pattern. Read the lines and clap with every bold syllable.

Ta**riq** jumped **up** to **catch** the **fly**ing **ball**

But **Le**ah **caught** it **first** be**cause** she's **tall.**

Poems often include other sound devices, such as **rhyme.** Words rhyme when they have the same sound in their ending syllable or syllables.

My TURN Choose a short poem from your classroom library and read it aloud to yourself. To describe the rhythm, count the stressed syllables you hear in the first two lines. Decide whether the pattern is regular. Then list all of the rhymes you hear.

Rhythm	Rhymes
Line 1 stressed syllables:	
Line 2 stressed syllables:	
Is this a regular pattern?	

Explore What Poetry Looks Like

Poetry is written in lines. Lines can be long or short. A poet, or writer of poetry, arranges lines in a pattern. Sometimes a poet groups lines into stanzas. Every stanza may have the same number of lines, or stanzas may have different numbers of lines.

Poems might have sentences that start with a capital letter and end with punctuation, but they do not always have sentences. Poets use punctuation for its effect, such as to encourage readers to pause or keep reading.

My TURN With a partner, choose a poem with stanzas from your classroom library and take turns reading the poem aloud. Then answer the questions.

1. What made you pause while you were reading? Was it the punctuation, the end of a line, or the end of a stanza?

    _____

    _____

    _____

2. How long were the pauses? Were all of the pauses the same length?

    _____

    _____

3. Are the stanzas the same or different? How do they compare in the number of lines, the length of lines, and punctuation?

    _____

    _____

    _____

    _____

    _____

Brainstorm Ideas

Poets think of ideas before they begin a poem. One way to gather ideas is called **brainstorming**. During brainstorming, the focus is generating ideas for writing.

My TURN Complete the sentences and the checklist to make choices about the elements of your poem.

- Topic, Theme, or Message:

  My poem could be about _____

  or _____

- Sound:

  My poem could sound like a poem I've read, such as _____

  _____

  That means it would sound

  _____

- Appearance:

  My poem could look like a poem I have read, such as _____

  _____

  That means it would have _____ lines and _____ stanzas.

Each element affects the others!

BRAINSTORMING FOR A POEM

☐ I will use rhymes.

☐ I will repeat words or phrases.

☐ I will use a regular rhythm.

Plan Your Poem

Choose a topic for your poem. Then, generate more ideas for your poem by **freewriting**. During freewriting, write without stopping to edit or revise.

My TURN Take five minutes to write anything that comes to your mind about your topic. Do not pay attention to spelling, grammar, lines, stanzas, or punctuation while freewriting.

After five minutes, stop and take a deep breath. Then look at what you wrote. Highlight words, images, and sounds you would like to emphasize. Finally, discuss your ideas with your Writing Club.

VOLCANIC
Activity

A volcano is a mountain or hill with a crater or vent. During a volcanic eruption, lava, gas, and bits of rock erupt through the crater.

View each piece of media. What stages can a volcano pass through?

Volcanoes are called **dormant**, or asleep, when they are quiet but could erupt in the future.

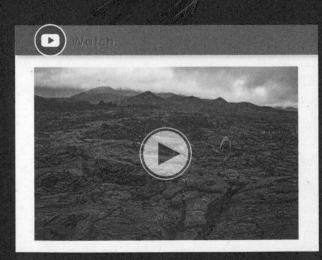

Watch

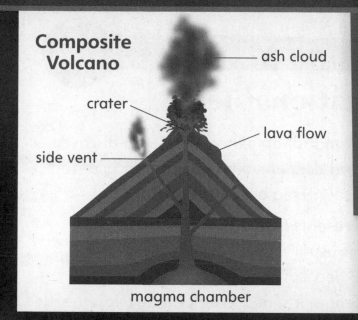

Composite Volcano
- ash cloud
- crater
- lava flow
- side vent
- magma chamber

An **active** volcano is one that still has the ability to erupt. When volcanoes erupt, they release heat, pressure, and substances from below Earth's crust. Thin, runny magma may be released in a slow lava flow. Thick, gooey molten rock can build up pressure that results in an explosion. This explosive eruption may throw ash, steam, poisonous gases, and enormous boulders into the sky.

A volcano that has not erupted in the last 10,000 years, or a volcano that is no longer connected to magma below the Earth's surface, is called **extinct**.

Weekly Question

In what ways do volcanoes impact Earth?

Quick Write What happens when a volcano erupts? Use evidence from the media to retell the process in a way that maintains its meaning and has a logical order.

Spotlight on Genre

Informational Text

Reading **informational text** can help you discover new topics and deepen your understanding of topics you have encountered before.

- The text presents facts.
- The tone is usually neutral.
- The main idea is not a claim to be supported.
- Details, definitions, and examples develop the idea.
- Photographs and captions demonstrate ideas.

Establish Purpose Knowing the genre of a text can help you set a realistic purpose for reading. Since an author's purpose in writing an informational text is to inform, what can you expect to gain from reading it?

What types of informational text have you read?

My PURPOSE _____

_____

_____

_____

TURN and TALK With a partner, discuss your purposes for reading. Make a plan to check in with your partner during and after reading. Decide how you will help each other determine whether you have achieved your purposes.

Types of Informational Texts

✓ Fact   ✗ Fiction

Reports
- ★ may contain charts, tables, or diagrams
- ★ present, analyze, and draw conclusions from data

Procedural, or "How-To," Texts
- ★ present steps in a process
- ★ describe assembly instructions
- ★ explain a recipe
- ★ provide rules of a game

Narrative Nonfiction
- ★ may include vivid descriptions
- ★ often focuses on people and events

Articles
- ★ can be informational or narrative nonfiction
- ★ may contain photos

Seymour Simon wants to develop "enthusiasm for exploring the world" in his readers. He attributes his direct, conversational approach to science topics to his twenty-three years as a science teacher.

Volcanoes

Preview Vocabulary

As you read *Volcanoes*, pay attention to these vocabulary words. Notice how they help you form mental images of important topics or ideas from the text.

	magma	face
reclaim	gushes	threatened

Read

Use the title of the text to identify its topic. Before you begin reading, write what you already know about this topic. Follow these strategies when you read **informational texts** for the first time.

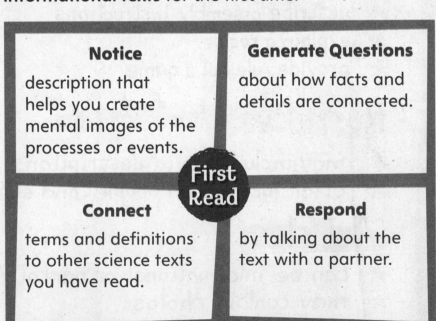

Notice description that helps you create mental images of the processes or events.

Generate Questions about how facts and details are connected.

First Read

Connect terms and definitions to other science texts you have read.

Respond by talking about the text with a partner.

VOLCANOES
by Seymour Simon

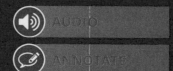

AUDIO

ANNOTATE

Analyze Main Idea and Details

Why does Seymour Simon include anecdotes, or brief stories, about people long ago?

Underline a main idea supported by these details.

1   Throughout history, people have told stories about volcanoes. The early Romans believed in Vulcan, their god of fire. They thought that Vulcan worked at a hot forge, striking sparks as he made swords and armor for the other gods. It is from the Roman god Vulcan that we get the word *volcano*.

2   The early Hawaiians told legends of the wanderings of Pele, their goddess of fire. Pele was chased from her homes by her sister Namaka, goddess of the sea. Pele moved constantly from one Hawaiian island to another. Finally, Pele settled in a mountain called Kilauea, on the Big Island of Hawaii. Even though the islanders tried to please Pele, she burst forth every few years. Kilauea is still an active volcano.

3   In early times, no one knew how volcanoes formed or why they spouted red-hot molten rock. In modern times, scientists began to study volcanoes. They still don't know all the answers, but they know much about how a volcano works.

4   Our planet is made up of many layers of rock. The top layers of solid rock are called the crust. Deep beneath the crust is the mantle, where it is so hot that some rock melts. The melted, or molten, rock is called magma.

5   Volcanoes are formed when magma pushes its way up through the cracks in Earth's crust. This is called a volcanic eruption. When magma pours forth on the surface, it is called lava. In this photograph of an eruption, you can see great fountains of boiling lava forming fiery rivers and lakes. As lava cools, it hardens to form rock that is also called lava.

CLOSE READ

Analyze Main Idea and Details

What main idea is supported with details in the text and the image on this page?

Underline the idea.

magma liquid rock beneath Earth's surface

CLOSE READ

Monitor Comprehension

When you monitor your comprehension, you keep track of what you do and do not understand.

Highlight an idea or detail that is essential to your understanding of volcanoes.

6   A volcano is a hill or mountain formed by erupted material that piles up around the vent. Mount Rainier in the state of Washington is an ice-covered volcano that last erupted in the nineteenth century.

7   Not far from Mount Rainier and another volcano, Mount Adams (top, right), is Mount St. Helens (bottom, left). Native Americans and early settlers in the Northwest had seen Mount St. Helens puff out some ash, steam, and lava in the mid-1800s. Yet for more than a century, the mountain seemed quiet and peaceful.

8   In March 1980, Mount St. Helens awakened from its long sleep. First there were a few small earthquakes that shook the mountain. Then, on March 27, Mount St. Helens began to spout ashes and steam. Each day brought further earthquakes, until by mid-May more than ten thousand small quakes had been recorded. The mountain began to swell up and crack.

9   Sunday, May 18, dawned bright and clear. The mountain seemed much the same as it had been for the past month. Suddenly, at 8:32 A.M., Mount St. Helens erupted with incredible force. The energy released in the eruption was equal to ten million tons of dynamite.

Monitor Comprehension

How can you use a text feature to improve your understanding?

Highlight details that help you understand what the image shows about force.

Analyze Main Idea and Details

<u>Underline</u> details that support a main idea in paragraph 10.

face surface; front or outer part

10   The eruption of Mount St. Helens was the most destructive in the history of the United States. Sixty people lost their lives. Measurable ash fell over a huge area of more than 75,000 square miles. Hundreds of houses and cabins were destroyed, leaving many people homeless. Miles of highways, roads, and railways were badly damaged. The force of the eruption was so great that entire forests were blown down like rows of matchsticks.

11   Compare the way Mount St. Helens looked before and after the eruption. The top of the volcano and a large segment of its north face slid away. In its place is a huge volcanic crater. In 1982, the mountain and the area around it were dedicated as the Mount St. Helens National Volcanic Monument. Visitor centers allow people to view the actively growing lava dome that now partially fills the crater.

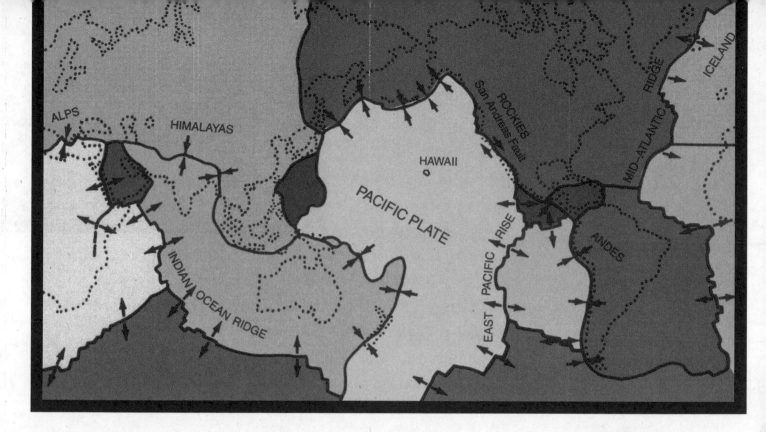

12   Volcanoes don't just happen anyplace. Earth's crust is broken into huge sections like a giant cracked eggshell. The pieces of the crust are called plates. The United States, Canada, Mexico, some parts of Russia, and the western half of the North Atlantic Ocean are all on the North American plate. Most of the world's volcanoes erupt in places where two plates meet.

13   Down the middle of the North Atlantic Ocean, two plates are slowly moving apart. Hot magma pushes up between them. A chain of underwater volcanoes runs along the line where the two plates meet. Some of the underwater volcanoes have grown so high that they rise from the ocean floor to above sea level as islands.

14   Iceland is a volcanic island in the North Atlantic. In 1963, an area of the sea near Iceland began to boil and churn. An undersea volcano was exploding and a new island was being formed. The island was named Surtsey, after the ancient Norse god of fire.

CLOSE READ

Analyze Main Idea and Details

Use details in the text to determine a main idea about the locations of volcanoes.

Underline details that support the idea.

Monitor Comprehension

What strategies could you use to improve your comprehension of a difficult text?

Highlight information you might need to reread, ask questions about, or include in a summary of how volcanoes create land.

reclaim take back

15   Ten years after the explosion that formed Surtsey, another volcano erupted off the south coast of Iceland on the island of Heimaey. Within six hours of the eruption, more than 5,000 people were taken off the island to safety. After two months, hundreds of buildings had burned down and dozens more had been buried in the advancing lava. Then the volcano stopped erupting. After a year's time, the people of Heimaey came back to reclaim their island with its new 735-foot volcano.

16   Many volcanoes and earthquakes are located along the margins of the large Pacific plate. Volcanoes and earthquakes are so numerous that these margins are called the "Ring of Fire." But a few volcanoes are not on the edge of a plate. The volcanoes in the Hawaiian Islands are in the middle of the Pacific plate.

17   These volcanoes have grown, one after another, as the Pacific plate slowly moves to the northwest to form the Hawaiian volcanic chain. Each volcano grew from the deep Pacific seafloor over several million years. Eruption followed eruption, and little by little, thin layers of lava hardened, one atop another. Thousands of eruptions were needed to build mountains high enough to reach from the deep sea bottom and appear as islands.

18   The largest Hawaiian volcano is Mauna Loa. It is seventy miles long and rises thirty thousand feet from the ocean floor. It is still growing and is one of Hawaii's most active volcanoes.

19   Hawaiian lava usually gushes out in red-hot fountains a few hundred feet high that feed lava rivers or lakes. Hawaiian volcanoes erupt much less violently than did Surtsey or Mount St. Helens. Only rarely does a Hawaiian volcano throw out rock and high clouds of ash.

20   Steam clouds billow as a flow of hot lava enters the sea. Hawaii is constantly changing as frequent eruptions of the Mauna Loa and Kilauea volcanoes add hundreds of acres of new land to the Big Island. Old lava flows are quickly weathered by the waves into rocks and black sand.

21   Hawaiian lava is fluid and flows quickly. In some lava rivers, speeds as high as thirty-five miles per hour have been measured. In an eruption in 1986, a number of houses were threatened by the quick-moving lava. Firefighters sprayed water on the lava to slow down its advance.

CLOSE READ

Vocabulary in Context

Skilled readers can use context clues, or words and sentences around a word, to determine a word's meaning. Use context clues to determine the meaning of the word *billow*.

Underline clues that support your definition.

gushes spouts; flows quickly

threatened endangered; put in a risky position

Analyze Main Idea and Details

Underline details that support an idea about the relationship between volcanic eruptions and volcanic rocks.

22   When lava cools and hardens, it forms volcanic rocks. The kinds of rocks formed are clues to the kind of eruption. The two main kinds in Hawaii have Hawaiian names. Thick, slow-moving lava called *aa* (AH-ah) hardens into a rough tangle of sharp rocks. Thin, hot, quick-moving lava called *pahoehoe* (pah-HO-ee-ho-ee) forms a smooth, billowy surface.

23   Earth scientists have divided volcanoes into four groups. Shield volcanoes, such as Mauna Loa and Kilauea, have broad, gentle slopes shaped like an ancient warrior's shield.

24   Cinder cone volcanoes look like piles of dry sand poured through an opening. They erupt explosively, blowing out burning red-hot ash and cinders. The ash and cinders build up to form the cone shape. The cinder cone on Pacaya volcano in Guatemala, Central America, has had frequent eruptions.

25   Most of the volcanoes in the world are composite or stratovolcanoes. Stratovolcanoes are formed by the lava, cinders, and ash from many eruptions. An eruption can be initially explosive, when ash and cinders fall to the ground. Later the eruption becomes less violent and lava slowly flows out, covering the layer of ash and cinders. Further eruptions add more layers of ash and cinders, followed by more layers of lava. Mount Shasta in California and Mount Hood in Oregon are stratovolcanoes. They are still active even though they have not erupted for many years.

CLOSE READ

Analyze Main Idea and Details

What main idea does Seymour Simon support with examples?

Underline the idea.

Monitor Comprehension

Highlight ideas that you might find surprising, confusing, or need to clarify.

26   A fourth kind of volcano is called a dome volcano. Dome volcanoes have thick, slow-moving lava that forms a steep-sided dome shape. After an eruption, the volcano may be plugged with hardened lava. The plug prevents the gases from escaping, like a cork in a bottle of soda water. As the pressure builds up, the volcano eventually explodes, as Mount St. Helens did. Lassen Peak in California is a dome volcano that erupted violently in 1915. You can see the huge chunks of volcanic dome rock near the summit.

27   Around the world there are many very old volcanoes that no longer erupt. Some of these volcanoes are dead and will not erupt again. These are called extinct. Others can be inactive for as long as 50,000 years and then reawaken. These are called dormant. Crater Lake Volcano in Oregon is currently considered dormant, but it is likely to erupt again. Almost seven thousand years ago, its predecessor, Mount Mazama, erupted and covered the ground for thousands of miles around in a blanket of pumice and ash. Toward the end of the eruption, the entire top of the volcano collapsed inward. A huge crater, called a caldera, formed and was later filled with water. Crater Lake reaches a depth of two thousand feet, the deepest lake in North America.

28   After a volcano erupts, everything is buried under lava or ash. Plants and animals are nowhere to be found. But in a few short months, life renews itself. Plants grow in the cracks between the rocks. Insects and other animals return. Volcanoes do not just destroy. They bring new mountains, new islands, and new soil to the land. Many good things can come from the fiery explosions of volcanoes.

Develop Vocabulary

Analogies compare two things that have something in common. For example, consider the analogy **up : down :: left : right**. The relationship between *up* and *down* is opposites. So is the relationship between *left* and *right*. This analogy could be read, "up is to down the way that left is to right." Other relationships in analogies include examples and parts of a whole.

My TURN Fill in the word to complete each analogy. On the line, explain the relationship between the words in each pair.

1. magma : lava :: _____ thoughts _____ : words

   Relationship: inside (magma and thoughts) to outside (lava and words)

2. face : volcano :: _____ : pie

   Relationship: _____

3. destroy : reclaim :: _____ : plant

   Relationship: _____

4. tiptoe : creep :: _____ : gushes

   Relationship: _____

5. warned : threatened :: asked : _____

   Relationship: _____

Check for Understanding

My TURN Look back at the text to answer the questions.

1. How can you tell that *Volcanoes* is an informational text?

2. How does Seymour Simon's use of photographs support your understanding of volcanoes?

3. What conclusion can you draw about the connection between volcanoes and earthquakes? Describe the connection, and use text evidence to support your conclusion.

4. People live on and near volcanoes. What advantages of living there outweigh the possible dangers? Synthesize information from the text and what you already know about why people live in certain places.

Analyze Main Idea and Details

Main ideas tell readers the most important information in a text. **Details,** or **supporting evidence**, add information about each idea. Analyze the author's main ideas and details to connect related information about a topic.

1. **My TURN** Go to the Close Read notes in *Volcanoes* and underline main ideas and supporting evidence about volcanoes.

2. **Text Evidence** Use the underlined text to analyze a main idea. Write a main idea and its supporting evidence. Then answer the question.

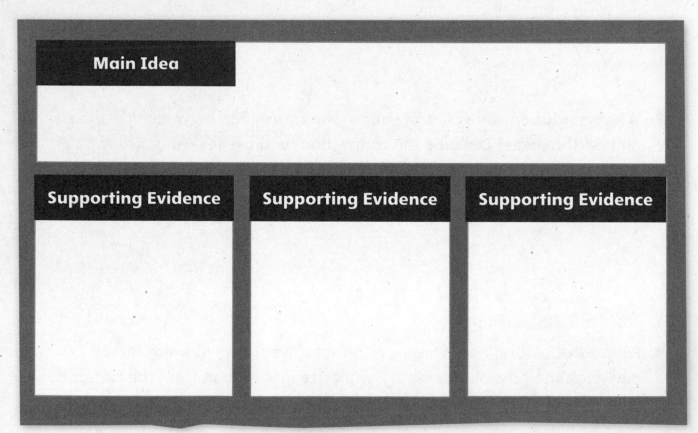

Main Idea	

Supporting Evidence	Supporting Evidence	Supporting Evidence

How does the supporting evidence relate to the main idea?

Monitor Comprehension

Monitor comprehension, or check your understanding of a text, as you read. When you do not understand something, stop reading to figure out why. To monitor comprehension as you reread *Volcanoes*, start by annotating, or marking, the unclear text so you can return to it. Then make adjustments to gain understanding. For example,

- Reread, slowly and carefully, to find connections among ideas.
- Use resources, including dictionaries, pictures, and your background knowledge, to determine the meaning of a word or an idea.
- Ask questions. Ask a person who knows more about the subject, or conduct research to get answers.

Once you have made adjustments, the unclear text should make sense, and you can continue reading.

1. **My TURN** Go back to the Close Read notes and highlight text that you do not understand.

2. **Text Evidence** Use your highlighted evidence to practice monitoring comprehension and deciding how to make adjustments.

Challenging Text	How to Make Adjustment
Word not defined: **vent**	Look up the definition
Difficult text:	
Unclear mental image:	
Unanswered question:	

Reflect and Share

Write to Sources What questions do you still have about the topic of volcanoes? Think about what interests you most about the texts you have read this week. Then write a letter to one of the authors. Ask your questions, and explain why you want to learn more about the subject. Use text evidence and domain-specific language to support your explanation.

- -

Use Domain-Specific Language Use domain-specific words to help your readers know exactly what you mean. For example, instead of writing "I liked reading about Hawaii," write about specific facts, such as "I liked learning how quickly Hawaiian lava can flow." Use these words in your response.

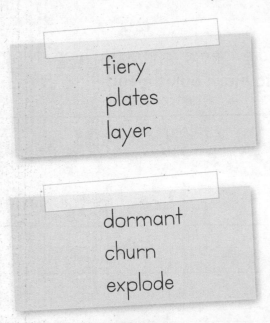

fiery
plates
layer

dormant
churn
explode

ash
dome
clouds

spout
force
cone

- -

Weekly Question

In what ways do volcanoes impact Earth?

Academic Vocabulary

A **synonym** has almost the same meaning as another word. An **antonym** has a meaning that is opposite.

My TURN For each underlined word,

1. **Write** a synonym from the word bank.

2. **Write** an antonym from the word bank.

3. **Revise** the original sentence using the antonym.

Word Bank

save   bored   destroy   name   disguise   astonished

Original Sentence	Synonym	Antonym	Antonym Sentence
Please label the carton clearly.	name	disguise	Please disguise the carton.
Laura amazed us with her juggling.			
They plan to preserve this swamp because it is a home to alligators.			

Suffixes -en, -ent, -ence

Add the **suffixes -en, -ent**, and **-ence** to roots and base words to change meanings and parts of speech.

-en	Means "to cause to be," "to cause to have," "to become," and "to come to have"
	Creates verbs in present tense and in past tense with *have, had,* or *has*
	Examples: *lengthen, darken, have written, had eaten, has broken*
-ent	Means "causing an action" or "being in a state"
	Creates adjectives
	Examples: *indulgent, confident, persistent*
-ence	Means "condition" or "action"
	Creates nouns
	Examples: *indulgence, confidence, persistence*

You can turn many nouns that end in **-ence** into adjectives that end in **-ent**.

My TURN Read and highlight the word in each sentence that has the suffix *-en, -ent,* or *-ence*. On the lines, give the word's part of speech and its definition.

1. An absorbent sponge helped me clean up the spilled water. __adjective__
   __capable of soaking up__

2. They confirmed the existence of extinct volcanoes. _____

   _____

3. Scientists have taken measurements of the lava's progress. _____

   _____

4. In legends, events may awaken a sleeping volcano. _____

   _____

Read Like a Writer

Authors write texts to convey a message, which is an idea they want readers to remember. Readers will remember a message if the author makes it meaningful to them. To do this, authors must understand who their readers are. Then authors choose literal language, or plain words and phrases, to connect their messages to readers' lives.

Model ! Reread paragraph 3 of *Volcanoes*.

1. Identify Seymour Simon uses literal language to tell how modern times are different from early times.

2. Question Why does this interest me as a reader?

3. Conclude This interests me as a reader because scientists still do not know all the answers. What scientists learn in the future may change our understanding of volcanoes.

Reread paragraph 11 of *Volcanoes*.

My TURN Follow the steps to explain the author's message in this part of the text.

1. Identify Seymour Simon uses literal language to describe

_____

_____

2. Question Why does this interest me as a reader?

3. Conclude This interests me as a reader because _____

_____

_____

_____

Write for a Reader

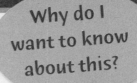

Authors want readers to understand and remember their messages. This requires knowing the audience and writing in a way that will interest readers. Often authors will use literal language to help readers connect to a text.

My TURN Think about how Seymour Simon makes ideas meaningful to readers. Now identify how you can hold your readers' interest in a similar way.

1. Write a message that you would like readers to remember about trying out for a sports team.

_____

_____

2. Imagine that your readers are all the fourth-graders at your school. What interests most of them about trying out for a sports team?

_____

_____

3. Write an informational passage that makes your message meaningful to readers. Make sure to include literal language in your passage.

_____

_____

_____

_____

_____

_____

Spell Words with -*en*, -*ent*, -*ence*

Adding the endings -*en*, -*ent*, and -*ence* as suffixes to roots and the ends of base words sometimes requires changing the spelling. For example,

> *bite → bitten* – drop the e, double the consonant, and add -*en*
>
> *indulge → indulgent* – drop the e, and add -*ent*

My TURN Read the words. Then sort the words by their endings.

SPELLING WORDS				
chosen	frozen	stolen	forgotten	driven
spoken	tighten	forbidden	undertaken	mistaken
present	presence	evident	evidence	confident
confidence	intelligent	intelligence	persistent	persistence

–en

_____

_____

_____

_____

_____

_____

_____

–ent

_____

_____

_____

_____

_____

–ence

_____

_____

_____

_____

_____

Capitalization Rules

Many historical events, languages, races, and nationalities have proper nouns for names. Proper nouns are capitalized.

Rule	Examples
Capitalize the main words in the names of historical events.	the American Revolution the Battle of San Jacinto
Capitalize the names of languages.	Swedish Arabic
Capitalize the names of races.	American Indian Native Hawaiian
Capitalize the names of nationalities.	Guatemalan Korean

My TURN Edit this draft by correcting capitalization for seven words.

English and spanish are the two most common languages spoken in Texas homes. The next two most common languages in Texas are vietnamese and chinese. This is because many immigrants came to Texas from Vietnam after the vietnam war ended in 1975. More asian immigrants came to Texas in the late 1970s, and most of them were of chinese descent.

Compose a Rhythm

Rhythm is a pattern of stressed syllables. Often, the pattern is regular. That means that the same pattern repeats in line after line. The best way to create rhythm is to experiment with saying words together aloud.

Learning Goal

I can use knowledge of the elements and structure of poetry to write a poem.

Lines	What to Notice
1. Lucy asked me where I went. 2. People left the circus tent.	Each line has 7 syllables. Say each line aloud and listen to the rhythm the stresses make.
Lucy asked me where I went when people left the circus tent.	Add the unstressed word *when* to line 2. This change adds a syllable, but it also keeps the rhythm the same and connects the ideas in the lines.

My TURN Say each word from the word bank aloud. Then experiment with putting the words together to create a rhythm. Do not worry about what the words mean. Finally, write a combination on the line. Underline the stressed syllables.

Word Bank

feather	begin	strong	soft
remember	September	listen	whisper
our	flower	decide	lovely

_____

_____

My TURN Apply rhythm when you compose a poem in your writing notebook.

Compose with Alliteration and Assonance

Repeated sounds help make a poem memorable. **Alliteration** is the repetition of consonant sounds at the beginnings of words.

Hilda **h**elped **H**aruki **h**old the **h**amster.

Assonance is the repetition of vowel sounds inside words.

W**e** s**ee** the b**ea**gle l**ea**p across the str**ea**m.

In lines of poetry with alliteration and assonance, the sounds only have to repeat once, not with every word.

My TURN Write four sentences. In each one, use the repeated sound indicated.

1. Alliteration of *tr* _____

_____

2. Assonance of long *o* _____

_____

3. Alliteration of *b* _____

_____

4. Assonance of short *u* _____

_____

My TURN Apply alliteration and assonance when you compose the draft of a poem in your writing notebook.

Compose with Similes and Metaphors

Similes and metaphors are figures of speech that make comparisons. Comparisons in poems often create unusual images in a reader's mind.

A **simile** compares two unlike things using the words *like* or *as*.

The **dog's expression** was *like* **a sly smile**. My **friend** is *as* nice *as* a **cake**!

A **metaphor** compares two unlike things without using *like* or *as*.

Baseball is **a summer afternoon**. The **fish** were **glowing slivers of moon**.

My TURN Use phrases from the phrase bank to create one simile and one metaphor. Remember to use *like* or *as* in the simile but not in the metaphor.

Phrase Bank	
horses running	grandmother's hug
thin ribbon	eyes twinkling
calm river	lonely rabbit
pearl necklace	green knee sock

Simile: _____

_____

_____

Metaphor: _____

_____

_____

My TURN Use similes and metaphors when you compose the draft of your own poem.

Compose with Rhyming Words

You may use rhymes to create predictable patterns of sound. Words **rhyme** when they have the same sound in their ending syllable or syllables. Rhyming words do not have to have matching spellings. Sounds make the rhymes.

fruit	boot	today	hooray
letter	better	president	hesitant
jingle	tingle	planetary	solitary

Sometimes phrases of more than one word can be used to make a rhyme.

comb your hair   go nowhere

My TURN Write at least one rhyming word under each bold word.

chopping	**tonight**	**flame**	**good**
_____	_____	_____	_____
_____	_____	_____	_____
_____	_____	_____	_____

My TURN Use rhyming words when you compose the draft of a poem in your writing notebook.

Some poems do not have rhymes.

Use Repetition

In poems, you may repeat words and phrases to emphasize ideas.

> Barely a thought
> I gave to being caught
> although caught was what I got
> when we played tag.
>
> Instead, running
> and laughing and swerving and laughing—
> were barely thoughts as I was caught!

Repetition of *caught* emphasizes what happened to the speaker.

Repetition of *and laughing* emphasizes fun.

Repetition of *barely*, *thoughts*, and *caught* echoes the first stanza and emphasizes the quickness of the game.

My TURN Write lines that contain each sample repetition.

Sample Repetition	My Three Lines
The phrase *in the boat* two times	
The same verb four times	

My TURN Use repetition to emphasize ideas when you compose your own poem. Discuss your poem with your Writing Club.

POLLUTANT
Emissions

Pollution, or substances that make land and air dirty or unsafe, takes many forms. Look at the diagram to learn more about sources of air pollution.

Clean air is important to health. Preventing air pollution can decrease many kinds of sicknesses, including asthma, bronchitis, eye disease, and skin cancer.

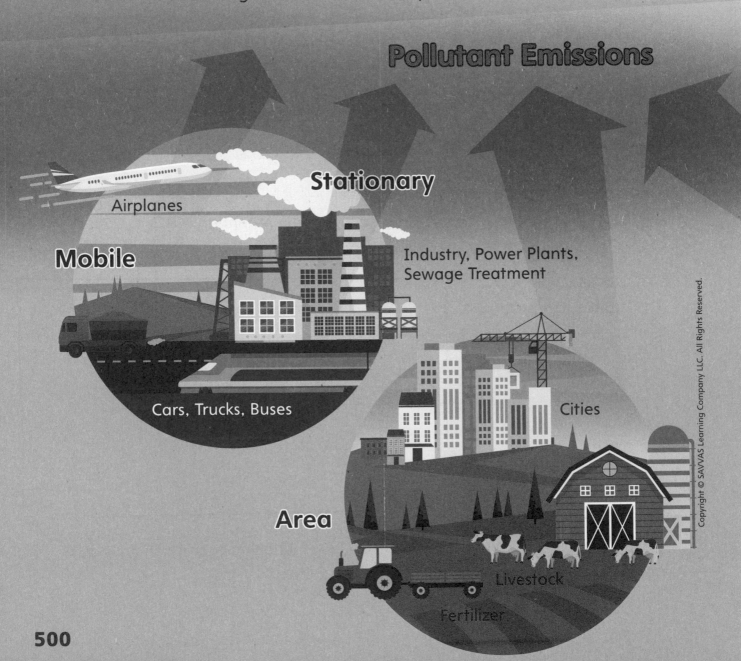

Pollutant Emissions

Stationary

Airplanes

Mobile

Industry, Power Plants, Sewage Treatment

Cars, Trucks, Buses

Cities

Area

Livestock

Fertilizer

Which source of pollutant emissions do you think humans have the *least* control over?

_____

_____

Which source of pollutant emissions do you think humans have the *most* control over?

_____

_____

Weekly Question

What daily actions can help reduce pollution?

TURN and TALK Talk with a partner about how your school and community are limiting dangerous emissions in your area. Use details from the diagram to support your discussion.

Natural

Lightning

Wildfires

Volcanoes

Learning Goal

I can learn more about the theme *Features* by analyzing the argument in an argumentative text.

Argumentative Text

Authors of **argumentative**, or **persuasive**, **texts** attempt to convince an audience to take action or to change beliefs or habits. Arguments include

- a **claim**, or opinion statement, that the author supports or defends.
- **reasons**, or statements of why the author makes his or her claim.
- **facts** and **details** that support reasons and make arguments stronger.

TURN and TALK With a partner, compare and contrast author's purpose in informational and persuasive texts. Use examples from what you have read.

Be a Fluent Reader Fluent oral reading requires practice. Fluent readers read smoothly and accurately. This week's text contains quotations, which record a person's words exactly and precisely.

When you read quotations aloud,

- ◎ Read the words with expression as if the person is actually saying them.
- ◎ Practice reading to avoid accidentally skipping small words such as *a*, *the*, and *of*.
- ◎ Pay attention to punctuation marks.
- ◎ Use what you know about spelling patterns to read words that are new to you.

Argumentative Text
Anchor Chart

Purpose

To make the reader think or act a certain way

Text Structure

order of importance, problem and solution, or cause and effect

Example:

1) Introduction
   a) Claim or opinion
2) One reason
   a) Supporting details
3) Another reason
   a) Supporting details
4) Opposing opinion or claim
   a) Reason that shows weakness of opposing opinion
5) Conclusion
   a) Restate claim or opinion

Features

vivid language, appeals to logic and emotion, addresses reader directly, a call to action

Nick Winnick has published books about a variety of topics, including animals, seasons, and green living. In the *Being Green* series, Winnick gives readers tips about forming eco-friendly habits.

from

The Top 10 Ways You Can Reduce Waste

Preview Vocabulary

As you read *The Top 10 Ways You Can Reduce Waste*, pay attention to these vocabulary words. Notice how they clarify and support the author's claim.

emissions	excessive
underlie watt	innovative

Read

Before you begin, preview the text and determine Nick Winnick's intended audience. Use these strategies to understand **argumentative texts**.

Notice
opinions, facts, and how they are connected.

Generate Questions
about main points and supporting details.

First Read

Connect
details in this text to events in your community, such as drives for recycling electronic devices.

Respond
by telling a partner which example or quotation you found most interesting.

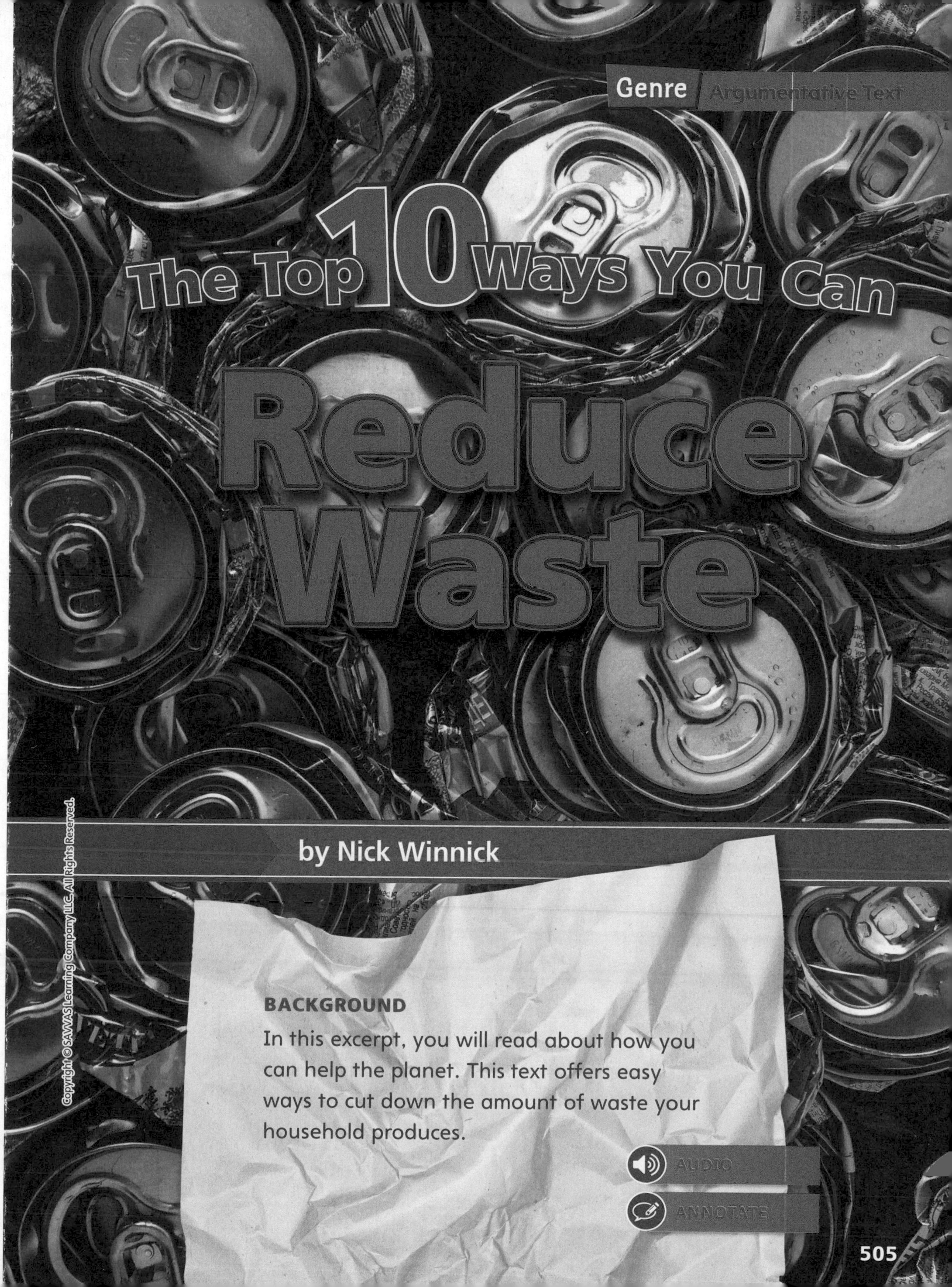

Genre | Argumentative Text

The Top 10 Ways You Can Reduce Waste

by Nick Winnick

BACKGROUND

In this excerpt, you will read about how you can help the planet. This text offers easy ways to cut down the amount of waste your household produces.

AUDIO

ANNOTATE

MAKING THE WORLD A GREENER PLACE

1 How can you make the world a greener place? You can help the planet by reducing your carbon footprint. A carbon footprint is the measure of greenhouse gases produced by human activities.

2 Greenhouse gases are created by burning fossil fuels. People burn fossil fuels for electricity, heating, and powering vehicles. One of the biggest causes of climate change is the greenhouse gas known as carbon dioxide. Many scientists believe that carbon emissions are more damaging to Earth than any other kind of pollution.

emissions substances released; anything given off by something else

3 There are many ways you can reduce your carbon footprint. One way is to walk or ride your bike instead of riding in a car. You can turn off lights when you leave a room to reduce energy waste. Reusing plastic shopping bags to carry other items is another way to help the environment. You can recycle newspaper so that fewer trees are chopped down to make new paper.

HOW CAN YOU REDUCE WASTE?

Analyze Argument

Identify and <u>underline</u> a reason that supports Nick Winnick's argument.

excessive a lot, or more than necessary

4   Reducing waste is one of the easiest ways you can help the environment. Once you decide to reduce the amount of waste you produce, you can learn many different ways to do it. Buying more items than you actually need can lead to excessive waste. Before making purchases, whether you are buying food or a new piece of electronic equipment, consider the waste the purchase will produce. Does the food item have an excessive amount of packaging? If it does have packaging, is that packaging recyclable or made from recycled materials? Do you need a new TV, or could you have an old one fixed or buy a used one? These are the types of questions to ask when you and your family are trying to reduce waste.

Analyze Argument

Identify and <u>underline</u> a reason that supports the author's claim.

LOOKING TO THE FUTURE

5   In the future, the world's population will likely grow much larger than it is today. How can the world support more people, yet still be kinder to the environment? The answer has a great deal to do with reducing waste.

WAYS TO REDUCE WASTE IN THE FUTURE

CLOSE READ

Summarize Argumentative Text

Highlight details that belong in a summary of this selection.

6 Think About People

Currently, there are nearly seven billion people on Earth. The population continues to grow, and every person on the planet produces waste. However, there are many simple ways that each person can cut back on the waste he or she produces.

> "This growing mountain of garbage and trash represents not only an attitude of indifference toward valuable natural resources, but also a serious economic and public health problem."
>
> *— Jimmy Carter, former U.S. president*

7 Be Efficient

Efficient energy products use less energy, but they work as well as, or better than, the items they replace. A good example is energy-efficient light bulbs. These bulbs have become popular because they give off the same amount of light as an incandescent light bulb. However, they last longer, use less electricity, and can be recycled.

8 Make Changes

The power to reduce waste lies in our own hands. Many people have started to make changes to become less wasteful in their everyday lives. These changes can have a ripple effect that benefits the world in many ways. For example, foods with less packaging are often more healthful. The next time you are in a grocery store, think about which foods create the most waste. Another example would be cleaning out a closet. Before throwing away an item, think about whether it could be donated to charity. Can you think of any other choices that create less waste and are beneficial to the planet in other ways?

Analyze Argument

Underline a reason Nick Winnick gives for his claim that people can help the planet by reducing waste.

IDEAS FOR WASTE REDUCTION

9   Think about all the times that you have heard people refer to the "Three Rs." The three Rs are "Reduce, Reuse, Recycle." Reducing is one of the most important parts of being green.

WAYS TO REDUCE THE WASTE YOU PRODUCE

CLOSE READ

Analyze Argument

Identify and <u>underline</u> facts that Nick Winnick uses to support an argument.

10 **Think Twice** Before you buy any item, ask yourself whether you really need it. A great deal of waste is created when people buy items they do not need or cannot use. It is a good idea to remember the following phrase whenever you are thinking of buying an item. "Buy what you need, and use what you buy."

"Our personal consumer choices have ecological, social, and spiritual consequences. It is time to re-examine some of our deeply held notions that underlie our lifestyles."
– *David Suzuki, biologist and environmentalist*

11 **"Precycle"** Another way to reduce waste is to precycle. Precycling refers to planning purchases with recycling in mind. For example, you may have a choice between two brands of eggs. They are the same price, but one comes in a Styrofoam container, and the other in a cardboard container. The cardboard can be recycled, and even if it should be thrown out, cardboard is biodegradable. The Styrofoam would have to be thrown away. It is not known exactly how long it takes for Styrofoam to break down, but it will last for at least 100 years. The eggs in the cardboard container are the better choice for the environment.

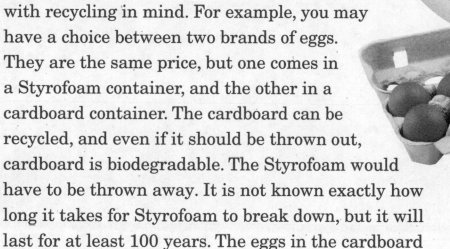

underlie form the foundation of

12 **Try a New Activity** Do you spend a great deal of time shopping with your friends? Some people think of shopping as a fun, leisure activity or as a hobby. One result of spending free time shopping may be buying items when you do not really need them. Trying a new activity, such as a sport or gardening, can reduce waste. There is very little waste created by a tomato that you have grown yourself.

PUTTING ITEMS TO
NEW USES

13   Reusing can be thought of as rescuing things that would otherwise be wasted. A water bottle might be recyclable, but it could be refilled and reused instead of buying another bottle of water. If a cell phone or a camera breaks, it may be possible to have it repaired rather than buying a new one.

WAYS TO REUSE ITEMS

14 **Ask Questions** Take a close look at an item you are thinking about throwing away. Maybe it is a bicycle with a broken gear shift or an old shirt that no longer fits. Ask yourself the following questions. "Can I still use this?" and "could someone else use this?" If the answer to either question is "yes," there are many ways you can reuse that item.

"A society is defined not only by what it creates, but by what it refuses to destroy."

– *John Sawhill, economist and conservationist*

15 **Find New Uses** Many disposable products can be used multiple times before they are thrown away or recycled. Plastic knives and forks can be washed and re-used for school lunches. Plastic shopping bags can be used as trash can liners or to pick up dog waste. Plastic water or soda bottles can be refilled and reused. What other items could be used more than once before they are discarded? Every time you re-use an item rather than buying or using something new for the same purpose, you are reducing waste.

16 **Repair or Donate** Repairing a damaged item can often be cheaper than replacing it. If you do not have a family member who knows how to do this, consider calling the store where you purchased the item for advice about having it fixed. Items you can no longer use or that you no longer need can be helpful to others. Many charities, such as Goodwill and the Salvation Army, can make sure that donated clothing and household goods get to people in need. A yard sale is another way to ensure your items continue to be used.

EFFICIENT ENERGY

17   Energy from many sources makes our world run. It powers cars, lights homes, and cooks food. Depending on how it is used, energy may be wasted. Wasted energy is one of the easiest problems to solve. New technologies and new ideas are helping to reduce wasted energy. These technologies may also save people money.

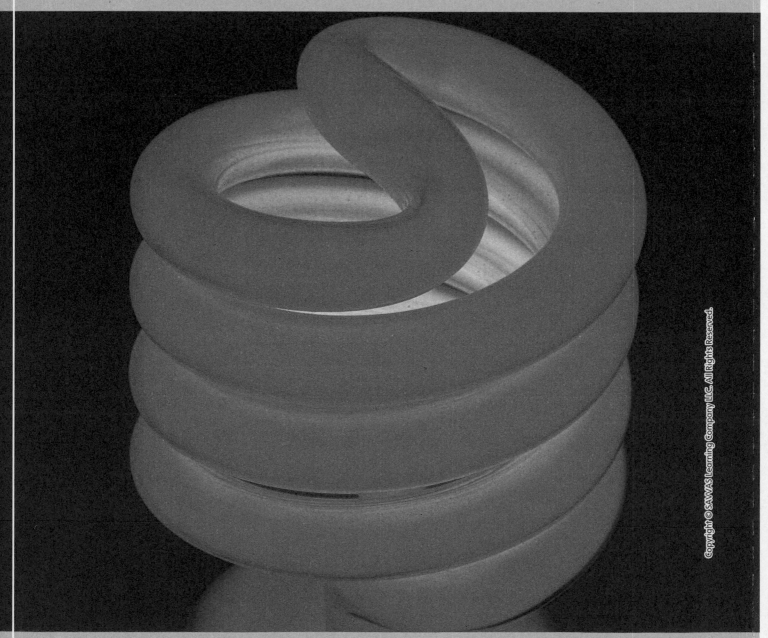

WAYS TO MONITOR ENERGY USE

CLOSE READ

18 **Use Power Strips** Did you know that some devices use power whenever they are plugged in, whether they are turned on or not? These energy-sucking devices are sometimes referred to as "vampires." Cell phone chargers, DVD players, microwave ovens, and coffee makers can be "vampires." There are a couple of different ways that you can slay these vampires. The simplest way is to unplug the devices. Many people choose to plug their devices into a power strip or bar. Power strips have several outlets with a single plug. They have switches that can be used to easily cut off power to every device plugged into the strip.

Vocabulary in Context

You can use **context clues** to determine the correct meanings of multiple-meaning words as they are used in a text.

<u>Underline</u> a phrase that helps you clarify the meaning of *drafts* as it is used here.

19 **Try Kill-A-Watt** Many families in the United States have saved money and energy by installing a power meter called a Kill-A-Watt. These meters attach to a home's electrical system. Kill-A-Watt meters display how much energy is being used and how much this energy costs. With this information, many people find it easier to keep track of how much energy they use.

watt unit of measurement for electrical power

20 **Keep Insulated** Think about the difference between hot chocolate in a cup and hot chocolate in a thermos. The liquid in the thermos stays hot longer because the thermos is insulated. The same idea is true for homes. In cold weather, well-insulated homes get warm faster and stay warm longer than homes with poor insulation. This means that less energy and less money is needed to heat well-insulated homes. Improving a home's insulation by sealing drafts and properly insulating the roof, walls, and floor, can be one of smartest financial and environmental decisions a family can make.

"Pollution is nothing but the resources we are not harvesting. We allow them to disperse because we've been ignorant of their value."

— *Buckminster Fuller, architect and inventor*

Analyze Argument

Underline a fact that supports a point that Nick Winnick is making.

innovative creative; using new ideas or methods

USING LESS
WATER

21   Earth may be covered by water, but only a small portion of that water is drinkable. Since all humans must drink water to survive, it is important not to waste this resource. Modern homes and businesses can use a great deal of fresh water, and, often, much of this water is wasted. Around the world, people are finding simple and innovative ways to save water.

WAYS TO REDUCE WATER USE

22 **Reuse Graywater** There are three major "types" of water in a modern home. They are drinking water, waste disposal water, and the water used for cooking, bathing, cleaning, and laundry, which is called graywater. Most of the water used in any home will become graywater. Many developers have begun

installing graywater treatment systems in homes. Using cleaning chemicals and filters, the graywater is treated until it can be used again for many household purposes. Homes with a graywater system can reduce their water use and their water bill by more than 50 percent. Even without a treatment system, you can reuse some graywater. Try collecting the water that runs in the shower while the water gets hot and then using it to water plants.

23 **Collect Rainwater** Many homes supplement their water intake by collecting rainwater. This can be as simple as draining your home's gutters into a bucket for watering the garden, or as sophisticated as a system that filters and pumps water into the home. Inexpensive rain barrels are available at most hardware stores. Most of these barrels have a screen that keeps out leaves and other debris. Some even have taps so that watering cans or birdbaths can easily be filled with water from the barrel.

24 **Modify Toilets** A great deal of the water used in any home is flushed down the toilet. However, there are ways to reduce the amount of water lost down the drain in your home. New low-flush toilets use much less water than older models, and many have an option to flush with more water when needed. If your family does not have a new toilet, you can try this simple trick instead. Open the back tank of your toilet, and place a brick or a sealed container of water in the tank. The toilet will keep the same level of water in the tank without using as much water with each flush.

"When the well is dry, we know the worth of water."
— *Benjamin Franklin, statesman, scientist, inventor, and author*

Summarize Argumentative Text

Highlight a sentence that includes a key idea about reducing waste without recycling.

MAKING COMPOST

25   Some types of waste can be harder to reduce than others. You cannot add spoiled food or old teabags to a recycling bin. Most families throw this kind of waste into the garbage. It is possible, however, to find a use for many types of spoiled or uneaten food.

"When plants die, they're recycled into basic elements [by organisms in the soil] and become a part of new plants. It's a closed cycle. There is no bio-waste."
— *Alice Friedemann, journalist*

WAYS TO USE COMPOST AT HOME

26 **Use Compost Containers** Fungi and bacteria can cause food to spoil. Most of the time, this spoiled food is thrown away. However, keeping some types of food in a special container can turn it into compost. Most composting is done outdoors. In addition to spoiled food, people put garden trimmings and parts of food

that cannot be eaten, such as cornhusks and eggshells, into a container in their garden. As these materials break down, they turn into a soil-like material that is helpful to plants. Every so often, some of the compost can be removed and used as fertilizer. Keep in mind that meat and dairy products cannot be composted.

CLOSE READ

Analyze Argument

<u>Underline</u> facts in paragraphs 26–28 that help you understand how composting reduces waste.

27 **Make Compost for Others** Many people do not have gardens, but almost everyone knows someone who does. If you do not have a use for compost at your home, ask your friends and family to see if anyone would like extra compost. Many gardeners would be happy for the help, and you could use some of your home's waste to make compost for them. Small compost buckets are inexpensive, can be kept in the house or garage, and are easy to transport to the person who will use the compost.

28 **Try Vermiculture** Not everyone can compost outdoors. People who live in apartments, for example, might not have this option. In many cases, people who wish to compost indoors use vermiculture. Vermiculture uses a colony of worms, such as earthworms, to break down food that would otherwise be wasted. Vermiculture can be difficult to use because the worms' habitat must be kept at a certain temperature and humidity level. However, the worms produce beneficial fertilizer for plants in small gardens or in window boxes.

Analyze Argument

Underline a sentence in which Nick Winnick makes an appeal to the audience.

HELPING YOUR COMMUNITY

29   Protecting the environment is a big job. Taking individual action is a great start, but a large group will see faster results. Think about ways that you could use what you have learned about reducing waste to help your community.

WAYS TO REDUCE WASTE IN A COMMUNITY

CLOSE READ

Vocabulary in Context

Use **context clues**, text evidence you find in and around a sentence containing a multiple-meaning word, to clarify the word's meaning.

<u>Underline</u> words and phrases that help you clarify the meaning of *pool* as it is used in paragraph 32.

30 **Hold Bottle Drives** In some states, people may receive money for turning in empty bottles and cans for recycling. The payment is 5 or 10 cents per can or bottle, which will add up over time. Bottle drives are a great way to earn money and help the environment. In a bottle drive, people go to homes and businesses in a community and ask residents to donate bottles and cans. Many groups, such as sports teams and charity organizations, use this method to earn money for their activities.

31 **Go Online** The Web can be a great resource for waste reduction. The Freecycle Network is a nonprofit group devoted to exchanging free items and keeping objects out of landfills. Some community sites have free classified sections where people can list items that they no longer need. These items can range from moving boxes to furniture. You can also find sites that list upcoming flea markets and garage sales. If you are interested in pursuing a listing, ask an adult for help.

32 **Pool Resources** One of the greenest ways to help your community is to keep items from being wasted in the first place. Imagine that you have old clothes, books, or sports equipment that you no longer need. You may not have enough to hold a yard sale of your own, but perhaps you can hold one with friends or neighbors. If all of you pool your resources and hold a sale together, you can earn money, provide your friends and neighbors with items they might need, and keep items from being thrown away.

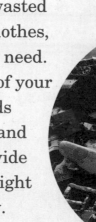

10 WAYS TO MAKE YOUR HOME GREEN

33   If you are interested in reducing waste, you can start in your home. Here are 10 simple ways to make a home more efficient.

34 Stop Air Leaks Heat is lost very quickly through air leaks. Windows, doors, light switches, and electrical outlets may be letting warm air escape. This means that more energy has to be used to heat the house. Sources of heat loss can be sealed with foam, caulking, or weatherstripping.

35 Turn It Off If you do not need it, do not run it. Any room without people in it should not have a light on and should not have electronics running.

36 Set Your Thermostat You can save money on heating costs and save energy by lowering your thermostat when you are out of the house or asleep. Hardware stores sell thermostats with timers that can be programmed to change temperatures at pre-set times.

37 Request the Test Certified home energy raters can test homes with a "blower door." This device pumps air into your home and helps to find poorly insulated or drafty areas. Finding and fixing these will help your home become more energy efficient.

38 Look for the ENERGY STAR Logo When your family is buying a new appliance, look for the ENERGY STAR logo. This logo identifies products that have been certified by the U. S. Environmental Protection Agency to be energy-efficient. Often, these products use 10 to 30 percent less energy than their competitors.

39 Go with the Low-Flow Installing  low-flow showerheads will save water. These are inexpensive and easy to install, and they can save money on water bills every year.

CLOSE READ

40 Use Coiled Fluorescent Light Bulbs (CFLs)
Replacing older incandescent bulbs  with CFLs, which are very energy efficient, will reduce your family's electric bill. If everyone in the United States made this change, the reduced need for electricity could mean that more than 5 billion tons (4.5 billion metric tons) of greenhouse gases would not enter the atmosphere.

Summarize Argumentative Text

To keep a summary brief, you might combine similar ideas while maintaining the meaning of the selection.

Highlight two ideas about reducing waste by adjusting a house's heating.

41 Clean and Maintain Your Furnace If your home  has a furnace, it is a good idea for your family to have it cleaned every second year. This improves the furnace's efficiency by between 5 and 10 percent. It also reduces heating costs and energy usage.

42 Plant a Tree A shade tree or bushes that will  grow tall in your front yard can save money on air conditioning in the summer. If your family plants a leafy tree, it will let sunlight through in the winter when its leaves have fallen off, helping to reduce heating costs.

43 Cover Your Water Heater Putting an inexpensive  insulated cover around your water heater keeps the water hot longer, which can save a great deal of energy. To save money, and reduce the risk of accidental burns, your family can turn your water heater's temperature down a few degrees.

Analyze Argument

How does Nick Winnick tie the idea of having a satisfying career to the idea of helping the environment? <u>Underline</u> text evidence that links this topic to his claim.

GREEN CAREERS

44   In order to have a clean and healthy world in the future, we need to start working toward it now. These are two of the potential careers for people who are interested in reducing waste.

Green Artist

45 **Career** Green artists combine their love of art with a passion for the environment. These artists may sculpt with recycled materials, create weavings with recycled fibers, design jewelry made from used glass, or find any other way to create art without harming Earth. Some green artists work in fashion design, creating clothing from organic cotton and other natural fabrics. Many green artists use their work to educate others about various environmental issues. Some of these artists work on their own. Others may work at design or retail companies.

46 **Education** A bachelor's degree in fine art will give a solid foundation for many artistic careers.

Green Contractor

47 **Career** Green contractors are builders and tradespeople who specialize in eco-friendly products and technologies. Green contractors install insulation, solar panels, graywater systems, and other technologies designed to make homes more energy efficient and environmentally friendly. These individuals often must learn specialized techniques associated with major construction trades, such as electrical work or plumbing.

48 **Education** All U.S. states require contractors to be licensed. The details of these licenses vary by state, but most licensed contractors must pass a multiple-choice exam.

TIME TO DEBATE

ISSUE Should cities fund door-to-door collection of materials for recycling programs?

49   Most people would agree that reducing waste is a good idea. However, there are many different ways to do so, and these specifics are often topics for heated debate. In the case of reducing waste, debate typically centers around the funding of waste management programs. Should a city's taxpayers, for instance, pay for door-to-door collection of recyclable materials? Should the city save that money and depend on people to drop off recyclable materials on their own?

CLOSE READ

Analyze Argument

Identify and <u>underline</u> the two opposing claims that are up for debate.

Fluency

Read paragraph 49 aloud to a small group. Remember to read with accuracy so that your audience understands what you are reading to them. Use what you know about spelling patterns to read words that are new to you.

PROS

1. Much less potentially recyclable material will be sent to landfills.

2. Easier participation will encourage more people to take part in local recycling programs.

3. Recyclable collection could be merged with other waste collection activities to save money.

CONS

1. Door-to-door collection will increase taxes for property owners.

2. There is an additional environmental cost in the form of more large trucks on the city's streets.

3. The bins used for recycling collection are unattractive.

Develop Vocabulary

Sometimes a word's definition is so specific that it will always appear in just one context, about just one topic. Other words have definitions that apply to more than one topic. For example, the word *innovative* may apply in any context where people are inventing new objects or ways of doing things.

My TURN Define each word, and then use it in a sentence about a topic from the list. In your sentence, underline the topic from the list.

Topic List		
gasoline engines	light bulbs	computers
noise	decaying leaves	science concepts

1. **emissions**
   Definition things given off
   Sentence Driving less will reduce emissions from <u>gasoline engines</u>.

2. **excessive**
   Definition
   Sentence

3. **underlie**
   Definition
   Sentence

4. **innovative**
   Definition
   Sentence

5. **watt**
   Definition
   Sentence

Check for Understanding

My TURN Look back at the text to answer the questions.

1. How do you know that this text is argumentative instead of informational? Give three examples to support your response.

2. Who is the audience for this text? How can you tell that Nick Winnick wrote for this audience?

3. How could you assess, or judge, how well Nick Winnick persuades readers to change their habits and reduce waste? Use text evidence to support your response.

4. Reread the circled quotation from Buckminster Fuller near paragraph 20. Do you think the quotation is always true, or can you think of examples to show that it is sometimes false?

Analyze Argument

Analyze an argument by identifying the author's claim, identifying supporting reasons, and evaluating the facts the author uses. Then determine how effectively the argument persuades the intended audience.

1. **MyTURN** Go to the Close Read notes in *The Top 10 Ways You Can Reduce Waste* and underline the author's claims and reasons.

2. **Text Evidence** Use the parts you underlined to complete the organizer. Then answer the question.

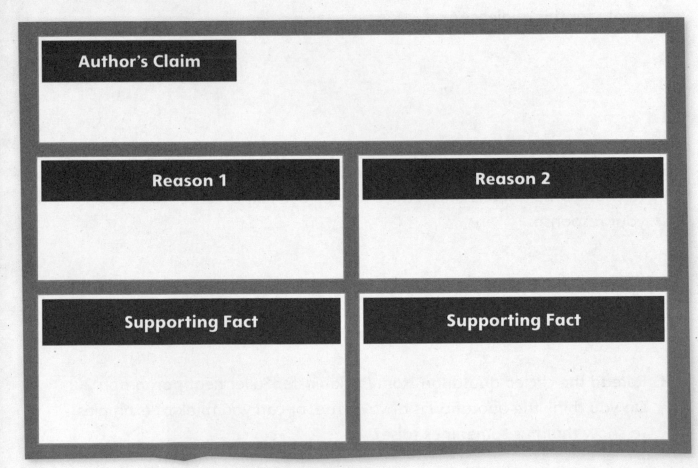

Author's Claim

Reason 1

Reason 2

Supporting Fact

Supporting Fact

My Analysis How well do Nick Winnick's reasons persuade his readers?

Summarize Argumentative Text

Summarizing an argument allows you to briefly tell the author's claim and most convincing reasons. You should also summarize the steps the author suggests that people should take. When you summarize, keep it short, use your own words, don't give your opinion, and use a logical order.

1. **My TURN** Go back to the Close Read notes and highlight information to include in a summary about ways to reduce waste at home.

2. **Text Evidence** Use your highlighted text to plan and compose a summary.

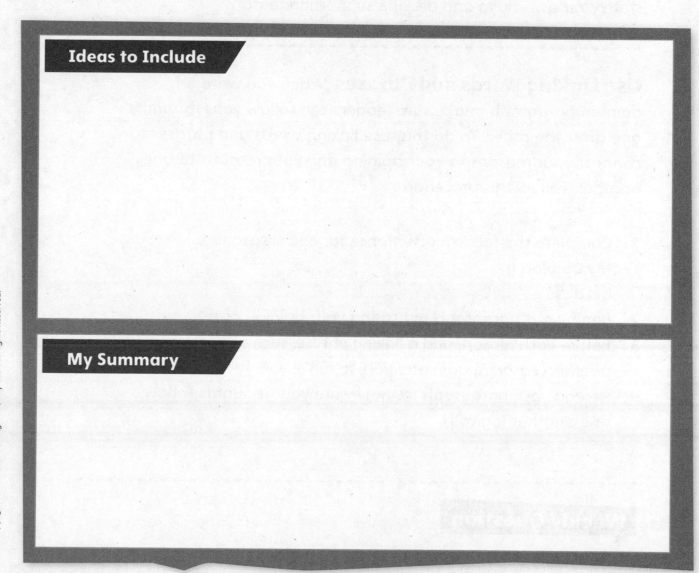

Ideas to Include

My Summary

Reflect and Share

Write to Sources How likely is it that people in your town would reduce waste in the ways Nick Winnick recommends? Think about the texts you have read this week and your own experiences with helping the environment. What usually encourages people to do these kinds of things? Form an opinion, and write an opinion paragraph. First, explain and evaluate authors' reasons and evidence from the texts you read. Then state your own claim and provide supporting reasons.

- -

Use Linking Words and Phrases When you write an opinion paragraph, make sure readers can follow your thoughts, one after the other. To do this, use linking words and phrases to connect your reasons to your opinion and your reasons to one another. Follow this procedure:

1. Complete the following sentence for each reason:
   My opinion is _____
   because _____.
2. Begin your paragraph by stating your opinion once.
3. Before each reason, add a linking phrase, such as *one reason is*, *another reason is*, or *in addition*, to make your reasoning clear.
4. Reread your paragraph to make sure your thoughts follow one another logically.

- -

Weekly Question

What daily actions can help reduce pollution?

Academic Vocabulary

Learning Goal

I can use language to make connections between reading and writing.

Context clues help readers figure out a word's meaning.

My TURN For each sentence,

1. **Highlight** a word or phrase that is a context clue to the meaning of the word in bold.

2. **Write** a sentence that explains how the word and the clue are related.

The student printed the name of each planet on a **label** for her model of the solar system.

Explanation: _____

_____

We were **amazed** when Henry said he had memorized the whole Earth science book.

Explanation: _____

_____

Workers may not take computers outside the **borders** of the space complex.

Explanation: _____

_____

What **consequences** would follow building a city on the moon?

Explanation: _____

_____

The museum promises to **preserve** the piece of moon rock Darryl donated.

Explanation: _____

_____

Syllable Pattern VCCCV

Words with the **syllable pattern VCCCV** have three consonants in a row.

- If the word is a compound word, divide it between the two word parts:

  half/way   board/walk   hour/glass

- If the word has a prefix or a suffix, divide it after the prefix or before the suffix:

  trans/form   re/heat   func/tion

- Do *not* divide digraphs, which are two letters that make one sound:

  king/dom   dol/phin   al/though

- Do not divide consonant blends:

  mon/ster   sur/prise   chil/dren

My TURN Read the following words by using the rules for syllable pattern VCCCV. Highlight the first syllable. Confirm your syllable breaks in a dictionary.

athlete   hundred   mushroom

control   improve   pumpkin

Read Like a Writer

Persuasive writers may use a first-person point of view to build a relationship with readers. This means using the pronouns *I, me, my, mine, we, us, our,* and *ours.* To strengthen the relationship, persuasive writers may also address readers as "you." This second-person point of view makes readers feel as if the author is speaking personally to them.

Model Read the text from *The Top 10 Ways You Can Reduce Waste.*

Energy from many sources makes our world run.

first-person point of view

1. **Identify** Nick Winnick uses the first-person point of view.

2. **Question** Why does he use this point of view?

3. **Conclude** He uses first-person point of view to remind readers that he and they live in the same world.

Reread paragraph 27 of the text.

My TURN Follow the steps to analyze the text. Describe how the author uses the literary device of point of view.

1. **Identify** Nick Winnick uses the _____ point of view.

2. **Question** Why does he use this point of view?

3. **Conclude** He uses _____

_____

_____

_____

Write for a Reader

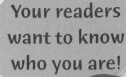

Your readers want to know who you are!

Writers choose a point of view to affect how readers relate to a text.

My TURN Think about how Nick Winnick's point of view in *The Top 10 Ways You Can Reduce Waste* makes you feel about his ideas. Now think about how you can use the literary device of point of view to influence your own readers.

1. Imagine you are running for class president. Write a sentence in the first-person point of view persuading readers to sign a petition to put you on the ballot.

_____

_____

2. Now write a persuasive sentence for the same reason using the second-person point of view.

_____

_____

3. Write a short letter to your classmates persuading them to elect you class president. Use the literary device of point of view to affect how your readers will relate to the letter.

_____

_____

_____

_____

_____

Spell Multisyllabic Words

Dividing words with three consonants together follows rules for the **syllable pattern VCCCV**. The rules depend on whether the word is a compound, has a prefix or suffix, or includes digraphs, which are two letters that make one sound. Check the syllable breaks of these multisyllabic words in a dictionary.

My TURN Read each word aloud to hear its sound spelling. Refer to a print or online dictionary to determine syllabication. Then correctly spell each word in the column that represents its syllable pattern.

SPELLING WORDS				
complex	fortress	extra	function	instant
arctic	conflict	partner	substance	extreme
apply	complaint	sculpture	emphasize	hindrance
technical	puncture	juncture	congress	simply

VC/CCV

VCC/CV

Title Capitalization

Follow rules for capitalizing words in the titles of historical documents, books, stories, and essays.

- Always capitalize the first and last words of the title.
- Capitalize all nouns, pronouns, verbs, adverbs, and adjectives.
- Capitalize the words *where*, *while*, *that*, *until*, *because*, *if*, and *since*.
- Capitalize prepositions that are five or more letters long.
- Do **not** capitalize the articles *a*, *an*, and *the*; the word *to*; or the conjunctions *and*, *but*, *or*, *nor*, *for*, *so*, and *yet*.

The following examples illustrate these rules.

Reaching for the Moon   "The Best Way to Run a Race"

Why the Sky Is Far Away   *The House That Jane Built: A Story About Jane Addams*

My TURN Edit this paragraph to correct fourteen errors in capitalization. Write three short lines (≡) under each letter that should be capitalized.

Benjamin Franklin, who helped draft the declaration of

independence, published *poor Richard's almanack* for twenty-five

years, beginning in 1732. His major work, now known as

The autobiography of Benjamin Franklin, was originally published

in French. The first English translation had the long title of *the*

private life of the late Benjamin Franklin, LL.D. *originally written by*

himself, and now translated from the French.

Compose with Line Breaks

Learning Goal

I can use knowledge of the elements and structure of poetry to write a poem.

Line breaks help readers read a poem. When a line stops, a reader takes a little pause. This affects the poem's sounds and the ideas and images it emphasizes. Look where the lines end in these examples.

Poem 1
Bread tastes better
when covered in butter
or jelly or honey
or melted cheese.

Poem 2
Bread tastes better when covered
in butter or jelly or honey
or melted
cheese.

In Poem 1, the first two lines emphasize *better* and *butter*. The repeated short *u* sound in *butter* and *honey* emphasizes these foods. In Poem 2, the first line ends in *covered*, which has the same short *u* sound as *butter* and *honey*. The one-word last line emphasizes that cheese is different from the other toppings.

Read each poem aloud and notice where you pause. Read each poem again and notice the rhythm.

My TURN Read the following sentences aloud. Next, experiment with breaking them into different lines. Mark the lines to show your favorite line breaks. Finally, answer the questions.

The sun beaming through my window this morning makes me happy. I will ride a pony at the birthday party this afternoon.

1. What sounds do your line breaks emphasize?

_____

2. What idea or ideas do your line breaks emphasize?

_____

Arrange Stanzas

A **stanza** is a group of lines in a poem. There is a longer pause at the end of a stanza than at the end of a line. The pause at the end of a stanza means that the mood or thought of the poem is changing.

Stanzas can have two or more lines. All stanzas do not have to have the same number of lines. Single lines can be mixed with stanzas. Stanzas do not have to end when a sentence ends.

My TURN Divide these lines into stanzas that have separate thoughts. Underline the last line of each stanza you create.

> A crowd waits at the bus stop.
>
> Buses come, six in a line.
>
> The crowd makes six lines.
>
> I find the line for mine.
>
> My line climbs six steps
>
> in the four-twenty-nine.
>
> The door squeaks and slams.
>
> I get home just fine.

My TURN Apply the skill of arranging stanzas when you compose a poem in your writing notebook.

Stanzas may separate ideas in unexpected ways.

Select Punctuation

Choose punctuation for the way it affects your poem's rhythm and pauses. For example, a comma forces the reader to pause or slow down.

Example	Explanation
Running and running and breathing hard I won the race.	The lack of punctuation makes the race sound as if it goes very quickly.
Running, and running, and breathing hard, I won the race.	Commas slow down the line, making the race sound difficult.

You can also choose punctuation for the way it affects ideas.

Example	Explanation
This is all. This is all?	With a period, this statement gives a final answer. With a question mark, the line asks for an answer.

My TURN Add punctuation to these lines to separate ideas and to control how fast the reader reads.

> Before the bell rings we are ready to go
>
> Our books are all closed and we've stacked them just so
>
> Our backpacks are packed and our jackets are on
>
> In just a few minutes we all will be gone

My TURN Choose appropriate punctuation when you compose your own poem.

Set a Rhyme Scheme

Some poems have rhymes. Rhymes at the ends of lines follow a pattern called a **rhyme scheme**.

My friend and I had a nice long **talk**	a
about what to do for **fun**.	b
Her father gave us some sidewalk **chalk**	a
and said, "Show me when you're **done**!"	b

Each rhyme at the end of a line is assigned a letter.

- *Talk* rhymes with *chalk*, and that rhyme is assigned the letter *a*.
- *Fun* rhymes with *done*, and that rhyme is assigned the letter *b*.
- The rhyme scheme is written as *abab*.

My TURN Find the rhyme scheme of the first stanza and write it on the line. Then add words to the second stanza that will give it the same rhyme scheme.

The tree was big
but the little twig
grew much, much taller
since it started out smaller.

Rhyme Scheme _____

The snowflake was small
but the big snow _____
flew for much _____
Its thrower was stronger.

My TURN Apply a rhyme scheme when you compose the draft of a poem in your writing notebook.

When you fit rhymes into a rhyme scheme, choose words that make sense in the poem.

Select a Genre

The genre of poetry has many subgenres. In other words, poetry comes in many forms. Some forms, like the ones in the chart, follow detailed rules.

Form	Rules	Example
Couplet	two rhymed lines giving a complete thought	We practice piano day after day Before Mr. Wu invites us to play.
Haiku	three lines, not rhymed first line with 5 syllables, second line with 7 syllables, third line with 5 syllables	Lightning BOOM thunder— look, twisting air is lifting roofs, dust, bicycles.

My TURN Read the following paragraph. Select a genre from the chart, and write a poem in that genre based on the paragraph.

Myeong loves to make birds out of modeling clay. She finds pictures of a bird she likes, such as a finch. Usually she finds more than one picture so she can see the bird from different angles. Then she uses tools to press, pinch, and cut the clay into exactly the right bird. When it is dry, she paints it.

My TURN Identify a topic, purpose, and audience. Then select any genre, and plan a draft by brainstorming ideas.

INTERACTIVITY

Preserving
BIODIVERSITY

The national parks of the United States contain some extreme environments. From animals in frosty landscapes to microorganisms in blistering hot springs, life makes its way in extreme environments.

from "Preserving Biodiversity" by the National Park Service

The National Park Service began because people—explorers, artists, politicians, and everyday citizens—recognized something valuable in the vast wildlands of undeveloped America. Today, we recognize the value of not only our lands, but the biodiversity that thrives upon them, as well.

Biological diversity (or biodiversity) includes all the living organisms on earth. . . .

To preserve biodiversity in parks for future generations, we must first discover the breadth of life forms that exist. In the past decade, numerous parks have teamed up with professional scientists, university students, school groups, volunteers and park partners for the purpose of biodiversity discovery. These efforts have identified species new to science, located species that have not been seen in parks in hundreds of years, and documented species that are able to survive in extreme conditions.

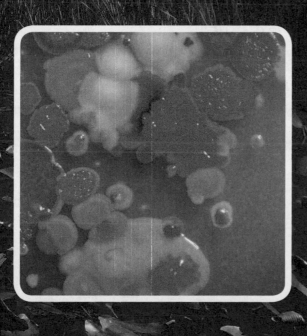

Weekly Question

What makes an extreme location a place to both protect and explore?

TURN and TALK What kinds of extreme environments do you know about? With a partner, make a plan to find answers to your questions in print or digital resources.

Spotlight on Genre

Informational Text

Authors of **informational texts** use text structure to organize ideas. When reading informational texts, look for:

- **Signal words**, such as *first*, *next*, *because*, *solution*, *such as*, and *like*
- **Topics**
- **Text features**, such as headings and subheadings

Informational texts commonly have one main text structure, but longer or more complex texts may incorporate more than one. Authors choose one or more text structures to support their purpose for writing.

Use text structure to build your understanding!

TURN and TALK Think about another informational text you have read. What was its text structure? Use the anchor chart to discuss text structure with a partner. Take notes to reinforce your understanding of how authors use text structure.

My NOTES _____

_____

_____

_____

_____

INFORMATIONAL TEXT ANCHOR CHART

Taking Notes on Informational Text Structures

1. Identify the topic.
2. Identify the text structure.
3. Choose a graphic organizer.
4. Evaluate details.

☆ **SEQUENCE of EVENTS**
OR Chronological Order

Beginning
↓
Middle
↓
End

COMPARISON and CONTRAST

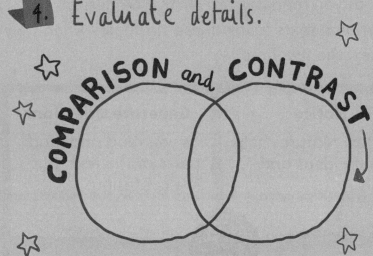

CAUSE AND EFFECT

WHY DID IT HAPPEN? → WHAT HAPPENED?

OR PROBLEM AND SOLUTION

Charles W. Maynard believes in the importance of wilderness. His more than forty publications include a series of books for young readers about the great mountain ranges of the world and a guide to hiking as a family.

The Himalayas

Preview Vocabulary

As you read *The Himalayas*, pay attention to these vocabulary words. Notice how they help you understand ideas related to Earth's features.

survey	subcontinent	
plateau	altitude	erosion

Read

Preview the headings and photographs to establish a "frame" as you read this text. Active readers of **informational texts** follow these strategies when they read a text the first time.

Notice
how text features help organize ideas and details.

Generate Questions
as you read and mark parts of the text that are confusing.

First Read

Connect
facts in this text to what you already know about Earth's features.

Respond
by discussing the text with a partner as you read.

THE HIMALAYAS

BY CHARLES W. MAYNARD

 AUDIO

 ANNOTATE

To determine the meaning of a word, look for **context clues** such as restatements or definitions given by Charles W. Maynard.

Underline a context clue that helps you determine the meaning of *abode*.

survey measurement of an area of land

ROOFTOP OF THE WORLD

1   The Himalayan mountain range includes the highest peaks in the world. Fourteen of the peaks rise more than 26,247 feet (8,000 m) above sea level. The Himalayas stretch for 1,550 miles (2,494 km) in central Asia. From China's border, they travel through Burma, Nepal, Tibet, and Bhutan, dip south to India, and spread west, ending in Afghanistan. These mountains form the boundaries between many countries on the continent of Asia.

2   The highest peak in the Himalayas, and thus in the world, is Mount Everest at 29,028 feet (8,848 m). Mt. Everest, on the border of Nepal and China, is named for Sir George Everest of Great Britain. Everest (1790–1866) led the survey of India from 1830 to 1843.

3   The name "Himalaya" comes from Sanskrit words that mean abode, or house, of snow. Sanskrit is an ancient language that was spoken in India. Because the highest mountains on Earth are in the Himalayas, these amazing mountains are also called the Rooftop of the World.

WHEN CONTINENTS COLLIDE

4   The Himalayas are young compared to other mountain ranges in the world. The Himalayas began forming from 60 to 65 million years ago. The Appalachian range in the eastern United States is from 250 to 300 million years old.

Explain Ideas

Underline the result of the movement of tectonic plates that you would include in an explanation of the height of the Himalayas.

5   The surface of Earth, called the crust, is made of huge slabs of rock called plates. These plates have moved slowly over millions of years, sometimes bumping into each other. When the plates bump together, the crust is pushed up and it forms mountains. Scientists call the movement of Earth's crust plate tectonics. About 50 million years ago, the Indian subcontinent began to bump into a land mass called Eurasia, which formed Europe and Asia. That event caused part of the Eurasian land mass to wrinkle, forming the Himalayas. These huge wrinkles are called fold mountains.

subcontinent large region that is part of a continent

The Himalayan mountains are part of the land in many countries, from China to Afghanistan. ▶

MOUNTAIN FACT EVEN TODAY, THE TECTONIC PLATES ARE STILL MOVING, AND THE HIMALAYAS ARE STILL GROWING. THE HIMALAYAS ARE GETTING TALLER BY ABOUT 1 INCH (2.5 CM) EVERY FIVE YEARS.

This picture of a huge, snakelike glacier in the Himalayas was taken from the space shuttle Atlantis. ▶

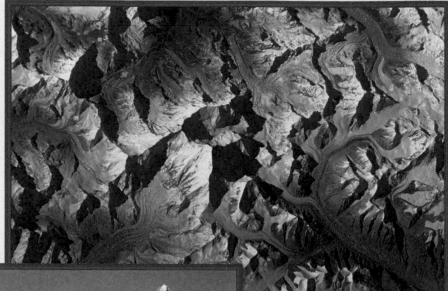

◀ Over time, this glacier on the Tibet side of Mt. Everest has carved out the large valley shown in this photograph.

The Ganges River in India was formed by a glacier, high in the Himalayas. The Ganges is sacred for people of the Hindu religion. ▶

Mountains Build Up and Wear Away

6   The peaks of the Himalayas were part of the ocean floor millions of years ago. Plate tectonic forces pushed the sea floors into high mountains. Some rocks near the highest peaks of the Himalayas are limestone. Limestone is a kind of rock that is made up of the fossils of sea creatures that lived and died millions of years ago.

Make Inferences

How are the bottoms of oceans and the tops of mountains related? Highlight details you can use to make an inference.

7   As the Himalayas rise, other forces are working to wear them down. Over millions of years, gigantic glaciers slowly carve large valleys through the high mountains. As the snow and ice of the peaks melt, they form rivers. India's great Ganges River begins in the Himalayas.

8   India's and Nepal's great plains lie south of the range. The high Tibetan plateau lies to the north. In between, the Himalayas have three different climate zones. The highest snow-covered peaks lie in the Great Himalayas. The Lesser Himalayas have peaks between 6,000 and 15,000 feet (1,829–4,572 m) tall and are covered with forests and fertile valleys. The lowest, southernmost peaks are the Outer Himalayas. They are called foothills, and they have wide valleys and rivers.

plateau large, high, flat area of land

Explain Ideas

<u>Underline</u> at least three examples of domain-specific vocabulary you might use to determine and explain the ideas in paragraphs 9 and 10.

altitude height or distance above sea level or Earth's surface

A LAND OF CONTRASTS

9   Wide differences of altitude in the Himalayas create the many climates found there. The valleys of the Outer Himalayas, such as those in India and Burma, are subtropical with hot days and plenty of rain. The valleys of the Lesser Himalayas have a temperate climate. Average summer day temperatures there are from 60°F to 77°F (16°C–25°C). Winters are cooler. The Kathmandu valley of Nepal, in the temperate zone, is populated with many farms and several cities.

10   Most of the year's rainfall of 60 inches (152 cm) comes with monsoon winds from June through September. The eastern Himalayas receive more rain. The Himalayas affect the climate of central Asia by blocking cold weather from the north and humid weather from the south. The high Plateau of Tibet, to the north in China, is dry and dusty. The winters there are cold and long.

MOUNTAIN FACT THE HIGHEST PEAKS IN THE GREAT HIMALAYAS ARE FROZEN WORLDS. SNOW AND ICE STAY ON THE GROUND YEAR-ROUND. EVEN THE VALLEYS ARE COLD AND DESERTLIKE, WITH NO TREES AND FEW PLANTS. ATOP MT. EVEREST THE OXYGEN IN THE AIR IS ONLY ONE-THIRD OF THAT AT SEA LEVEL. IT IS DIFFICULT FOR PLANTS, ANIMALS, AND HUMANS TO LIVE THERE.

VARIED VEGETATION

11   The altitudes and climates in the Himalayas support many types of plant life. Rainfall, temperatures, and oxygen all affect the species of trees and plants that live in the mountains and in the valleys. The Outer Himalayas, once covered with a rich, tropical forest, have been harvested. The land is now either farmed or used to graze goats and other livestock. Pine, oak, and poplar trees grow in the Lesser Himalayas. People have cut down many of these trees, which has caused erosion. Tree roots are necessary for keeping soil in place on steep mountainsides. They keep the soil from washing away in rain or blowing away in high winds. Even though many of the steep slopes no longer have trees, beautiful wildflowers color the mountainsides. Orchids, lilies, anemones, poppies, and rhododendron flowers flourish among the mountains and valleys of the Lesser Himalayas. The tree line in the Great Himalayas is about 16,000 feet (4,877 m). Trees will not grow above this level because of the high altitude and the cold.

CLOSE READ

Explain Ideas

<u>Underline</u> details that would allow you to explain key ideas about *erosion* to someone.

erosion process of wearing away or breaking down land over time

The snowcapped peak Annapurna is seen in the distance from this fertile valley in Nepal. ▶

AMAZING ANIMALS

Make Inferences

Highlight details that support an inference you can make about humans and the animals of the Himalayas.

12   Leopards, tigers, deer, and Indian rhinoceroses were once plentiful in the forests of the Outer Himalayas. When people cut down the trees for lumber, the forests changed and so did the types and numbers of animals that lived in them. Black bears, leopards and other cats, and the muntjac, a deer known for making a barking sound, now live in the few existing forests.

13   The Great Himalayas, a land of few people, are home to wolves, snow leopards, small, bushy-tailed marmots, and musk deer. A kind of tiny black spider lives as high as 22,500 feet (6,858 m).

14   The yak is a Tibetan ox that lives on high plateaus and in the mountains. It likes the cold, dry climate. People raise yaks to carry heavy loads and to pull carts. Yaks are a source of milk and meat. Yak hair is woven to make rope and cloth, and yak skin is used for leather.

MOUNTAIN FACT
THE WILD YAK IS A HUGE ANIMAL WITH LONG, BROWN-BLACK HAIR FORMING A THICK COAT. MALE YAKS CAN BE 6 ½ FEET (2 M) TALL AT THE SHOULDERS. THEY CAN WEIGH MORE THAN 2,000 POUNDS (907 KG).

A yak, shown here with a Tibetan family, is a common sight in the Himalayas. ▶

MANY MOUNTAIN CULTURES

15   About 40 million people live in the Himalayas. The Himalayas pass through the Indian states. The Himalayas also lie in the kingdoms of Nepal and Bhutan, as well as in Tibet.

16   Many of the people who live in the southern countries of the Outer Himalayas and Lesser Himalayas are of Indian origin and practice the Hindu religion. North of India, most Tibetan people are Buddhist. Nepal has 35 separate ethnic groups.

17   Most people of the Himalayas are farmers who grow fruits and grains and who herd livestock. The Sherpa people live in Nepal's Great Himalayas. The Sherpas are tribespeople who came from Tibet and settled in the steep-sided valleys of the Himalayas. Sherpas are known as the best guides for climbers of these mountains.

Make Inferences

Highlight details you can use to make an inference about climbing the Himalayas.

On Top of the World

Make Inferences

What inference can you make about the difficulties of climbing and studying the Himalayas?

Highlight details that support your inference.

18   The Himalayas were some of the last mountains on Earth to be explored. Ancient spice and silk trade routes between China and India wound through the high mountain passes between India and Tibet. A Spanish priest drew one of the first maps of the area in 1590. In 1852, British surveyors claimed that Peak XV was the highest peak in the world. It was later named Mt. Everest.

19   After several attempts, George Mallory and Andrew Irvine set out to climb Mt. Everest on June 8, 1924. They never returned. On May 29, 1953, Tenzing Norgay, a Sherpa, and Edmund Hillary, of New Zealand, became the first to reach Everest's peak. Since then, many climbers who have tried to scale this mountain have died from the freezing temperatures and the low oxygen. However, hundreds have reached Everest's peak, the top of the high Himalayas.

Mountain Fact In 1999, an expedition searched for clues to the 1924 disappearance of George Mallory and Andrew Irvine. The team found George Mallory's body at more than 25,000 feet (7,620 m). After removing a few articles from his pockets, the team buried Mallory on the north face of Mt. Everest.

Top: Mallory and Irvine are photographed at the beginning of their attempt to climb Everest. ◀

Bottom: A woman climbs a frozen waterfall in the Khumbu range of the Himalayas. ▶

Explain Ideas

<u>Underline</u> details in paragraph 20 that help you explain why and how the Himalayas are being protected.

MAPPING AND PROTECTING THE HIMALAYAS

20   One early challenge to exploring the Himalayas was mapping its many high, snow-covered peaks. Today aircraft and satellites make exact maps possible. Geologists, geographers, and other scientists are still working to understand the Rooftop of the World better. Some areas of the Himalayas are being protected by several governments so that endangered plants and animals will be saved. The Sagarmatha National Park of Nepal is one example of this effort. The entire park is located above 9,700 feet (2,957 m).

▲ *Edmund Hillary (left) and Tenzing Norgay (right) were eating breakfast before setting out to climb Mt. Everest.*

The government of Nepal set aside this special place to protect animals, plants, and mountain scenery. The Sherpa people are allowed to live in the national park. Although only a few people will ever climb the mountains, people come from all over the world to look with wonder at these mysterious high peaks and their steep valleys, large glaciers, and swift rivers. The Himalayas remain among Earth's most wonderful places.

THE ABOMINABLE SNOWMAN

21   People who follow the Hindu and Buddhist religions in the Himalayas consider these mountains to be sacred. The Ganges, a sacred river to the Hindu people, begins from the snows of the Himalayas. The mountains were the "abode of the gods" to people who believed that the most powerful gods lived on the snowy peaks.

22   The Sherpas and Tibetans tell legends, or tales, about the yeti, who is also known as the Abominable Snowman. It is said that the name "yeti" comes from the Sherpa words *yah*, meaning rock, and *teh*, meaning animal. The yeti is believed to be a large, hairy creature that is bigger and stronger than a human.

23   There are no photographs or other proof to show that the yeti lives in the Himalayas. However, stories are told of yeti that attack and kill yaks in the high meadows. The religious beliefs and the stories about the yeti show that many people consider the Himalayas to be special mountains with many mysteries yet to be solved.

CLOSE READ

Explain Ideas

Underline an idea in paragraphs 21–23 that you can explain using details from the text.

Develop Vocabulary

Concrete words refer to things a person can sense or measure, such as a book. Abstract words name things that cannot be touched, such as ideas. Many concrete nouns can be used in figurative language or as verbs. For example, you can use the noun *pencil* as a verb: I will *pencil* that in on my calendar.

My TURN Use each concrete word from the word bank either as a verb or in a figurative or abstract way. You may add an ending to a word you are using as a verb. Then define the word the way you used it.

Word Bank				
survey	subcontinent	plateau	altitude	erosion

1. **Sentence** Bethany surveyed the crowded gymnasium.

   Definition looked around

2. **Sentence**

   Definition

3. **Sentence**

   Definition

4. **Sentence**

   Definition

5. **Sentence**

   Definition

Check for Understanding

My TURN Look back at the text to answer the questions.

1. Is *The Himalayas* informational text or argumentative text? How can you tell?

2. Charles W. Maynard refers to the Himalayas as "young compared to other mountain ranges in the world." How does this explain the fact that the tallest mountain in the world is in the Himalayas?

3. If you were a scientist, what experiment could you conduct to learn more about the environment of the Himalayas? What question would your experiment answer, and how could you find the answer?

4. How do the photographs and diagrams in *The Himalayas* help explain why people around the world are interested in learning more about these mountains?

Explain Ideas

Explaining key ideas means making them clear by giving examples and defining vocabulary. You can use specific details from a text to explain ideas, such as what happens and why.

1. **My TURN** Go to the Close Read notes in *The Himalayas* and underline details that help you determine key ideas.

2. **Text Evidence** Imagine that you are being asked to explain ideas based on specific details in the text. Use your evidence to complete the diagram.

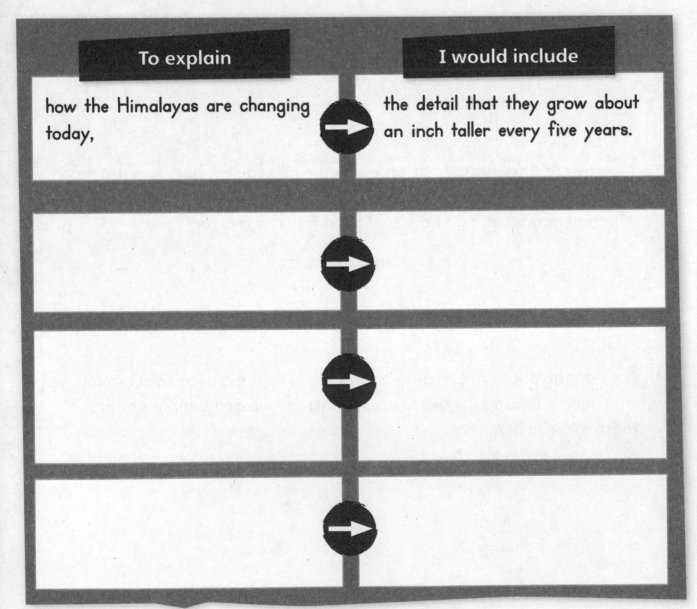

To explain	I would include
how the Himalayas are changing today,	the detail that they grow about an inch taller every five years.

Make Inferences

To make inferences, put evidence from a text together with what you already know to develop a deeper understanding of an idea or a concept.

1. **My TURN** Go back to the Close Read notes and highlight evidence that helps you make inferences about the Himalayas.

2. **Text Evidence** Paraphrase your highlighted text to support an inference about climbing and studying the Great Himalayas. Use evidence to support your understanding of the text.

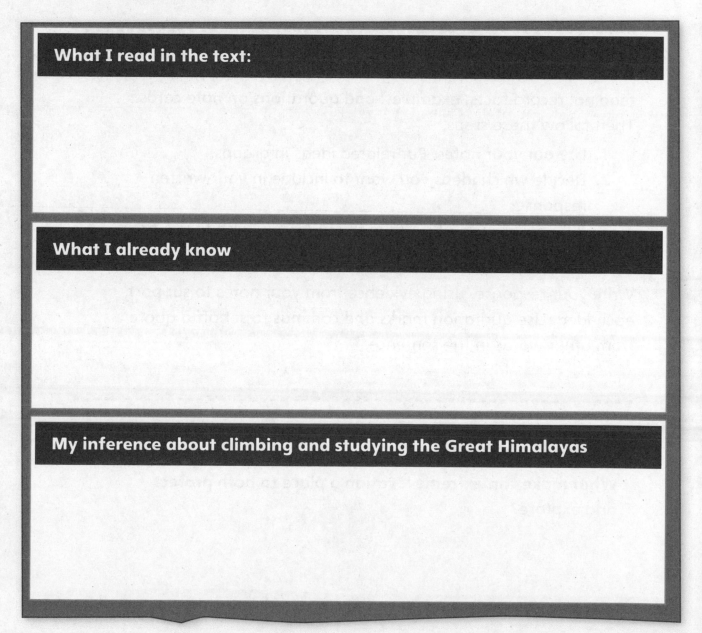

What I read in the text:

What I already know

My inference about climbing and studying the Great Himalayas

Reflect and Share

Write to Sources The Himalayas are one set of mountains on Earth. Every continent on the planet has mountains that formed due to tectonic forces. Exploring and studying mountains can be dangerous. Why do some people take the risks involved to explore the landforms of Earth? Use evidence from the texts you have read this week to write and support an appropriate response.

- -

Use Text Evidence As you gather evidence from your reading, record facts, examples, and quotations on note cards. Then follow these steps.

1. Lay out your notes. Put related ideas in groups.
2. Decide which ideas you want to include in your written response.
3. Put your groups of notes in the order you wish to use for your response.

Write your response, using evidence from your notes to support each idea. Use quotation marks and commas to set off a quote from other words in the sentence.

- -

Weekly Question

What makes an extreme location a place to both protect and explore?

Academic Vocabulary

Figurative Language A simile is a kind of figurative language that compares two unlike things using the word *like* or *as*. You may use similes to draw attention to ideas you want to express. For example, a park ranger might say, "Antelopes flood this valley like boats coming into harbor before a storm." This simile compares two unlike things, antelopes and boats, and draws attention to how antelopes move.

Word Bank

umbrella   dandelion   crayons   goldfish

MyTURN For each numbered word,

1. **Choose** a word from the word bank.

2. **Write** a sentence with a simile that uses both the numbered academic vocabulary word and the word you chose.

3. **Identify** the idea the simile expresses.

1. label   The label "Fluffy" is as scary as a dandelion.
   Idea: "Fluffy" is not a scary name.

2. border _____
   Idea: _____

3. consequences _____
   Idea: _____

Prefixes *dis-*, *over-*, *non-*, *under-*

The prefixes *dis-* and *non-* both mean "opposite of." The prefix *over-* may mean "on top of," "use more of," or "too much." The prefix *under-* may mean "beneath" or "less of."

Word with Prefix	Meaning Prefix Adds	Meaning of Word
discover	opposite of cover	find
overpower	use more power	defeat
nonfiction	opposite of fiction	factual text
underfoot	below the feet	on the floor

My TURN Read each bold word and write its definition. Then use a prefix to make and define a word that has the opposite definition.

Word	Definition	Make and Define Its Opposite
overcharge	charge too much	undercharge—charge too little
competitive		
agree		
undersize		

High-Frequency Words

High-frequency words are words you will see in many different texts. Read these high-frequency words: *wonder, bottom, exactly, trouble, symbols, engine.* Try to identify them in your independent reading.

Read Like a Writer

Authors use print features such as headings and subheadings to help readers find information.

Model ! Read this text from *The Himalayas*.

> **Many Mountain Cultures** ▶ ⋯⋯ heading
>
> About 40 million people live in the Himalayas.

1. Identify Charles W. Maynard uses the heading "Many Mountain Cultures."

2. Question What will I learn about in the text under this heading?

3. Conclude I will learn about the different cultures to which 40 million people belong.

Read this text.

> **Mapping and Protecting the Himalayas**
>
> One early challenge to exploring the Himalayas was mapping its many high, snow-covered peaks.

My TURN Follow the steps to analyze a heading.

1. Identify Charles W. Maynard uses the heading _____

_____

2. Question What will I learn about in the text under this heading?

3. Conclude I will learn about _____

Write for a Reader

What am
I about to
read?

Print features such as contents lists, chapter titles, headings, and subheadings help readers understand a text's structure. They tell readers what sections of the text are about.

My TURN Think about how headings in *The Himalayas* by Charles W. Maynard help you know what you will be reading. Now think how you can use headings in your own writing to let readers know what they will be reading.

1. For a section you are writing about the flavors of vegetables, what heading could you use that will help readers?

_____

2. Write a short passage about the best sandwich you have ever eaten. After you write the passage, write a heading that will tell readers what the passage is about.

   Heading: _____

   _____

   _____

   _____

   _____

   _____

   _____

   _____

   _____

Spell Words with *dis-, over-, non-, under-*

Dis-, over-, non-, and *under-* are word parts that can function as prefixes. Adding one of these word parts as a prefix to a base word does not change the spelling of the base word.

My TURN Read the words. Then sort and spell the words in alphabetical order.

SPELLING WORDS

disobey	disconnect	disinfect	disembark	disappoint
nonexistent	nonsense	nonrenewable	nonverbal	nonliving
overreact	overachieve	overwhelm	overcast	overcharge
underachieve	understatement	underarm	underdog	underline

_____   _____

_____   _____

_____   _____

_____   _____

_____   _____

_____   _____

_____   _____

Comma Rules

A compound sentence is made by joining two or more sentences. A comma follows the content of the first sentence. Next comes a coordinating conjunction: *for, and, nor, but, or, yet,* or *so.* Last comes the content of the second sentence. The entire compound sentence ends with a period.

First Sentence and Comma	Coordinating Conjunction	Second Sentence
Laredo is too far away,	**so**	we will stay overnight in San Antonio.
Adnan found Dina,	**and**	they came back to the lunch table.

My TURN Edit the paragraph by deleting two commas where they do not belong and adding three commas that are missing in compound sentences.

West Texas has more than forty mountain ranges and, you can explore parts of seven of them. The ranges formed in different ways. For example, the Guadalupe Mountains look like other mountains but, they are the remains of an ocean reef. You can visit the Hueco Mountains that formed when Earth's crust stretched or you can visit the Davis Mountains that formed when a volcano collapsed.

Use Verbs

Progressive verb tenses show actions in progress.

- The past progressive tense shows an action that was happening in the past: *We were hiking*.

- The present progressive tense shows an action that is happening right now: *We are hiking*.

- The future progressive tense shows an action that will be happening in the future: *We will be hiking*.

Some helping verbs, called *modal verbs*, help writers express attitudes. These verbs always come before another verb. Here are some examples.

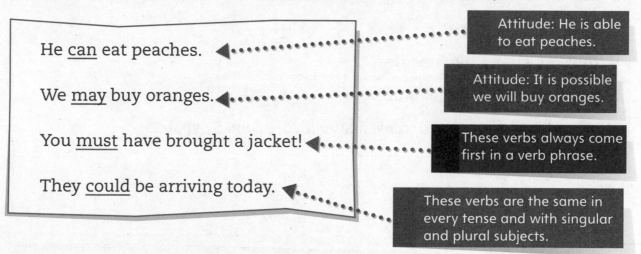

He <u>can</u> eat peaches. ◄ ········ Attitude: He is able to eat peaches.

We <u>may</u> buy oranges. ◄ ········ Attitude: It is possible we will buy oranges.

You <u>must</u> have brought a jacket! ◄ ········ These verbs always come first in a verb phrase.

They <u>could</u> be arriving today. ◄ ········ These verbs are the same in every tense and with singular and plural subjects.

Common modal verbs include *can, could, may, might, must, should, will,* and *would.*

My TURN Choose a verb from the box to correctly complete each sentence.

Verbs			
gliding	can	may	will
must	resting	hearing	should

1. The swans were _____ on the pond.

2. We _____ finish by the due date.

Revise for Structure

Changing the structure of a poem changes its effect on readers. The change might involve

- putting ideas in a different order
- adding or removing rhymes
- adding, deleting, or rearranging concrete words
- making rhythms more obvious

> *First Structure: Unrhymed quatrain, four lines with similar rhythms*
>
> Beware of kittens!
>
> They have tiny teeth
>
> that are sharp, like needles,
>
> and will make you leap up!
>
> *Second Structure: Haiku, three lines with 5, 7, and 5 syllables*
>
> Tiny kitten teeth
>
> sharp, startling as needles.
>
> Get ready to jump!

My TURN Revise this poem so that it has the structure of an unrhymed quatrain, a rhymed quatrain, or a haiku.

> Listen to that wind, playing with the crack
>
> in the window. A whistle, an oboe,
>
> flute, horn, oboe again, and then the strings
>
> climb the scale to a shriek. Here comes the storm!

My TURN Revise for structure when you revisit drafts of your own poems.

Revise for Word Choice

Choosing new words for a poem clarifies its ideas. It also changes the poem's effect on readers. Revising for word choice might involve

- adding and deleting concrete words
- rearranging sensory details for coherence
- using new words to create clear rhythm and images
- adding or removing rhymes

Original Poem

We are third from the sun, a ball of rock.

Venus and Mars come from similar stock.

Our air is different. It keeps us alive.

It's why we have oceans, with whales that dive.

Poem Revised for Word Choice

This stony planet, the third from the sun,

is, unlike near others, a lively one

with air, with water, with animals too

that scurry and dive under skies so blue.

This change makes the poem sound more formal and less personal.

Ideas have been rearranged. "Unlike near others" refers to Venus and Mars. "Lively" is a short way of referring to life. The image of animals "that scurry and dive" says more about life on Earth than the original poem because it alludes to animals that live on land as well as in water.

My TURN In your writer's notebook, revise for word choice to create coherence and clarity in one of your own poems.

Edit for Adjectives

An **adjective** describes a noun or pronoun. A **comparative adjective** compares **two** nouns. A **superlative adjective** compares **three or more** nouns.

Rule	Comparative	Superlative	Examples
Add -*er* and -*est* to short adjectives	*longer*	*longest*	A week is *longer* than a day. In North America, the *longest* day is in June.
Use *more* and *most* with long adjectives	**more adventuresome**	**most adventuresome**	Andre is **more adventuresome** than Lim. This year Dinara is the **most adventuresome** camper.

Adjectives usually come before the word they describe. When you use two or more adjectives to describe one thing, you can put the adjectives in order according to the example below that shows where they often appear before a noun.

closest to noun	color	**red** box
next closest	shape	**square red** box
next closest	age	**old square red** box
next closest	size	**tiny old square red** box
farthest	opinion	**beautiful tiny old square red** box

My TURN Edit drafts of your own poems for adjectives. Follow the rule for adding -*er* and -*est* to spell adjectives correctly.

Adjectives give useful details.

Edit for Prepositional Phrases

A **preposition** is the first word in a **prepositional phrase**. A prepositional phrase ends with a noun or pronoun called the **object of the preposition**. The prepositional phrase tells about another word in the sentence.

Mother strolls to the window and looks at the trees, then asks, "After the game, would you work with me please?"

To the window tells where Mother is going. At the trees says what Mother sees. After the game says when the two people would work. With me reveals who will work together.

Review the meanings of several prepositions.

Preposition	Sample Meanings	Preposition	Sample Meanings
of	coming from; being one member or part	between	with one on either side
with	having; in the company of	over	across; above; on top
before	in front of	to	in the direction of
after	behind in order	in	within the area of; by means of
during	while something is happening	without	not having
through	in one side and out the other; by way of	at	in a particular place; to or toward; in the field of
among	surrounded by	into	to the inside or middle

My TURN Edit drafts of your own poems for prepositional phrases. Share some of your favorite prepositional phrases with your Writing Club.

INTERACTIVITY

THE TROUBLE
with Ocean Trash

WHAT IS IN THE OCEAN? Some items commonly found in the ocean are:

- microplastics (tiny pieces that broke off of larger items, or mini beads designed for use in personal care products)
- plastic beverage bottles
- plastic bags
- disposable utensils and plates
- straws and stirrers

HOW DOES IT GET THERE? Things we throw away have to go somewhere. Wind and rain can move litter and items in landfills.

Weekly Question

What happens to what we throw away?

WHAT CAN WE DO?

- Refuse and reduce. Limit the number of disposable items you use by carrying a refillable bottle or cup. Avoid single-use utensils.
- Reuse. Do not throw away something after using it once. Find a way to use it again. Be creative!
- Recycle. Find out more about recycling rules in your community. Follow the rules and help others do so, too.
- Write. Communicate with legislators in your area about how to craft laws that will protect our oceans.
- Dispose responsibly. Do not litter. Use containers with lids; do not let trash blow away or wash away in the rain.

Illustrate What methods or processes does your community use to limit the amount of waste you create? Draw and label your response.

Spotlight on Genre

Informational Text and Video

Just like print texts, **digital**, or electronic, **texts** can take many forms. Web sites, individual pages on Web sites, links on pages within a Web site, images and videos on Web sites, and e-books are all examples of digital texts.

Common characteristics:

- They must be accessed on an electronic device.
- They are interconnected, often linking multiple resources in one text.
- They are navigable, using features such as time stamps and thumbnails in videos to orient the user.

Read, look, listen!

TURN and TALK With a partner, compare and contrast the features of informational printed text and digital text. Describe how you would refer to the specific location of evidence in each kind of text. Take notes on your discussion.

My NOTES _____

_____

_____

_____

_____

DIGITAL TEXT
ANCHOR CHART

Features

Address or URL
- is the location of the digital text
- is usually an Internet address
- could be a location on a computer

Link or hyperlink
- goes to a different part of the text
  or
- goes to a different text

Image
- can be zoomed in
- can be edited and changed

Video
- can be paused, rewound, and watched again
- usually includes audio

Rukhsana Khan is a children's author and storyteller. She grew up in the small town of Dundas, Ontario, where she dreamed of becoming a writer. Her greatest hope is that her stories help create understanding among cultures and reduce conflict in the world.

Trashing Paradise

Preview Vocabulary

As you read *Trashing Paradise*, pay attention to these vocabulary words. Notice how they give precise information about key concepts.

marred	disposable	crude oil
toxic	phenomenon	

Read

Before you begin reading, preview the text. Notice that an **informational text** in print is static, or unchanging. If you wanted to find more information about the topic of this text, how would you locate and access resources? Use these strategies when you read the text the first time.

Notice facts and examples that clarify concepts.

Generate Questions before and during reading. Make a plan to answer these questions by rereading or by researching.

First Read

Connect information in this text to other texts you have read this week.

Respond by discussing with a small group.

Trashing
Paradise
by Rukhsana Khan

 AUDIO

 ANNOTATE

Compare and Contrast Accounts

Identify and <u>underline</u> the concept that is the main topic of this text.

marred damaged; made ugly; marked

1 Close your eyes and imagine yourself on the tropical island of Bali, in Indonesia. Picture blue skies and palm trees. Think of white sand that runs through your fingers like powder. The smell of orchids and coconuts mingles with a gentle breeze from the Indian Ocean. Gigantic aqua waves curl offshore. People swim, surf, snorkel, and soak in the tropical vibes.

2 That's the Bali many people see in their mind's eye. It's the Bali that existed for most of the island's history.

3 Now picture another version of Bali. This one is marred by trash. Waste is piled high on roadsides. It floats in the aqua ocean and washes up on the white-sand beaches. The smell of garbage replaces the scent of flowers. Unfortunately, this is the reality of Bali today. Garbage, particularly in the form of plastic waste, is turning this onetime paradise into an environmental nightmare.

4   For most of its history, Bali really was a paradise. The Balinese people created little or no trash. They used cloth bags to carry what they needed. They used banana leaves, coconut shells, and other natural items as wrappings and plates for their food. Most of what they threw out was biodegradable. That means it decomposed, or rotted. It didn't create pollution. Bali's environment was in balance.

5   Then convenience came to Bali. It came in the form of disposable plastic containers, plastic bags, and other nonbiodegradable products. Soon everyone was drinking from plastic bottles. Store clerks were putting even the smallest purchase—say, a pack of chewing gum—into its own plastic bag.

6   The same thing was happening all around the world, of course, including the United States. Plastic, in particular, proved hard to resist. It's durable, lightweight, and waterproof. Almost overnight, plastic bags became a basic convenience of modern life. Few knew about or took the time to ask about the consequences of convenience.

CLOSE READ

Vocabulary in Context

Context clues, such as word restatements, examples, and antonyms, can help you understand a word's meaning.

Use sentences in paragraphs 4 and 5 to determine the meaning of *biodegradable*.

Underline clues that support your definition.

disposable single-use; designed to be thrown away

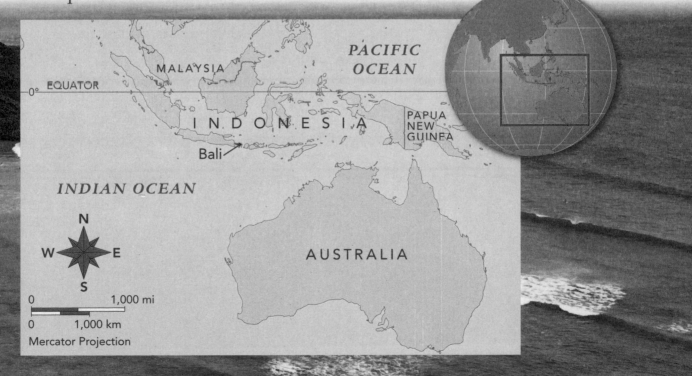

CLOSE READ

Compare and Contrast Accounts

Underline details about how plastic is different from other materials. Is this information also presented in "Bye Bye Plastic Bags on Bali"?

crude oil unrefined liquid petroleum

7   Plastic is made from chemicals. Scientists take the chemicals from crude oil found deep inside the ground. Then they change the chemicals through reactions with other chemicals. That's how they make polyurethane and other types of plastic. To make plastic bags, polyurethane is formed into pellets. Then the pellets are melted into a thin film. Machines cut the film into bags. The problem is that all plastics are different from anything that occurs in nature. That means nature doesn't have an easy way to break them down. In fact, it can take hundreds or thousands of years for plastic to biodegrade. And in some cases, it never does.

Disposable plastic items do not break down the way objects made of natural materials do.

8　For several reasons, Bali has felt the effects of this increase in the use of plastic more harshly and more visibly than many other places.

9　One reason is that Bali is a small island. At a little more than 2,000 square miles, it's about the size of the state of Delaware. Someone could easily drive around the whole island in a day. Trash can pile up quickly in such a small place.

10　Another reason is that the Balinese are used to disposing of things by simply dropping them on the ground. When people carried food in banana leaves, this was fine. A dropped banana leaf soon breaks down and mixes with the soil. A dropped plastic container won't. However, longstanding habits are hard to break. In addition, many people simply don't consider the damage they're doing to the environment.

11　Tourists are a third reason for the trash problem—a *huge* reason. More than 3 million tourists visit Bali each year. They account for a large percentage of the hundreds of tons of plastic waste the island produces each day. They drink from countless plastic bottles or plastic bags. (Many small restaurants serve soft drinks in plastic bags, with straws, for convenience.) They get take-out food in plastic containers. They carry souvenirs in plastic bags. Often, they dispose of their trash thoughtlessly. They drop it out of their rental cars. They leave it sitting on the beach. Because they don't live on Bali, many tourists feel no responsibility to keep the island clean.

CLOSE READ

Use Text Evidence to Explain Concepts

Highlight text evidence that would help you explain why throwing trash on the ground is dangerous for Bali.

Use Text Evidence to Explain Concepts

Highlight text evidence that helps you explain why the amount of trash on Bali is increasing.

12   Then again, there really isn't any good way to dispose of garbage on the island. That's the fourth reason for Bali's trash troubles. According to one source, 75 percent of rubbish isn't picked up by any trash service. Bali's refuse collection and disposal services simply can't keep up with all the garbage produced by residents and tourists. How much garbage? According to the nonprofit R.O.L.E. (Rivers, Oceans, Lands, Ecology), an Indonesian organization that works to protect the environment, the average person on Bali produces about 6 pounds of potentially harmful solid waste per day. That's more than twice as much as the average person in Indonesia's capital city, Jakarta.

13   For the most part, the Balinese—like many other people around the world—have not developed adequate systems for waste management. Instead, they hide or eliminate trash in any way they can.

14   Many Bali businesses, such as hotels and restaurants, burn litter, including plastics, in public places. Bali isn't unique in this practice; experts estimate that 40 percent of the world's waste is eliminated through burning. To put it mildly, that's not a safe solution. Plastic products are made of polyethylene, a type of gas. Burning plastic releases toxic chemicals called dioxins into the air, which carries them short or long distances to contaminate both land and water. These toxins are linked to illnesses such as cancer, birth defects, and breathing disorders in both wildlife and people. Burning waste also releases carbon dioxide into the air. Studies link high levels of carbon dioxide to climate change.

15   Other businesses and individuals in Bali simply dump trash in rivers or on the side of the road. In many cases, they don't want to pay the fees required to use legal dumping spots.

CLOSE READ

Compare and Contrast Accounts

<u>Underline</u> details in the text that help you explain the downsides of burning trash. Consider how this information builds on details presented in the video.

toxic poisonous

Without safe, reliable ways to dispose of trash, Bali suffers from the buildup of discarded objects.

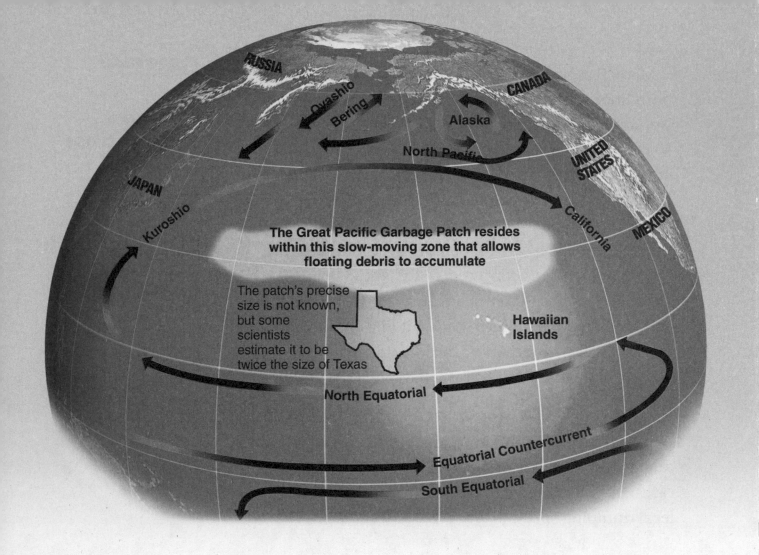

The Great Pacific Garbage Patch resides within this slow-moving zone that allows floating debris to accumulate

The patch's precise size is not known, but some scientists estimate it to be twice the size of Texas

Hawaiian Islands

North Equatorial

Equatorial Countercurrent

South Equatorial

CLOSE READ

Vocabulary in Context

Use **context clues** in paragraph 18 to determine the meaning of *marine life*.

<u>Underline</u> examples that support your definition of the term.

16   R.O.L.E. reports that every 24 hours, the Balinese dispose of almost 530,000 cubic feet of trash along roadways and at illegal dump sites. That's enough waste to fill six Olympic-size swimming pools. Beachside hotels often bury trash under the sand. Soon the tide comes up and washes the trash into the ocean. River trash often heads out to sea too. There it mingles with the trash that is washed or blown into the water from Bali's shore.

17   Much of the trash eventually washes back onto the shore. Some of it will float far from the island, perhaps ending up in the Indian Ocean Garbage Patch in the North Pacific Ocean. This area of floating trash is at least 2 million square miles in size. About 90 percent of it is plastic. The patch is one of five spread across Earth's oceans.

18   Trash has a deadly effect on marine life. Plastic is the worst offender by far. Plastic doesn't biodegrade in the ocean. Sunlight and waves break some plastic items into smaller and smaller pieces, but they never disappear entirely. These tiny pieces are about the size of the plankton and algae that many sea creatures feed on. When birds or fish consume these plastic bits, they can get sick and die. If people eat the fish that consume the plastic, they can get sick too.

19   Many animals mistake larger pieces of plastic for food too. Leatherback sea turtles are one example. These turtles have been around for more than 100 million years, but today they are endangered, partially because they mistake plastic bags in the water for jellyfish, their favorite food. When they try to swallow a plastic bag, they suffocate. Scientists also have found traces of plastic in the turtles' eggs. Birds also eat large pieces of plastic, confusing things such as bottle caps with food. Mother birds even mistakenly feed plastic pieces to their babies. Sometimes the birds' stomachs fill up with plastic. This signals to the birds that they are full, so they stop eating real food. Then they starve.

20   Seals, manta rays, and black-tipped sharks have all been found with plastic in their stomachs. Plastic bags also wrap around these sea animals so they can't swim. Bags even suffocate the beautiful living coral on the floor of the Indian Ocean.

CLOSE READ

Compare and Contrast Accounts

<u>Underline</u> details in paragraphs 19 and 20 that tell you why plastic is dangerous to animals. How does this reason for resolving plastic bag pollution compare to the reasons presented in the video?

Plastic trash can be dangerous to marine life.

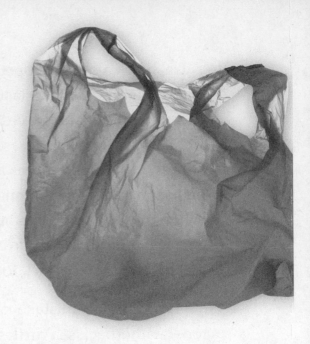

Compare and Contrast Accounts

<u>Underline</u> a key idea about Bali's tourism economy that is supported by details in both texts.

21   Nature does its share to make Bali's trash problem worse, or at least more obvious. Because Bali is a tropical island, it's greatly affected by the tides and by seasonal weather patterns. During Bali's rainy season, much of the island's trash washes out to sea. Then, during the winter season, from December to February or March, wind, waves, and strong currents drive the trash back to shore. It washes up on the sand or bobs nearby in the water. That's why winter in Bali has come to be known as "trash season." The cycle repeats every year. However, the amount of trash that goes out and comes back in gets bigger and bigger. It never goes away entirely.

22   Needless to say, all this garbage is bad for Bali's tourism business. No one wants to swim, snorkel, surf, or sunbathe at trash-infested beaches. A decrease in tourists might help slow the buildup of trash, but it would also damage the island's economy. Much of Bali's economy is based on tourist dollars. Tourists support many stores, restaurants, hotels, and other businesses on the island.

23   Those who fish—whether to feed their families or to make a living—suffer from the trash problem too. Anyone aware of the effects of plastic on fish will hesitate to eat seafood from the waters surrounding Bali. In addition, plastic gets tangled in fishing nets. It also damages boat propellers and other equipment.

24   The Balinese government was slow to address the island's trash problem. It was also seemingly slow to understand the causes. Bali's governor, Made Mangku Pastika, called the issue a "natural phenomenon." He blamed the rains and the tides for the repeated cycle of trash washing out and back in again, but he didn't address the problem of where the trash came from in the first place. Understandably, he didn't want to point the finger of blame at tourists, or hotels, or restaurants, or any one group. However, to bring about change, everyone on the island had to become aware of the problem. And they had to understand their role in creating it.

Use Text Evidence to Explain Concepts

Highlight text evidence you can use to explain the government's reaction.

phenomenon something that can be studied or observed; event

Compare and Contrast Accounts

Identify and <u>underline</u> details that tell you what inspired the Wijsen sisters to do something about the trash. How does this information show that *Trashing Paradise* is a secondhand account?

25   Because the government wasn't doing anything, it was up to individuals to take action. In 2013, a pair of sisters named Melati and Isabel Wijsen, then ages 13 and 10, stepped up to help their island. They were appalled by the plastic waste piling up and washing up around them. They wanted to convince people to change their trash-making ways. At first they weren't sure how to tackle such an enormous issue. Then the girls decided to focus on one crucial part of the problem: plastic bags. In Melati and Isabel's view, the bags were not only deadly but also entirely unnecessary.

26   The sisters named their project Bye Bye Plastic Bags. They found a group of like-minded kids to work with them. Then they created petitions and developed educational presentations to raise awareness. They spoke at markets and festivals. They held beach cleanup events. They gave out net bags and bags made of recycled newspaper and other organic materials to replace plastic.

27   Then Melati and Isabel made a video to showcase the problem. The nonprofit organization TED (which stands for Technology, Entertainment, and Design) saw the video. They contacted the girls and asked them to give a talk in London. The talk was recorded and viewed by people around the world.

28   Melati and Isabel got people to pay attention. That was the first, crucial step to making real change in Bali. The sisters talked to the head of the United Nations and to Jane Goodall, who gave advice about how to grow a network of followers and activists. Finally, they even got the governor of Bali on their side. He signed a pledge that Bali would become plastic-bag free by 2018. In 2016, officials at Bali's airport started making sure that tourists weren't bringing plastic bags to the island.

29   Melati and Isabel's project spread from Bali to other parts of Indonesia. Today, many Indonesian cities are working to eliminate plastic bags. In a number of places, people must pay a fee to get a plastic bag at a store. This policy has proved very effective in getting people to bring their own cloth or recycled bags when they shop.

CLOSE READ

Use Text Evidence to Explain Concepts

Highlight details that help you explain how the Wijsen sisters had an effect.

Use Text Evidence to Explain Concepts

Highlight additional details that you could use to explain effects of what the Wijsen sisters started.

30   The sisters are now focused on creating an educational book for elementary school students. It will be filled with information about pollution, waste management, and alternatives to plastic bags and other plastic products. Melati noted, "Change doesn't happen if no one is educated."

31   Many other individuals and organizations are now taking action too. For example, groups of surfers and companies that sell surfing equipment have organized regular beach-cleanup days on Bali. In one recent event, they cleaned up more than 1 million pounds of trash from Bali's Kuta, Legian, Seminak, Jimbaran, and Kedonganan beaches. Other organizations, such as the nonprofit group Bali Fokus, are sharing the message "Free Bali from plastic." They're encouraging both residents and tourists to find alternatives to waste products. Bali Fokus and other local organizations are also working to develop better waste management facilities for the island.

Individuals can join together and work to make a positive change in the environment.

32   Bali's future depends on the work of these individuals and groups. It also depends on the cooperation of Bali's residents and its visitors. Environmentalists now urge tourists to plan ahead to make their visit as eco-friendly as possible. Before booking a room, for example, tourists should check to make sure their hotel follows proper waste-management procedures. Because foreigners shouldn't drink local water (which might make them sick), they should also check to see whether hotels have dispensers for boiled water, which is safe to drink. That way they can avoid buying bottle after bottle of water from the local stores.

33   Every choice and every change, small or large—from refusing a plastic drinking straw to building a new waste-treatment facility—can help make Bali a cleaner place to visit and to live. If everyone works together, one day the island may again become a real-life paradise.

Compare and Contrast Accounts

Underline the author's main point in the text.

Melati and Isabel Wijsen were only ten and thirteen years old when they launched their campaign to ban plastic bags in Bali. "Don't ever let anyone tell you that you're too young," Melati tells others who want to make a difference with their actions.

Bye Bye Plastic Bags on Bali

Preview Vocabulary

As you view "Bye Bye Plastic Bags on Bali," pay attention to this vocabulary word. Notice how it connects to a key concept in the video.

> initiative

View and Compare

Before you begin, establish a purpose for viewing. As you watch, compare the **video** to *Trashing Paradise*. Consider the focus and the kind of information provided in both texts.

Notice
Is the video a firsthand or a secondhand account? How do you know?

Generate Questions
during and after viewing to deepen your understanding of the topic.

First Read

Connect
facts and examples in this video to what you learned from *Trashing Paradise*.

Respond
by planning a video of your own in which you address questions to Melati and Isabel Wijsen.

Bye Bye Plastic Bags on Bali

by Melati and
Isabel Wijsen

BACKGROUND

Melati and Isabel Wijsen asked themselves how they could make a
positive impact on the world. They identified a problem and proposed
a solution. In 2013, these sisters launched a successful campaign to
propose and pass a law banning plastic bags on Bali. This video helped
the Wijsens become known internationally as founders of a global
activism initiative. See SavvasRealize.com to access the link to the video.

CLOSE READ

Compare and Contrast Accounts

Identify why the
speakers created this
video. How is this
account similar to and
different from *Trashing
Paradise*? Is the video a
firsthand or secondhand
account?

initiative an act,
process, or program
that starts something

 AUDIO

Develop Vocabulary

In informational text, authors choose words to affect how readers interpret, or think about, facts. Words have dictionary definitions that are called **denotations.** Words also have **connotations.** These are feelings that readers have when they see the words.

Connotations depend on readers' experiences. A word may have a positive connotation for some readers and a negative connotation for other readers.

My TURN Read each word in context and its denotation. Write whether the word's connotation is negative, neutral, or positive. Then answer the question.

Word in Context	Word in Context	Word in Context
Now picture another version of Bali. This one is **marred** by trash.	It came in the form of **disposable** plastic containers.	Burning plastic releases **toxic** chemicals called dioxins into the air.
Denotation	**Denotation**	**Denotation**
damaged, made ugly, marked	single-use, designed to be thrown away	poisonous
Connotation	**Connotation**	**Connotation**

Question:

How do the three connotations affect your interpretation of plastic containers?

Check for Understanding

My TURN Look back at the texts to answer the questions.

1. What characteristics do the informational text *Trashing Paradise* and the digital text "Bye Bye Plastic Bags on Bali" share?

2. How did tourists and residents make Bali less inviting than it once was? Give examples from the texts to support your answer.

3. Why should people around the world learn about the trash problem in Bali and about the Wijsen sisters? Use at least one quotation from a text to support your answer.

4. If you were in charge of communicating facts about a new, convenient way to dispose of trash, would you create a written informational text or a digital text? Explain your choice, using an example from each text to support your answer.

Compare and Contrast Accounts

To compare and contrast two accounts of the same topic or event, readers tell how the texts are similar and different. Readers also determine whether each text is a firsthand or secondhand account. A firsthand account is told by someone who has experienced the event. A secondhand account is told by someone who knows about the event but was not there at the time.

1. **My TURN** Go to the Close Read notes in *Trashing Paradise* and "Bye Bye Plastic Bags on Bali." Underline and note details that show how the texts approach the topic.

2. **Text Evidence** Use your underlined text to compare and contrast the accounts of the topic in the chart.

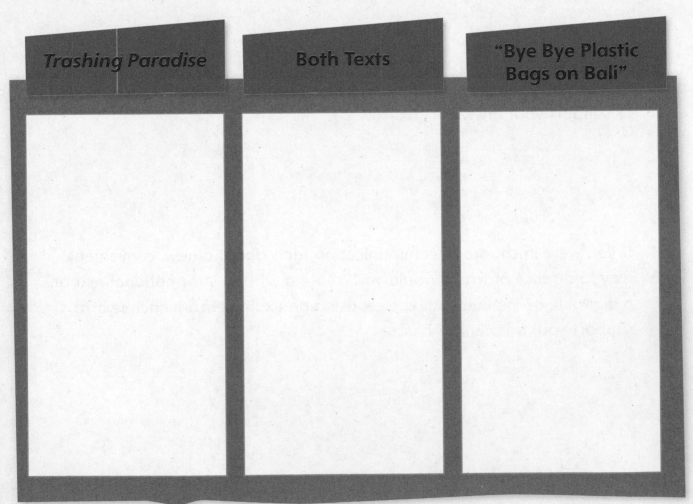

Trashing Paradise	Both Texts	"Bye Bye Plastic Bags on Bali"

Use Text Evidence to Explain Concepts

To explain concepts in a text, readers use specific details, facts, and examples to clarify and relate to abstract ideas.

1. **My TURN** Go back to the Close Read notes and highlight ideas that help explain concepts.

2. **Text Evidence** Sort your highlighted text evidence into the correct category. Then use text evidence to explain one concept to a partner.

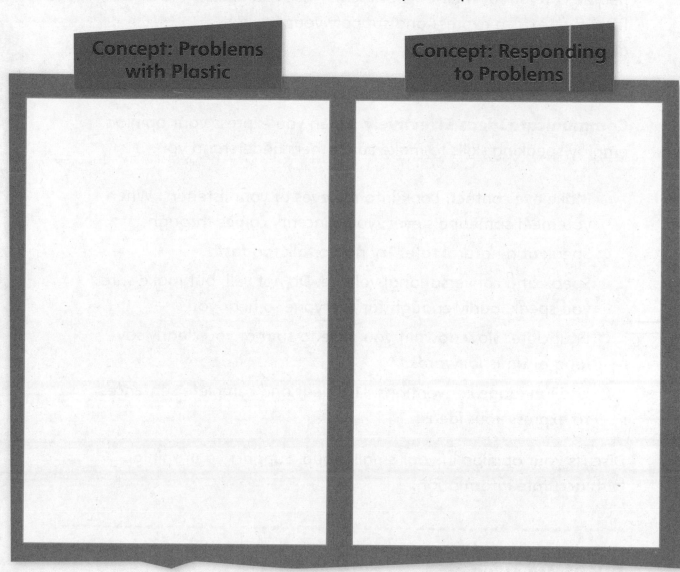

Concept: Problems with Plastic

Concept: Responding to Problems

Reflect and Share

Talk About It In *Trashing Paradise* and "Bye Bye Plastic Bags on Bali," you learned about actions that Bali residents Melati and Isabel Wijsen took because they were appalled at all the trash they saw. What other texts have you read in which people's environments inspired them to take action? Why do people care about their environments? Use examples from the texts to express and support your opinion about why people care.

- -

Communicate Ideas Effectively When you express your opinion, employ speaking skills to make sure others understand you.

- Make eye contact. Look into the eyes of your listeners. When you meet someone's eyes, your sincerity comes through.

- Speak at a natural rate. Try not to talk too fast.

- Speak at a conversational volume. Do not yell, but make sure you speak loudly enough for everyone to hear you.

- Enunciate. Slow down if you have to so that you clearly say long or unusual words.

- Use language conventions. Use clear and complete sentences to express your ideas.

Discuss your opinion in your small group. Support your opinion with accurate information.

- -

Weekly Question

What happens to what we throw away?

Academic Vocabulary

Parts of Speech A word's meaning changes slightly with its part of speech. For example, as a verb, *walk* means to move with one's legs. As a noun, *walk* refers either to a surface on which one walks or to the activity of taking a walk. A word's context helps you determine its part of speech.

My TURN For each sentence,

1. **Identify** the bold word's part of speech—noun, verb, or adjective—on the line.

2. **Write** your own sentence using the word in the same way.

_____ **1.** The **border** between Canada and the United States runs down the center of the St. Clair River.

_____

_____

_____ **2.** Sarnia, Ontario, **borders** the river on the east.

_____

_____

_____ **3.** Please check the nutrition **label** on the bag of rice.

_____

_____

_____ **4.** The researcher **labels** each sample as it is collected.

_____

_____

Word Parts *sub-*, *inter-*, *fore-*

The **Greek and Latin word parts** *sub-*, *inter-*, and *fore-* often give clues to a word's meaning. For example,

- *sub-* means "under," "near," or "part of"

  In *subzero*, which means "under zero," the word part is added to *zero*.

- *inter-* means "between"

  In *interchange*, which means "to exchange," the word part is added to *change*.

- *fore-* means "before" or "in front of"

  In *forewarn*, which means "warn people before something happens," the word part is added to *warn*.

My TURN Use your knowledge of word parts as a clue to each word's meaning. Write your definitions on each line. Then use a print or digital dictionary to check your definitions.

Word	Definition
foreground	
subway	
intercommunication	
subgroup	
forethought	

Read Like a Writer

The **author's purpose** is the reason an author has for writing. An author may select literal, or plain and exact, language to achieve his or her purpose. The purpose may be to entertain, to inform, to persuade, or to express ideas and feelings. In a single text, the author may have more than one purpose.

Model Read this text from *Trashing Paradise*.

> To make plastic bags, polyurethane is formed into pellets. Then the pellets are melted into a thin film. Machines cut the film into bags. The problem is that all plastics are different from anything that occurs in nature. That means nature doesn't have an easy way to break them down.

author's language

1. **Identify** Rukhsana Khan uses literal language to explain how plastic bags are made. Then she calls attention to a problem.

2. **Question** What purpose does her language suggest?

3. **Conclude** The primary purpose is to inform because facts and details are used.

Reread paragraph 21 of *Trashing Paradise*.

My TURN Follow the steps to analyze the passage. Explain the author's purpose based on her choice of words.

1. **Identify** Rukhsana Khan uses literal language to explain

_____

_____

2. **Question** What purpose does Rukhsana Khan's language suggest?

3. **Conclude** Her language suggests _____

Write for a Reader

On her Web site, Rukhsana Khan says, "My stories have all depended on what demanded to be written at the time I was writing them." Authors write for a purpose, and they choose their words to achieve their purpose.

My TURN Think about how Rukhsana Khan's use of literal language suggests her purpose for writing *Trashing Paradise*. Now think about how you can use literal language to communicate your own purpose for writing.

1. Imagine that you want to inform readers that the school's water will be turned off for an hour so that a broken pipe can be repaired. What words could you use to clearly communicate your purpose?

_____

_____

2. Write an announcement for your classmates about an upcoming one-hour period without water. Use literal language to reveal your purpose.

_____

_____

_____

_____

_____

_____

_____

Spell Words with *sub-, inter-, fore-*

Greek and Latin word parts offer clues to the meanings of words. The word part *sub-* means "under," "near," or "part of." The word part *inter-* means "between." The word part *fore-* means "before" or "in front of." Knowing these Greek and Latin word parts can help you spell words that contain *sub-*, *inter-*, and *fore-*. Use a dictionary to confirm the full meaning of a word.

My TURN Read the words. Sort and spell the words in alphabetical order.

SPELLING WORDS

submarine	submerge	international	forehead
interfere	subfreezing	interception	foreperson
forearm	suburb	interpreter	forecast
subdue	interaction	foremost	substandard
interface	foreground	subheading	subvert

Dialogue Punctuation

Dialogue is written conversation. The words characters speak are called direct speech. Direct speech always appears in quotation marks.

Follow these rules to punctuate dialogue.

Rule	Example
Use quotation marks at the beginning and end of each speaker's words.	"Please help me collect plastic bags for recycling."
When direct speech begins in the middle of a sentence, put a comma before the quotation starts.	Adnan asked, "Can every plastic bag be recycled?"
When regular text interrupts a complete sentence of dialogue, follow the interruption with a comma.	"Mr. Jackson," I said, "can you tell us if the recycling company will accept all kinds of plastic bags?"
Put punctuation that ends a quotation inside the quotation marks.	"I'm glad you asked!" Mr. Jackson said.

My TURN Edit this draft to correctly punctuate the dialogue.

Our guide pointed out the grove of palm trees.

This one is a date palm she said from which people harvest dates.

Zeke asked   What do dates look like?

The guide smiled and said   I just happen to have a few to show you!

Add and Delete Ideas for Coherence and Clarity

Poets add and delete ideas so their poems have the rhythms, rhymes, and meanings they want. For example, they delete and add words, parts of lines, and lines so that their poems become clearer.

Learning Goal

I can use knowledge of the elements and structure of poetry to write a poem.

Unclear Idea Deleted

My golden retriever is hoping to run
~~up over there~~ to the lake.
She wags her long tail and says, "This will be fun!
Come along, just for my sake!"

Clearer Idea Added

My golden retriever is hoping to run
over the fields and to the lake.
She wags her long tail and says, "This will be fun!"
Come along, just for my sake!"

My TURN Cross out the least clear idea in each couplet. Add an idea to make the couplet clearer.

The teacher told us twice

The place we will go is nice.

Bleating goats and noisy geese

Make it hard to nap in peace.

My TURN Add and delete ideas as needed when you revise the draft of a poem in your writing notebook.

Prepare for the Celebration

A poet's goal is to end up with exactly the sounds, images, and ideas he or she wants, with nothing extra to confuse readers. Therefore, as poets complete their poems, they read them both silently and aloud to make sure they are just right.

My TURN Write your poem in cursive. Make sure you can read every word. Then read your poem aloud. Make changes if you need to. Read the poem aloud again.

Follow the process in this checklist to prepare your completed poem.

MY POEM IS COMPLETE WHEN

- ☐ I have chosen line breaks.
- ☐ I have chosen punctuation.
- ☐ I have arranged lines in stanzas if I want to.
- ☐ I have made choices about rhythm, repeated letter sounds, and rhymes.
- ☐ I have read my poem out loud to make sure it sounds the way I want it to.
- ☐ I have repeated these steps until I am happy with my poem.
- ☐ I have made final corrections and written a clean copy in legible cursive.

Trust your ears!

Publish and Celebrate

Before you publish, consider the audience that would most enjoy your poem. Is it other poets, classmates, younger students, or someone else? Poets often read their published work aloud to a group. Making an audio recording is another way to publish your poem. Arrange a reading, make a recording, or publish your poem in a suitable way for your audience.

My TURN Complete these sentences about your writing experience.

The audience I will publish my poem for is _____

_____

_____

I will publish my poetry by _____

_____

_____

The form of poetry I liked using the most was _____

_____

My most descriptive word choices were _____

_____

_____

Prepare for Assessment

My TURN Follow a plan as you prepare to write a poem that appropriately responds to the prompt. Use your own paper.

1. Study the prompt.

You will receive an assignment called a writing prompt. Read the prompt carefully. **Highlight** the type of writing you must do. <u>Underline</u> the topic you are supposed to write about.

Prompt: Write a short poem about an astronaut's view of planet Earth.

2. Brainstorm.

List at least six things that are unique about the way an astronaut sees Earth. Circle three ideas that you think will capture readers' interest.

3. Freewrite your poem.

For five minutes, write about the three ideas you circled. Do not pay attention to spelling, grammar, lines, stanzas, or punctuation.

4. Draft your poem.

Determine the form of your poem. Apply your choices about rhythm, alliteration, assonance, rhyme, similes and metaphors, line breaks, stanzas, and punctuation.

> When you read your poem silently to yourself, tap out the rhythm.

5. Revise your poem.

Find ways to strengthen the structure, word choices, and ideas in your poem.

6. Finalize your poem.

Present your poem by reading it aloud. Apply the skills and rules you have learned to polish your poem.

Assessment

My TURN Before you write a poem for your assessment, rate how well you understand the skills you have learned in this unit. Go back and review any skills you mark "No."

		Yes!	No
Ideas and Organization	◐ I can understand what poetry looks like and sounds like.	☐	☐
	◐ I can brainstorm and freewrite to get ideas for a poem.	☐	☐
	◐ I can select a form for a poem.	☐	☐
	◐ I can create rhythms and repetition in a poem.	☐	☐
	◐ I can use alliteration and assonance in a poem.	☐	☐
	◐ I can choose line breaks and stanzas for a poem.	☐	☐
	◐ I can determine the rhyme scheme of a poem.	☐	☐
Craft	◐ I can use similes and metaphors in a poem.	☐	☐
	◐ I can use punctuation for effect.	☐	☐
	◐ I can revise the structure of a poem.	☐	☐
	◐ I can revise word choice in a poem.	☐	☐
	◐ I can add and delete ideas for clarity.	☐	☐
Conventions	◐ I can use adverbs correctly.	☐	☐
	◐ I can use prepositional phrases correctly.	☐	☐
	◐ I can use modal verbs correctly.	☐	☐

UNIT THEME

Features

TURN and TALK

Connect to Theme

In this unit, you learned many new words for talking about Earth's *Features*. With a partner, review each selection to find and quote a sentence from the text that best illustrates the academic vocabulary word. Be prepared to tell why you chose that sentence from each text.

from The Top 10 Ways You Can Reduce Waste

preserve

_____

_____

_____

_____

BOOK CLUB

WEEK
2

Volcanoes

label

_____

_____

_____

VOLCANOES
by Seymour Simon

BOOK CLUB

WEEK
1

from Planet Earth

amazed

_____

_____

_____

Planet Earth
by Christine Taylor-Butler

BOOK CLUB

The Himalayas

border

_____

_____

_____

BOOK CLUB

Trashing Paradise and "Bye Bye Plastic Bags on Bali"

consequences

_____

_____

_____

_____

Essential Question

My TURN

In your notebook, answer the Essential Question: Why is it important to understand our planet?

BOOK CLUB

Project

Danger AHEAD!

Activity

Extreme weather can lead to extreme results. Storms and environmental events such as tornadoes, blizzards, hurricanes, and floods can destroy and reshape Earth's features. What storm or environmental event do you think poses the greatest danger? Write an opinion article to share your answer and support it with facts.

 RESEARCH

Research Articles

With your partner, read "Warning! Warning!" to generate questions about how warning signs in nature can predict extreme weather. Then make a research plan for creating your opinion article.

1 **Warning! Warning!**

2 **Too Tied to Technology?**

3 **Living Near a Volcano**

Generate Questions

COLLABORATE After you read "Warning! Warning!" use the information in the article to generate questions about warning signs in nature and how to predict weather. List three of your questions here.

1. _____

2. _____

3. _____

Use Academic Words

COLLABORATE In this unit, you learned many words related to the theme of *Features*. Work with your partner to add more academic vocabulary words to each category. If appropriate, use this vocabulary when you plan, research, and create your opinion article.

Academic Vocabulary	Word Forms	Synonyms	Antonyms
label	labeled labeling mislabeled _____	name describe tag	unmarked untitled unnamed
amazed	amaze amazing amazement _____	shocked astonished surprised	bored uninterested expected
border	borders bordering bordered _____	limit boundary edge	center middle focus
consequences	consequence consequential inconsequential _____	results effects costs	causes reasons roots
preserve	preserves preserved preserving	protect save conserve	destroy damage harm

A Clear Claim Close-Up

The claim in an opinion article almost always shows up in the first paragraph, but it might not be the first sentence.

People write **argumentative texts** to persuade readers to think or do something. Look for these features when you read opinion articles:

• a claim,
• reasons and evidence that support the claim, and
• a logical order, such as order of importance.

 RESEARCH

COLLABORATE With your partner, read "Too Tied to Technology?" Then answer these questions about the text.

1. What is the writer's claim?

_____

_____

2. What evidence does the writer use to persuade readers?

_____

_____

_____

3. Does the writer present the strongest evidence first or last? How does this make the argument more persuasive?

_____

_____

_____

_____

Plan Your Research

COLLABORATE Before you begin to research dangerous weather, you need to make a research plan. Use this chart to write a claim and plan how you will look for evidence.

Definition	Examples
CLAIM A claim is a statement of the writer's perspective or opinion. An effective claim • defines a writer's goal, • is clear and specific, and • is supported by facts and other evidence. Read the two examples to the right. Then, with your partner, write a claim for your opinion article about dangerous weather.	This writer is writing an argumentative text about caves. • Caves are super cool! *Too general and vague* • Mammoth Cave is the most impressive geographic feature in the United States. *Clear and specific* My dangerous weather claim:
EVIDENCE Information that supports your claim is evidence. You might include • facts • statistics • quotations • examples	**Fact:** A famous shaft in Mammoth Cave is called the Bottomless Pit. **Statistic:** More than 400 miles of cave have been explored at Mammoth. **Quote:** Cave guide Stephen Bishop said Mammoth Cave is "grand, gloomy, and peculiar." **Example:** Caves are impressive because there is little or no natural light inside.

With your partner, list some possible sources in which to look for evidence that supports your dangerous weather claim.

REACH Out to a PRO

Experts can help you gather evidence to support your claim. You might contact one of these weather experts:

- a local weather forecaster
- a weather scientist

Locate a Contact Address You can find e-mail addresses on professional or educational Web sites.

Write Your E-mail When you write your e-mail:

- Use a polite, formal tone.
- Generate one or two specific questions.
- Clarify your questions to be sure they make sense.

EXAMPLE Layna sent this e-mail to a tour guide.

New Message	X

To a_graner@nps.email

Subject Information for a School Report ◄••••••••••••••

> The subject tells the reader what the e-mail is about.

Dear Abel Graner,

My partner and I are writing an article about Mammoth Cave. Since you are an expert on Mammoth Cave, we would like to include some of your ideas in our article.

> The writer explains why she is writing.

What is the most amazing thing about working in Mammoth Cave? What is the strangest thing that ever happened during one of your tours?

> The writer asks specific questions that only this expert can answer.

Thanks for reading this note.

COLLABORATE With your partner, think of two types of experts you could write to when gathering evidence for your dangerous weather opinion article. Then generate questions with your partner.

	Expert 1	Expert 2
Type of Expert and Expertise		
Where to Look for E-mail Address		
Specific Questions Only This Expert Can Answer		

Work together to write polite, clear e-mails to the experts. When you get a response, talk about which evidence could best support your claim.

Defend YOUR Claim

An **opinion article** tries to persuade readers to believe a claim. Well-structured opinion articles follow this basic plan:

- The **introduction** presents the writer's claim, or opinion statement.
- The **body** of the article presents evidence to support the claim.
- The **conclusion** restates the claim and leaves readers with something to think about.

The body paragraphs can present evidence in different ways. Some articles present the strongest evidence first. Other articles build up to the ideas that provide the best support. When writers present their strongest support first or last, they are using order-of-importance organization. Writers include transitions to help readers follow the organization, or structure, of their argument.

COLLABORATE Read the Student Model. Work with your partner to recognize the characteristics of argumentative texts.

Now You Try It!

Discuss the checklist with your partner. Work together to follow the steps as you compose your opinion article.

Make sure your opinion article

- ☐ states a specific claim
- ☐ presents facts, statistics, quotes, or examples as evidence
- ☐ follows a clear structure, such as order of importance
- ☐ includes a strong conclusion that restates your claim

Student Model

In the United States, you can see wild waterfalls, huge deserts, or super-deep canyons. Of all the geographic features, though, Mammoth Cave National Park in Kentucky is the most impressive.

Underline the sentence that states the writer's claim.

Mammoth Cave is the longest cave system in the world. It includes more than 400 miles of underground passages. More than 2 million visitors come to this national park each year.

Highlight two statistics.

Some of the caves are big enough for people to walk in. Others you have to crawl to explore. Some are too small for people to enter at all.

One early cave guide, Stephen Bishop, called Mammoth Cave "grand, gloomy, and peculiar." Abel Graner is a guide there today. "The cave is my favorite place in the world," he says, "but it's not for everyone. I've seen people faint because they got scared. But some people love it as much as I do."

Underline two quotations.

Mammoth Cave is unlike almost any other place in the United States. The underground caves include cool rock formations like stalactites and stalagmites.

Highlight the sentence that restates the claim.

If you want to see the most inspiring place in the United States, you should definitely put Mammoth Cave at the top of your to-visit list!

Student Model

Super Sources

Great research includes a variety of sources. When you look for information, ask yourself: When was this material created, and who created it?

- **Primary sources** are created at the time of an event. People who see an event and document it produce primary sources.
- **Secondary sources** are created after an event is over by people who did not see the event themselves.

This chart gives some examples of primary and secondary sources.

Primary Sources	Secondary Sources
• a diary written by someone who lives near a volcano	• an encyclopedia article about volcanoes
• a photograph of a volcano erupting	• a diagram showing the parts of a volcano
• a newspaper article written at the time of a volcanic eruption	• a magazine article that describes the causes and effects of an eruption
• a speech given by a leader to persuade citizens to leave a dangerous place	• a biography of a leader written by a modern author
• a movie filmed as a volcano erupts	• a documentary about the volcano

COLLABORATE Read the article "Living Near a Volcano." Then draw a T-chart on a separate sheet of paper. Work with a partner to identify primary and secondary sources used in the article. Record them in your T-chart.

Read this paragraph. Then answer the questions.

Stephen Bishop, Cave Expert

by Elena Nunez

Stephen Bishop was an enslaved person in his teens when he first came to Mammoth Cave in 1838. He soon became one of the greatest experts on this underground area. Bishop explored many parts of the cave that no one had ever seen before. He began to lead tours through the caves. Bayard Taylor, one of the people he guided, wrote that Bishop was "the model of a guide—quick, daring, enthusiastic, persevering, with a lively appreciation of the wonders he shows." Bishop became a free man in 1856, but he died just one year later.

1. Identify the primary source named in the paragraph. How can you tell this is a primary source?

Primary Source: _____

How I can tell: _____

_____

_____

2. Is the paragraph by Elena Nunez a primary or secondary source? Why?

_____

_____

Finding FACTS In Online Archives

An **online archive** is a collection of articles and other resources. Many newspapers, magazines, and Internet sites have online archives you can search.

Use the same search methods you use when choosing keywords to look for information in an online search engine. Place phrases in quotation marks to find results that include an exact phrase.

When you find information, place quoted material in quotation marks or use your own words to paraphrase the ideas you find. Cite your sources.

Layna searched for articles about Mammoth Cave in *The Daily Times* online archive. This sample shows her results.

Click *Newest* to see the most recent sources first. Click *Oldest* to see the oldest sources first. Click *Relevance* to see the sources that are most connected to your search first. Choose the date range for your search.

The Daily Times Online Search

Your Search: "Mammoth Cave"

Sort by: Newest Oldest **Relevance** ◄···

Date Range:

All Since 1900

Past 24 hours

Past 7 Days

Past 30 Days

Past 12 Months

Result Type

All Types

Article ◄····

Blog Post

Multimedia

BIG DISCOVERIES IN MAMMOTH CAVE
Geologist Dr. Shannon McBridge shares findings of a recent study of rock formations in Mammoth Cave National Park.
July 29, 2015

Specific Dates MAMMOTH CAVE SCRAPBOOK ◄···
Images collected by reporters over the last 25 years.
September 7, 2012

Choose the kinds of results your search will include.

Click a title to view that source.

COLLABORATE With your partner, think about how you can use online archives to find more information for your opinion article. Complete the planning chart to guide your research.

Name of Online Archive:	Search Key Words:
	Date Range:
Archive Web Address (URL):	What types of results are we looking for?
Name of Online Archive:	Search Key Words:
	Date Range:
Archive Web Address (URL):	What types of results are we looking for?
Name of Online Archive:	Search Key Words:
	Date Range:
Archive Web Address (URL):	What types of results are we looking for?

Revise

Revise Claim and Evidence Reread your opinion article with your partner. Have you

☐ clearly stated your claim?

☐ included strong facts, statistics, quotations, and examples?

☐ used order-of-importance organization and transitions to structure your ideas?

Adding Support and Transitions

The writers of the Student Model opinion article added more information about Abel Graner and his work in Mammoth Cave. They also added an introductory phrase to make the order of their support clear.

One early cave guide, Stephen Bishop, called Mammoth Cave "grand, gloomy, and peculiar." Abel Graner is a guide there today.∧"The cave is my favorite place in the world," he says . . . He loves to take visitors on both electric-light tours and tours where the only light comes from paraffin lamps people carry.

The most important reason you should see Mammoth Cave is that it ∧~~Mammoth Cave~~ is unlike almost any other place in the United States. The underground caves include cool rock formations like stalactites and stalagmites.

Edit

Conventions Read your opinion article again.
Have you used correct conventions?

- [ ] spelling
- [ ] punctuation
- [ ] capitalization of names and places
- [ ] quotation marks around ideas quoted from research
- [ ] correct comparative and superlative adjectives (such as *better*, *best*, *more*, and *most*)

Peer Review

COLLABORATE Exchange opinion articles with another group. Use the chart to review an article. Write the claim and then note the key evidence. Rank the evidence from most to least persuasive. Compare your ranking with the order the writers used to share these ideas.

CLAIM	
EVIDENCE	

Time to Celebrate!

COLLABORATE Now you will present your opinion article to another group. To prepare, decide if your presentation will be oral, multimedia, or a video. As you present, remember to make eye contact with your audience and speak at a natural rate and volume. If your topic is serious, remember to use formal English when you present. Listen to your audience's comments and questions after you finish.

How persuasive did your audience find your claim and article? Write some of their reactions here.

_____

_____

_____

_____

Reflect on Your Project

My TURN Think about your opinion article. What parts of your article do you think are strongest? Which areas might you improve next time? Write your thoughts here.

Strengths

_____

_____

_____

Areas of Improvement

_____

_____

Reflect on Your Goals

Look back at your unit goals. Use a different color to rate yourself again.

Reflect on Your Reading

Which idea from the unit would you most like to share with a friend or family member who did not read the same texts? Why?

_____

_____

_____

_____

_____

_____

Reflect on Your Writing

Review the writing you did for this unit. Which writing are you proudest of and want to put in your portfolio for this year? Why?

_____

_____

_____

_____

How to Use a Glossary

This glossary can help you understand the meaning, part of speech, pronunciation, and syllabication of some of the words in this book. The entries in this glossary are in alphabetical order. The guide words at the top of each page show the first and last words on the page. If you cannot find a word, check a print or digital dictionary. You would use a dictionary just as you would a glossary. To use a digital resource, type the word you are looking for in the search box at the top of the page.

Example glossary entry:

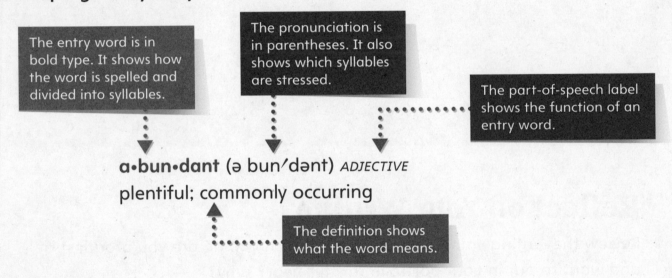

The entry word is in bold type. It shows how the word is spelled and divided into syllables.

The pronunciation is in parentheses. It also shows which syllables are stressed.

The part-of-speech label shows the function of an entry word.

a•bun•dant (ə bun′dənt) *ADJECTIVE*
plentiful; commonly occurring

The definition shows what the word means.

My TURN Find and write the meaning of the word *challenge*.

Write the syllabication of the word. _____
Use the pronunciation guide to help you say the word aloud.
What other words do you know that share the same base word as *challenge*?

TURN and TALK With a partner, discuss how you can use a print or digital dictionary to find the meaning of a word that is not in this glossary.

Aa

a·bun·dant (ə bun′dənt), *ADJECTIVE*. plentiful; commonly occurring

ac·cen·tu·at·ed (ak sen′chü ā tid), *VERB*. highlighted; called attention to

ac·com·plish (ə kom′plish), *VERB*. achieve; succeed

a·dopt·ed (ə dop′tid), *VERB*. started to use a selected idea or method

al·ti·tude (al′tə tüd), *NOUN*. height or distance above sea level or Earth's surface

a·mazed (ə māzd′), *ADJECTIVE*. awed; impressed; struck

as·ton·ish·ment (ə ston′ish mənt), *NOUN*. a feeling of great surprise

Bb

bar·gain (bär′gən), *NOUN*. an agreement between people about what each will give or receive

bor·der[1] (bôr′dər), *NOUN*. line or boundary

bor·der[2] (bôr′dər), *VERB*. to form a separating edge

Pronunciation Guide

Use the pronunciation guide to help you pronounce the words correctly.

a in *hat*	ō in *open*	sh in *she*
ā in *age*	ȯ in *all*	th in *thin*
â in *care*	ô in *order*	ᴛʜ in *then*
ä in *far*	oi in *oil*	zh in *measure*
e in *let*	ou in *out*	ə = a in *about*
ē in *equal*	u in *cup*	ə = e in *taken*
ėr in *term*	ù in *put*	ə = i in *pencil*
i in *it*	ü in *rule*	ə = o in *lemon*
ī in *ice*	ch in *child*	ə = u in *circus*
o in *hot*	ng in *long*	

both·ered (boŦH′ərd), *ADJECTIVE.* annoyed or upset with

buoy (bü′ē), *NOUN.* an object that floats on the surface of water

Cc

chal·lenge (chal′ənj), *NOUN.* a thing that requires skill or thought

cir·cu·lates (sėr′kyə lāts), *VERB.* moves through a system

com·mend·a·ble (kə men′də bəl), *ADJECTIVE.* worthy of praise

com·po·sure (kəm pō′zhər), *NOUN.* the calm control of oneself

con·flict (kən flikt′), *VERB.* goes against; interferes with

con·fused (kən fyüzd′), *ADJECTIVE.* unable to understand

con·se·quen·ces (kon′sə kwen səz), *NOUN.* results; effects

cool (kül), *ADJECTIVE.* interesting or stylish

cre·ate (krē āt′), *VERB.* make or produce something

crude oil (krüd oil), *NOUN.* unrefined liquid petroleum

Dd

de·ceived (di sēvd′), *VERB.* caused a person to believe something that is not true

ded·i·ca·tion (ded′ə kā′shən), *NOUN.* an official ceremony for something created for a special purpose

deed (dēd), *NOUN.* something that is done; an action taken

dis·pos·a·ble (dis pō′zə bəl), *ADJECTIVE.* single-use; designed to be thrown away

drought (drout), *NOUN.* a long time of low or no rainfall

Ee

e•mis•sions (i mish′ənz), *NOUN.* substances released; anything given off by something else

er•o•sion (i rō′zhən), *NOUN.* process of wearing away or breaking down land over time

ex•ces•sive (ek ses′iv), *ADJECTIVE.* a lot, or more than necessary

ex•change (eks chānj′), *NOUN.* return

ex•pand (ek spand′), *VERB.* communicate in detail; make larger

Ff

face (fās), *NOUN.* surface; front or outer part

fes•ti•val (fes′tə vəl), *NOUN.* organized series of special events and performances

flocked (flokt), *VERB.* moved in a group

frus•trat•ed (frus′trā tid), *ADJECTIVE.* feeling annoyed at being unable to change something

Gg

grudge (gruj), *NOUN.* a strong feeling of dislike toward someone who treated you badly

gush•es (gush′iz), *VERB.* spouts; flows quickly

Hh

her•i•tage (her′ə tij), *ADJECTIVE.* related to important traditions from the past

Ii

il•lus•trate (il′ə strāt), *VERB.* show

im•pul•sive•ly (im pul′siv lē), *ADVERB.* suddenly; without careful thought about the consequences

in•fer•nal (in fėr′nl), *ADJECTIVE.* unpleasant; related to the underworld

i•ni•ti•a•tive (i nish′ə tiv), *NOUN.* an act, process, or program that starts something

in•no•va•tive (in′ə vā′tiv), *ADJECTIVE.* creative; using new ideas or methods

in•sist•ed (in sis′tid), *VERB.* demanded or required something forcefully

in•spi•ra•tion (in′spə rā′shən), *NOUN.* something that gives someone the desire to do something

in•stinc•tive•ly (in stingk′tiv lē), *ADVERB.* without thinking about how to do it

in•ter•pret (in tėr′pret), *VERB.* figure out

in•tri•cate (in′trə kit), *ADJECTIVE.* complicated; very detailed

ir•ri•ta•ble (ir′ə tə bəl), *ADJECTIVE.* easily made angry or annoyed

Ll

la•bel¹ (lā′bəl), *NOUN.* identification tag

la•bel² (lā′bəl), *VERB.* to categorize, name, or describe

Mm

mag•ma (mag′mə), *NOUN.* liquid rock beneath Earth's surface

man•tle (man′tl), *NOUN.* the layer of Earth between the crust and the core

marred (märd), *VERB.* damaged; made ugly; marked

mis•er•a•ble (miz′ər ə bəl), *ADJECTIVE.* deeply unhappy or uncomfortable

mis•led (mis led′), *VERB.* caused to believe something untrue

mol•ten (mōlt′n), *ADJECTIVE.* melted; hot enough to be in liquid form

Oo

o•bliged (ə blījd′), ADJECTIVE. grateful; thankful

or•nate (ôr nāt′), ADJECTIVE. highly decorated; complex and fancy

Pp

par•a•pet (par′ə pet), NOUN. a low wall at the edge of a structure, such as a bridge

par•tic•i•pate (pär tis′ə pāt), VERB. take part of or in

per•form•ance (pər fôr′məns), NOUN. a public presentation to entertain an audience

phe•nom•e•non (fə nom′ə non), NOUN. something that can be studied or observed; event

pla•teau (pla tō′), NOUN. large, high, flat area of land

plunge (plunj), VERB. dive; sink rapidly; drop quickly

pre•dict (pri dikt′), VERB. announce in advance

pre•serve¹ (pri zėrv′), NOUN. a protected area for plants or animals

pre•serve² (pri zėrv′), VERB. to maintain; to keep or save

Rr

re•claim (ri klām′), VERB. take back

re•cov•er (ri kuv′ər), VERB. return to normal health or strength

rep•u•ta•tion (rep′yə tā′shən), NOUN. the opinion that many people have of someone

re•veal (ri vēl′), VERB. make known

riled (rīld), VERB. irritated; aggravated

Ss

sa•tis•fied (sat′i sfīd), ADJECTIVE. pleased or happy with something

GLOSSARY

sa•vor•ing (sā′vər ing), *VERB.* completely enjoying

sen•si•tive (sen′sə tiv), *ADJECTIVE.* capable of responding to stimulation; easily affected

shrewd (shrüd), *ADJECTIVE.* clever; showing good judgment

snooz•ing (snüz′ing), *VERB.* dozing; sleeping lightly

sub•con•ti•nent (sub kon′tə nənt), *NOUN.* large region that is part of a continent

sub•sid•ed (səb sī′did), *VERB.* stopped; died down

sur•vey (sər vā′), *NOUN.* measurement of an area of land

Tt

tem•per•a•ments (tem′pər ə mənts), *NOUN.* personalities; usual attitudes or behaviors

threat•ened (thret′ənd), *VERB.* endangered; put in a risky position

thrill•ing (thril′ing), *ADJECTIVE.* exciting and pleasing

thud (thud), *NOUN.* a dull sound

tox•ic (tok′sik), *ADJECTIVE.* poisonous

tra•di•tion•al (trə dish′ə nəl), *ADJECTIVE.* established; customary

trance (trans), *NOUN.* dreamlike state

trilled (trild), *VERB.* made a pleasant, repetitive, high-pitched sound

Uu

un•bid•den (un bid′n), *ADJECTIVE.* not asked for

un•der•lie (un′dər lī′), *VERB.* form the foundation of

Ww

watt (wät), *NOUN.* unit of measurement for electrical power

wa•ver•ing (wā′vər ing), *ADJECTIVE.* changing

Text

Abrams Books

Trombone Shorty by Troy Andrews and Illustrated by Bryan Collier. Text copyright © 2015 Troy Andrews and Bill Taylor. Illustrations copyright © 2015 Bryan Collier. Used with the permission of Express Permissions on behalf of Abrams Books for Young Readers, an imprint of Harry N. Abrams, Inc., New York. All rights reserved.

Bye Bye Plastic Bags on Bali

Bye Bye Plastic Bags on Bali used with permission from Bye Bye Plastic Bags.

Isabel F Campoy

I Will Be a Chemist: Mario José Molina by Alma Flor Ada from The Poetry Friday Anthology for Science, 2014. Pomelo Books. Used with permission of the author.

Candlewick Press

Weslandia. Text copyright © 1999 by Paul Fleischman. Illustrations copyright © 1999 by Kevin Hawkes. Reproduced by permission of the publisher, Candlewick Press.

Paul Fleischman

Weslandia by Paul Fleischman. Published by Candlewick Press. Used with permission from the Paul Fleischman.

Hachette UK Ltd

"Race to the Top" by Geraldine McCaughrean in The Crystal Pool, first published in the UK by Orion Childrens Books, an imprint of Hachette Childrens Books, Carmelite House, 50 Victoria Embankment, London Imprint, EC4Y 0DZ.

HarperCollins Publishers

Volcanoes, Text Copyright (c) 1998 by Seymour Simon. Used by permission of HarperCollins Publishers.

Houghton Mifflin Harcourt Publishing Company

Pandora from The Beautiful Stories of Life: Six Greek Myths, retold by Cynthia Rylant. Text copyright© 2009 by Cynthia Rylant. Reprinted by permission of Houghton Mifflin Harcourt Publishing Company. All rights reserved.

Thunder Rose by Jerdine Nolen, illustrated by Kadir Nelson. Text Copyright © 2003 by Jerdine Nolen, Illustrations Copyright © 2003 by Kadir Nelson. Reprinted by permission of Houghton Mifflin Harcourt Publishing Company. All rights reserved.

Lee & Low Books

Mama's Window by Lynn Rubright. Text Copyright © 2008 by Lynn Rubright. Permission arranged with Lee & Low Books, Inc., New York, NY 10016. All rights not specifically granted herein are reserved.

Lindgren & Smith Inc. Artists Representatives

Tales Like Rumpelstiltskin, Titeliture, How Ijapa the Tortoise Tricked the Hippopotamus and Oniroku, illustrations ©StefanoVitale/lindgrensmith.com

Scholastic Library Publishing

Planet Earth by Christine Taylor-Butler. All rights reserved. Reprinted by permission of Children's Press an imprint of Scholastic Library Publishing, Inc.

Judy Sierra

Tales Like Rumpelstiltskin, Titeliture, How Ijapa the Tortoise Tricked the Hippopotamus and Oniroku, used with permission from Judy Sierra.

Simon & Schuster, Inc.

From Out of My Mind by Sharon M. Draper. Copyright © 2010 Sharon M. Draper. Reprinted with the permission of Athenaeum Books for Young Readers, an imprint of Simon & Schuster Children's Publishing Division. All rights reserved.

Smith & Kraus Publishers

La Culebra (The Snake) by Pamela Gerke from Multicultural Plays for Children, Volume 2. Reprinted by permission from Smith & Kraus Publishers.

The Rosen Publishing Group Inc.

The Himalayas by Charles Maynard, 2004. Reprinted by permission from Rosen Publishing.

University of New Mexico Press

From The Circuit by Francisco Jiménez. Copyright © 1997 University of New Mexico Press, 1997.

Weigl Publishers Inc.

The Top 10 Ways You Can Reduce Waste 4-11, 18-28, 30. Reproduced by permission from AV2 Weigl, The Top 10 Ways You Can Reduce Waste (New York, NY AV2 by Weigl, 2011)

Photographs

Photo locators denoted as follows Top (T), Center (C), Bottom (B), Left (L), Right (R), Background (Bkgd)

10 (BL) Rawpixel/Shutterstock, (Bkgd) Jim West/Alamy Stock Photo; **20** Susan Walsh/AP Images; **21** (R) Classen/Shutterstock; **26-27** Fotolia; **44** (Bkgd) Darezare/Shutterstock, (T) Zoonar GmbH/Alamy Stock Photo, (BL) Jim Richardson/National Geographic Creative/Alamy Stock Photo, (BR) Ivoha/Alamy Stock Photo; **44** (Bkgd) Elena Veselova/Alamy Stock Photo; **45** (T) Steve Skjold/Alamy Stock Photo, (B) Igor Vorobyov/123RF; **78** (Bkgd) Amy Harris/REX/Shutterstock, (B) Kzenon/Shutterstock; **79** (T) Dreamer Company/Shutterstock, (B) Scharfsinn/Shutterstock; **112** Photo by Patty Brown; **118** (T) Simon Tang/Shutterstock, (C) Iam Prawit/Shutterstock, (BL) Zeljko Radojko/Shutterstock, (BC) Thanakorn Hongphan/Shutterstock, (BR) Regreto/Shutterstock; **119** (T) S.Borisov/Shutterstock, (B) UfaBizPhoto/Shutterstock; **136** Copyright by Francisco Jimenez. Used with author's permission.; **137** (Bkgd) Library of Congress Prints and Photographs Division [LC-DIG-highsm-21738], 123RF; **138** Nsf/Alamy Stock Photo; **140** Bettmann/Getty Images; **141** Underworld/Shutterstock; **143** Jaroslaw Pawlak/Alamy Stock Photo; **144** Rappensuncle/E+/Getty Images; **146** Randy Vaughn-Dotta/Design Pics Inc/Alamy Stock Photo; **147** Age Fotostock/Alamy Stock Photo; **149** Caimacanul/Shutterstock; **166** (Bkgd)

Radka1/Shutterstock, (T) Michael Harder/Alamy Stock Photo, (C) Zev Radovan/BibleLandPictures/Alamy Stock Photo, (B) Blend Images/Shutterstock; **167** (T) Igor Kyrlytsya/Shutterstock, (B) Pingvin_house/Shutterstock; **195** Aisyaqilumar/Fotolia; **200** (T) Wavebreakmedia/Shutterstock, (B) Tyler Olson/Shutterstock; **202** Poznyakov/Shutterstock; **204** Pinkcandy/Shutterstock; **206** (L) Dotshock/Shutterstock, (C) Bruce Rolff/123RF, (R) Liudmila Matvienco/123RF; **209** Jaren Wicklund/123RF; **218** (Bkgd) Jag_cz/Shutterstock, (T) Ssuaphotos/Shutterstock, (C) Marekuliasz/Shutterstock, (B) Fer Gregory/Shutterstock; **219** (T) Lightspring/Shutterstock, (B) Cosma/Shutterstock; **256** (Bkgd) Senee Sriyota/Shutterstock, (T) Ian Allenden/123RF, (B) Shojiro Ishihara/123RF; **257** Viachaslau Bondarau/123RF; **328** Imtmphoto/Shutterstock; **368** (Bkgd) Flas100/Shutterstock, Manbetta/Shutterstock, Robert_S/Shutterstock, (T) Yurlick/Shutterstock, (C) Scottchan/Shutterstock, (BL) Ollyy/Shutterstock, (BC) Iakov Filimonov/Shutterstock, (BR) Rob Byron/Shutterstock; **369** Aslysun/Shutterstock; **410** (Bkgd) Ron and Joe/Shutterstock; **414** Dennis Hallinan/Alamy Stock Photo; **416** Richard Cavalleri/Shutterstock; **417** Library of Congress, Music Division; **418** Focal Point/Shutterstock; **420** (Bkgd) Tramvaen/Shutterstock, (R) MTaira/Shutterstock; **423** Darrin Henry/Shutterstock; **426** (Bkgd) Triff/Shutterstock, (BL) Nobra/Shutterstock; **432-433** (Bkgd) Harvepino/Shutterstock, Kokliang/Shutterstock; **432** (T) Jixin Yu/Shutterstock, (B) Designua/Shutterstock; **437** Johan Swanepoel/Shutterstock; **438** Mopic/Shutterstock; **439** Spencer Sutton/Science History Images/Alamy Stock Photo; **440** (TL) Merkushev Vasiliy/Shutterstock, (BR) Spencer Sutton/Science History Images/Alamy Stock Photo; **441** (B) Claus Lunau/Science Source; **442** Designua/123RF; **443** (TL) B.A.E. Inc./Alamy Stock Photo, (BR) Snowbelle/Shutterstock; **444** dalmingo/Shutterstock; **446** Stocktrek/Stockbyte/Getty Images; **447** Ma Ping/ XINHUA/AP Images; **448** Carsten Peter/National Geographic/Getty Images; **449** (TR) SPL/Science Source; Christian Darkin/Science Source; **466** Ammit/123RF; **467** Kasimova/Shutterstock; **470** (TL) Charles Harbutt; **471** Douglas Peebles/Corbis/Getty Images; **472** J.D.Griggs/U.S. Geological Survey; **473** Hawaii Volcanoes National Park /National Park Service; **474** David Fossler/Shutterstock; **475** InterNetwork Media/DigitalVision/Getty Images; **476** (L) Rick Hoblitt/U.S. Geological Survey Cascades Volcano Observatory, (R) Solomonjee/Shutterstock; **478** Images & Volcans/Science Source; **479** J.D.Griggs/U.S. Geological Survey; **480** Seymour Simon; **481** Hawaii Volcanoes National Park/National Park Service; **483** George Burba/Shutterstock; **505** (Bkgd) Valeria Evteeva/EyeEm/Getty Images, (B) Prapass/Shutterstock; **507** Elena Elisseeva/Shutterstock; **508** (C) Michael Blann/Stone/Getty Images; **509** (TC) Richard I'Anson/Lonely Planet Images/Getty Images, (CL) Tuanyick/Shutterstock, (BR) Rob Simmons/NASA; **510** (C) Taxi/Getty Images; **511** (TC) Jamie Grill/The Image Bank/Getty Images, (CR) Alex Staroseltsev/Shutterstock, (BR) Charriau Pierre/The Image Bank/

Getty Images; **512** (C) Mark Viker/The Image Bank/Getty Images; **513** (TC) Brian Chase/Shutterstock, (CR) Anki21/Shutterstock, (BR) Ralf Herschbach/Shutterstock; **514** (C) Stuart Dee/The Image Bank/Getty Images; **515** (TL) Anthony Berenyi/Shutterstock, (C) Electronistock/Alamy Stock Photo, (BR) Ugorenkov Aleksandr/Shutterstock; **516** (C) Tim Graham/The Image Bank/Getty Images, (BL) Newphotoservice/Shutterstock; **517** (C) Nils-Johan Norenlind/Nordic Photos/Getty Images, (BR) Shmeliova Natalia/Shutterstock; **518** (C) Barbro Bergfeldt/Shutterstock; **519** (TC) Alzbeta/Shutterstock, (CR) J. Bicking/Shutterstock, (BR) Peter Anderson/Dorling Kindersley Ltd.; **520** (C) Jupiterimages/Photolibrary/Getty Images; **521** (TC) Dylan Ellis/The Image Bank/Getty Images, (CR) Rob Marmion/Shutterstock, (BR) Apple Tree House/Photodisc/Getty Images; **522** (TL) Greg McGill/Shutterstock, (CL) Feng Yu/123RF, (CR) John Lamb/The Image Bank/Getty Images, (BL) Ben Arnoldy/The Christian Science Monitor/Getty Images, (BR) Justin Sullivan/Getty Images; **523** (TC) Boris Sosnovyy/Shutterstock, (CR) Alan Myers/Alamy Stock Photo, (BL) Africa Rising/Shutterstock, (BR) Lisa F. Young/Shutterstock; **542-543** (Bkgd) Antonio Balaguer Soler/123RF; **543** (T) David Osborn/Shutterstock, (C) Kokoulina/Shutterstock, (B) KuLouKu/Shutterstock; **547** Microstock Man/Shutterstock; **549** Serban Bogdan/Shutterstock; **550** (T) NASA, (BR) Frans Lemmens/Corbis Unreleased/Getty Images, (C) Daniel Prudek/Shutterstock; **553** Jerry Kobalenko/Alamy Stock Photo; **555** Andrew Errington/The Image Bank/Getty Images; **557** (TL) Chronicle/Alamy Stock Photo, (BR) Bobby Model/National Geographic/Getty images; **558** (BC) Keystone Pictures USA/Alamy Stock Photo; **576** (T) Musicalryo/Shutterstock, (C) Thailerderden10/Shutterstock, (CL) Yurchenko Yulia/Shutterstock, (T) Rich Carey/Shutterstock, (B) Kanvag/Shutterstock; **577** (Bkgd) Arsen Luben/Shutterstock; **577** (R) Tawatchai.m/Shutterstock, (C) Aha-Soft/Shutterstock; **581** (Bkgd) Yuxuan Wang/Moment/Getty Images, (T) Lisa S./Shutterstock, (C) Paris Spellson/Alamy Stock Photo, (B) Dusit Kachatong/Shutterstock; **585** Mike Lane/NHPA/Photoshot/Newscom; **586** (L) Micah Wright/Age Fotostock/Alamy Stock Photo, (R) Charles O. Cecil/Alamy Stock Photo; **587** Peter-Verreussel/iStock/Getty Images; **588** Maschietto/MCT/Newscom; **589** Paulo Oliveira/Alamy Stock Photo; **593** RibeirodosSantos/iStock/Getty Images; **594** Agung Parameswara/Getty Images; **596, 597** Used with permission from Bye Bye Plastic Bags.

Illustrations

19, 259, 371, 435 Ken Bowser; **23-27** Shane Rabenscheid; **47, 81, 169, 295, 469, 503** Olga & Aleksey Ivanov; **49-61** Ale + Ale; **121, 331, 545** Ilana Exelby; **171-177** Jui Ishida; **221, 383-391, 579** Valeria Cis; **225, 233, 333, 373, 383** Karen Minot; **292-293** Ian Joven; **297** Marilyn Smith/AnimalsClipart.com; **298-309** Jago; **333, 351** Fabricio Vanden Broek; **373-381** Martin Wickstrom; **414, 420** Rob Schuster; **467** Jun Park; **583** Mapping Specialists